LEARNING
TO LIVE
TOGETHER

LEARNING TO LIVE TOGETHER

Interchurch partnerships as ecumenical communities of learning

Lothar Bauerochse

WCC Publications, Geneva

in cooperation with EMW, the
**Association of Protestant Churches
and Missions in Germany**

Originally published in German as *Miteinander leben lernen: Zwischenkirchliche Partnerschaften als ökumenische Lerngemeinschaften*, Erlangen, Verlag der Ev.-Luth. Mission, 1996

English translation by Cynthia Lies

Cover design: Rob Lucas

ISBN 2-8254-1343-7

Printed in Switzerland

Contents

vii   *Preface*
      KONRAD RAISER

1   **I. Partnership in Mission: The Historical Development of a Concept**

2   1. The early modern mission as the mission of the non-church fathers

4   2. Finding partners

10   3. Partners as equals:
       Jerusalem 1928 and Tambaram/Madras 1938

26   4. Partners in mission: Whitby 1947

39   5. The participation of the partners in the *missio Dei:*
       Willingen 1952, Achimota 1958, Mexico City 1963

61   6. The threat to partnership from the poverty of the South and the wealth of the North: Bangkok 1973, Melbourne 1980

75   7. Koinonia – the eucharistic community of sharing:
       El Escorial 1987, San Antonio 1989, Canberra 1991

88   8. Partnership – the transformation of a concept: the yield of the historical review

96   **II. Experiencing Ecumenism: Partnerships and Their Importance for Congregations and Dioceses, Regional Churches and Their Mission Departments**

97   1. The formation of partnerships

99   2. The aims of partnership

104   3. The partnership work of the regional churches and their mission departments

106   4. Motives and experience in partnership work

108   5. The importance and meaning of partnership for the life of the congregations and the dioceses

112   6. Mission and partnership

114   **III. Partnership as a Community of Learning: Learning Processes in Ecumenical Partnerships**

114   1. Learning in the partnership: basic comments

119   2. Intercultural learning in the partnership

131   3. Ecumenical learning in the partnership

159   **IV. Practising Ecumenical Existence: Considerations for a New Orientation with a Systematic Perspective**

162   1. The challenge to *Konvivenz:* partnerships as a way of practising ecumenical existence

167   2. The foreign partners: how we see the others in interchurch partnerships

174   3. Festivity and celebration: reflecting on the identity of the community

177   4. Foreigners become brothers and sisters: towards an African understanding of partnership

183   5. Practising ecumenical existence: perspectives for a new orientation of partnership work

Preface

For more than fifty years, "partnership" has been a key term used to characterize the ecumenical relationships between churches and Christians in the North and the South. In spite of its ambiguities, the concept has remained in current use and attempts to replace it by a term with more immediate ecclesial connotations have failed.

With the title of his book, "Learning to Live Together", Lothar Bauerochse, a religion journalist with a regional radio station in Germany, offers an interesting interpretation of partnership which poses a challenge to much of the practice which has developed under this title. His interpretation is rooted in a very careful re-reading of the ecumenical discussion around the notion of partnership, especially in the context of the International Missionary Council and later the Commission on World Mission and Evangelism of the World Council of Churches. This historical analysis, which brings to light many unknown and unexpected features, takes up the first half of the book. Since nothing comparable has been done so far, the author's research is particularly valuable for contemporary ecumenical discussions about missionary cooperation and ecumenical sharing of resources.

The other half of this publication is devoted to a more empirical analysis of findings from four case studies focusing on partnership links between church communities in Germany and in Africa, as well as on the experience of the three well-known international frameworks of missionary cooperation, i.e. the Evangelical Community of Apostolic Action (CEVAA), the Council on World Mission (CWM) and United in Mission (UIM). His analysis shows that many of the so-called "partnerships" are not guided by a clear objective beyond the desire to get to know each other; that the relationships are distorted by the influence of money being transferred from the Northern to the Southern partners; and that therefore the potential opportunities for genuine ecumenical learning across the differences of culture are not really being used. Building on his fuller understanding of partnership, Lothar Bauerochse is therefore able to formulate a set of very helpful and practical guidelines and suggestions which will be useful far beyond the specific contexts on which his analysis is based.

The original German edition of the book contains extensive empirical and case-study material which is only of limited interest to readers in the English-speaking world. However, considering the significance of the notion of partnership in developing criteria and models of ecumenical relationships of cooperation, including links between local communities in different cultural contexts, the reflections and proposals presented in this book are of more general importance, and it is hoped that they might inspire new initiatives of learning to live together in the worldwide ecumenical community. If it is true that the ecumenical movement has the potential of developing an alternative to economic and financial globalization, this is the critical context in which this alternative has to prove its viability.

KONRAD RAISER
General Secretary
World Council of Churches

I. Partnership in Mission
The Historical Development of a Concept

Ecumenical partnerships, as well as direct contacts between congregations and church districts in Germany on the one hand and countries in Asia, Africa and Latin America on the other, are part of church and mission relationships. For this study I examined four partnership case studies. All are coordinated and supported by German mission agencies. To clarify the concept of partnership I have decided to start with the history of mission and ecumenism. The first part of this book deals with the great world mission conferences and with several of the ecumenical movement's other conferences and study programmes, looking at them particularly with regard to interchurch relations. I start with the first world mission conference in Edinburgh in 1910 – where for the first time delegates became aware of problems that would shape future relations between the missionary societies of the North and the newly formed churches of the South – and I continue through to the world mission conference in San Antonio 1989 and the assembly of the World Council of Churches in Canberra 1991. I deliberately go beyond the concept of "partnership" and ask more generally about "interchurch relationships". This enables me to give a more chronological perspective, as "partnership" was mentioned only occasionally before 1947, and not at all in German-language texts. This can also sharpen our awareness of the conflicts arising between the churches of the North and the South, between the "old" and the "new" churches, as they used to be called in missionary circles.

I confine myself to the negotiations and results of the world mission conferences, as they were and still are the real forum for raising questions of mission theology and mission practice. At these conferences the principal question discussed was about the relationships between the independent churches of the South and the missionary societies (or later the churches) in the North and how they corresponded to recognized missiological thinking. The term "partnership" was used very prominently at several of these conferences.

In this historical retrospective there are three main sets of questions. I ask first of all when and in what contexts "partnership" was mentioned in a stricter sense, and what was understood by this term. I am able to show that the understanding of partnership within the mission movement was subject to historically determined change. Occasionally I indicate which aspects of an understanding of partnership can be relevant to district and congregational partnerships. Second, I try to evaluate which statements are made about the relationship between the "partners", i.e. the churches and the missionary societies, where there is no explicit mention of partnership. How are "partners" described? What is the perceived position of the newly-emerging churches of the South? What is the quality of the relationship? What expectations and demands are made for structuring interchurch relationships? Which roles and tasks are given to each side? Finally, the world mission movement not only speaks of "partnership" but also of "partnership in mission". We must therefore ask how far the concept of partnership is qualified by these terms and what is understood by the word "mission". The theological understanding of mission has undergone radical change in the course of the 20th century. This development will also be described briefly, along with questions about the consequences of this change for partnership relations between churches, congregations and districts.

Such a historical review serves not only towards developing a much clearer profile for the concept of partnership, but also to remind us of ecumenical insights already gained, some quite a long time ago. Often these insights were not transferred, or not adequately translated, into day-to-day missionary practice and have been buried and forgotten. Historical recollection can be an important aid in understanding current problems and difficulties in partnership relations between congregations and districts and can also provide a stimulus for developing new forms of such relationships.

1. The early modern mission as the mission of the non-church fathers

To be able to perceive clear changes in "interchurch relationships" occurring in the history of mission, we must first take a brief look at the beginnings of modern Protestant mission. The specific feature of this mission is that it originally thought in terms that excluded the churches, in both the Anglo-Saxon and the continental areas. The model for the missionaries was that of the "fathers".

THE PIETISTIC APPROACH TO MISSION

The roots of the modern world mission movement are to be found in the pietism of the 18th century. In Germany the first person to be mentioned here is Ernst August Franke. When European sailors came home and told of foreign continents and foreign peoples, pietistic circles reacted by setting themselves the task of proclaiming the gospel of Jesus Christ to these foreign people in far-away places. When his two students, Bartholomeus Ziegenbalg and Heinrich Plütschau, set out for Tranquebar on the east coast of India, this marked the beginning of the Danish-Halle Mission, and indeed the beginning of modern world mission in Germany.

The pietistic mission did not aim for mass baptisms and the growth of churches but rather for "the salvation of individual souls" (like Cornelius in Acts 10). Entirely in accordance with their own form of religious observance, these missionaries wanted to lead *individuals* to personal conversion. As Zinzendorf put it, they were to win "souls for the Lamb". The English-speaking mission also reflected a basically non-church foundation. Its declared intention was to "spread the kingdom of God" and to this end it made use not only of preaching but also of church institutions (universities, secondary schools and hospitals) to a far greater extent than the European missions.

This independence from the churches has two sides: on the one hand, the missionary societies themselves kept a certain distance from the institutional churches in their own countries; on the other hand, initially at least, they had no thought of founding churches in the mission areas. Mission circles had organized themselves in associations and societies outside the institutional churches, but were also totally convinced that they themselves were the true church. The content of their missionary work was to bring together selected congregations in all parts of the world in accordance with the pietistic idea of "ecclesiola". The congregations which came into being in the mission areas were looked after by the missionaries, who themselves were not pastors in the institutional churches in their homelands. The mission leadership, although legally in charge of a "society", understood themselves as church leaders.

In view of later developments it is important not to lose sight of this: in almost all countries the early pietistic mission was a mission outside the institutional churches. It was a mission of societies and associations, whose members considered the institutional churches to be weak and lacking in faith. There can be no talk of "interchurch relations" at this time.

THE DISCOVERY OF THE CHURCH AS A MISSION AIM

Only later, and as a consequence of their own work, did the missionary societies have to face the question of independent churches in the mission field. In the middle of the 19th century the Englishman Henry Venn (1796-1873) and the American Rufus Anderson (1796-1880) coined the "classic basic requirement" of the so-called "three-selfs" for determining the independence of a church: "To be able to regard a church in the mission field as independent it must be self-supporting, self-governing and self-propagating."

Gustav Warneck (1834-1910) made the concept of church the basic axiom for German missiology. After the publication of his five-volume work, *Protestant Doctrine of Mission* (1892-1902), "church planting" became the essential aim of mission work: "By Christian mission we understand the whole activity of Christendom aimed at planting and organizing the Christian church among non-Christians." Warneck was thinking of a church that puts down roots in foreign soil, a people's church that permeates the whole population as yeast permeates bread dough, finally bringing all the people of the country into itself, an independent church, which in turn is a missionary church.

It was mainly pragmatic reasons that led Warneck to formulate such a position. Churches had come into existence in the mission field as a result of mission work. It was now necessary for mission theory to consider how they should be treated. Here too there can only be limited talk of "interchurch relations", for the churches in the mission field existed in relationship to European and American missionary societies, not to churches. This was the situation at the beginning of the 20th century when the ecumenical mission movement met for its first and so far largest ecumenical world mission conference in Edinburgh in 1910.

2. Finding partners

EDINBURGH 1910

The world mission conference in Edinburgh in June 1910 can be considered the beginning of "mission ecumenism". It was the first really worldwide gathering of responsible people from the missionary societies and it became a model for all future world mission conferences and for many ecumenical assemblies. It was, however, a conference of missionary representatives from the North. Out of over 1300 delegates, only 17 came from the countries of the South and even they were representing missionary societies, not indigenous churches.

> This is a clear reflection of the fact that even in Edinburgh it was still the middle of the colonial age. From a political point of view it was not yet time for the transformation of the colonies to independent states. And the leadership of missions or churches in the mission field was still fully in the hands of the Western missionary societies or the missionaries they had sent out.

THE PERCEPTION OF THE CHURCHES IN THE MISSION FIELD

These Western missionary representatives spoke "as befitted the times" of "our mission fields", of "mission churches" and of "natives" as "helpers of our missionaries". Nevertheless in the later reports it was always stressed how important the delegates from the mission field were for the conference discussions and negotiations, even though the churches from which they came, the so-called "young churches", were still regarded as "churches 'in being'".

In the German report at the end of the section on the "striking personalities" of the conference, several representatives from the mission fields are named.

> If anyone came to Edinburgh with the antiquated idea that the heathen Christians were all more or less dependent children who would always need the maternal care of the missionaries, then he could be taught something completely different in Edinburgh.

For some people it was a surprise that the Japanese, Chinese and Indians present were "treated as having fully equal rights", and were even the "absolute darlings of the congress". This showed an attitude not so much of recognition and respect as of benevolent paternalism. The mood of the conference is often described as euphoric. The well-known slogan of the Student Christian Movement ("the evangelization of the world in this generation") met with a very positive response. Edinburgh was understood, at least by the Anglo-Saxons who dominated the conference, as the meeting of the general staff before the decisive battle, the meeting at which they would assess their forces, consider the most effective way of deploying them, and study the enemy's front-line and inner mood.

The question of North-South relations was already on the agenda at Edinburgh. For one thing, the subject of the second day of the conference was "The Church on the Mission Field". And what is more, at an evening session Bishop Roots from China, President K. Ibuka from Japan and the Anglican V.S. Azariah, who went on to become the first Indian bishop, briefly gave their views on the subject of "The Problem of Cooperation between Foreign and Native Workers". Azariah's speech especially caused quite a sensation at the conference. It was celebrated as a "masterpiece of oratory" and even reckoned to be one of the "most impressive speeches of the whole conference", but it also aroused the anger of several delegates from the North.

The commission on the missionary church was introduced by its president, the Rev. J. Campbell Gibson, with the remark that one should no longer speak of the "native church", "as the word native has become a term of contempt". One should instead speak of "church". Gibson asked the delegates "not to make any difference in estimation between the church in the Christian and in the non-Christian world". Here we have the first indications that a new relationship was in the process of developing between the churches in Europe and America and above all with those in Asia, but it required new forms of language to express it.

The commission dealt with the questions of how to promote the independence of the native church and whether the missionary work supported with foreign money had also to be kept under foreign control. What attitude should the mission adopt towards the independent indigenous church: one of independence, of cooperation, or of service? In his statement to the commission the American Presbyterian, William Adams Brown, made it clear that while the independence of the churches in the mission areas had been a declared aim of the mission, at the same time its achievement aroused anxieties amongst the missionary societies at their own success:

> We always wanted a native church; but now that it is here, we do not know how we should behave towards it. Originally there was only mission. Today however, now that there is a church out there which takes responsibility for itself, we do not want to behave in the way that we have always talked; the missionary boards exercise too much power. For this reason a certain unease and irritability is stirring in the mission church. Why do we want to keep God's people on earth in our hands? A fourfold error prevails among us:
> 1) our own aim fills us with fear;
> 2) we are of the opinion that the mission churches should become like our churches;
> 3) we feel ourselves responsible for all their future mistakes;
> 4) we do not want to trust their future leadership to Christ.
> The workings of the Spirit are not limited to the country of the whites. Our only right to be in Asia and Africa is that we are allowed to hasten to the assistance of our brothers in the Lord. We must learn to recognize the rights of the church of God in the non-Christian countries.

The explosive force of radical change can be felt in this statement. The churches' insistence on independence, strongest in China, Japan and India and influenced by the growing national self-confidence, demanded of the missionary societies that they reduce their influence and limit their area of responsibility. The supporters of church independence in the South stressed that the Christian faith and the church could not be allowed to remain foreign bodies in Asian society; in addition the splintering into various denominations which the Western missionary societies had brought with them was a burden for the young churches and had to be lifted through the independence of national churches. Sceptics or opponents of independence feared that the churches would distance themselves, drift into sectarianism and lose their links to the worldwide community of churches.

With this, the commission had touched on the essential themes of the discussion about new forms of interchurch relationships. In this respect we can really say that "what we know today as partnership relations between churches in various parts of the world... was discovered here". However the problems were only touched upon, they were not discussed in depth, nor were any decisions taken. And so it is also the case that the "white man's self-assurance" remained unbroken in Edinburgh. Above all, the white men still remained among themselves and talked about the young churches, not with them. The representatives of Asian and African Christians were only allowed to speak on the fringe of the conference, especially in the short evening speeches already mentioned.

STATEMENTS FROM THE CHURCHES IN THE MISSION FIELDS

The speeches made by Ibuka of Japan and Azariah of India are particularly worth analyzing in detail. They describe the problems in interchurch relations between North and South clearly and from the perspective of Asian Christians. Ibuku, Azariah and Bishop Roots from China all raise the same issue: how and to what extent should the responsibility for church work and missionary work be transferred from the missionaries to indigenous church leaders?

Here is Roots' answer: "Just as soon and so far as the native workers and the native church are able to sustain that responsibility and do that work." He said missionaries should work towards this aim. By so doing they would make themselves unneeded, and could then withdraw entirely. He described the churches in the South at this point in time as "no longer children, but not quite yet grown up; they are adolescents".

Ibuka described a model of cooperation being discussed in his country. In it, the foreign mission and the native church were "co-workers for a common end" – a model which today would probably be called "a relationship in partnership". "It means an equal share in the general care or supervision of a certain kind of evangelistic work carried on by the missions related to the church."

According to Ibuka such cooperation was controversial. The opponents were against the limitation of the missions' responsibility and argued firstly that the mission had always worked in the interests of native Christians and would continue to do so. It was therefore not necessary for native workers to share responsibility. The limitation of the mission's independence should be avoided. Secondly, the money came from American churches and therefore the mission must take sole responsibility for it. Thirdly, the Japanese workers were needed for other tasks. They had no time for this committee work; and anyway they had neither the training nor the experience for such work.

The supporters of shared responsibility replied that the church had become independent. It had its own history and was in a fully valid sense church, a church active in evangelism, building up an effective administration and becoming increasingly self-sufficient financially. Secondly, the Japanese co-workers had qualities comparable to those of the missionaries; the money did not necessarily have to be administered by Americans, but above all by reliable personnel. Finally and centrally: the missionary work must take place within the church, the mission should not be permitted to cut itself off.

Ibuka made it clear that in the background was the growing self-confidence of the Japanese church. "Finally," he explained. "the synod is not demanding anything different from what every general assembly or synod in America or Scotland would demand if the situation were reversed."

V.S. Azariah made a further specific point. He named substantial elements, in that 1910 presentation, of what would later be summarized in the term "partnership in mission". Azariah was not sparing with his criticism:

> At least in India the relationship is all too often not what it ought to be, and things must change and change speedily if there is to be a large measure of hearty cooperation between the foreign missionary and the Indian worker.... A certain aloofness, a lack of mutual understanding and openness, a great lack of frank intercourse and friendliness exists throughout the country.

What Azariah hoped for was a friendly relationship between missionaries and native Christians, not the sort of relationship which teachers and pupils have. Friendship, according to Azariah, is more than "condescending love". He did not dispute that the foreign missionaries loved the country and the people, and were self-sacrificing. Friendship, however, was more than the love of a benefactor. Azariah demanded a change in the relationship: once the children are grown up, fathers must become friends. This sort of friendship was also possible between the races and cultures. Azariah called upon the missionaries to try and develop a natural relationship with their Indian fellow-Christians in a practical way, to visit them in their houses and to invite them into theirs. "In India we have a new generation of Christians who no longer wish to be treated as children", he said.

With reference to the official relationships Azariah explained that as long as the missionary remained the paymaster and his Indian co-worker the servant, neither self-confidence nor individuality could grow in the Indian church. Independent thought and action were frequently suppressed. Missionaries had to give up some of their responsibilities and privileges. The phrase "our money, our control" must disappear. A change of this sort could not be brought about suddenly, but had rather to be brought about step by step.

Finally Azariah went into a third aspect, the spiritual level of the relationship. In his judgment many missionaries had not tried to reach the hearts of the Indians. They had gained no understanding of the special "religious atmosphere" in India; to that extent external institutions and Christian behaviour patterns had remained foreign to many Indians. What Azariah then demanded must have sounded revolutionary to those who heard him at the time, for he rejected the idea that missionaries had sole responsibility for the proper understanding of the gospel, and spoke of the need for a church community of living and learning:

> It is in this cooperation of joint study at the feet of Christ that we shall realize the oneness of the body of Christ. The exceeding riches of the glory of Christ can be fully realized not by the Englishman, the American, and the continental alone, nor by Japanese, the Chinese and the Indians by themselves – but by all working together, worshipping together and learning together the Perfect Image of our Lord and Christ.

He closed his speech with the sentences, often quoted later, which put the finger on the heart of the matter: "You have given your goods to feed the poor. You have given your bodies to be burned. We ask also for love. Give us friends!"

The aspects of the discussion about the relationship between the missions and the churches already described are of such fundamental importance that we should review them. The aim of the previous section was to show how soon the conflicts in North-South relations broke out between the missionary societies and the churches. Edinburgh was no more than an indication of the problems, but also no less. The problems appeared from the moment that churches began to exist in the mission areas. In the "days of innocence", as the conference in Edinburgh is sometimes called, these problems were already being mentioned, although at first only in passing. Christians from Asia (later also from Africa) stated their interests and made increasing demands for independence. The missionary societies were to a large extent totally unprepared for this, and the majority of them were at first quite incapable of knowing how to deal with it. This applied, with certain exceptions, both to individual missionaries, who could not or would not grasp how the understanding of their roles was changing, and to the missionary societies and their governing bodies, who tried to secure their influence into the future.

The crucial problems and points of conflict were many: Who bears the responsibility for the work? Who makes the decisions, particularly about the use of financial resources? With the emergence of a native church leadership group, these were the first urgent challenges. But there were also questions of how far the missionary societies would permit the churches to develop their own theology, an indigenous spirituality, a creed or liturgy appropriate to their own circumstances. How far could the societies even see this as an opportunity for Christians of the North to learn something new and enriching? And, finally, how far were the foreign missionaries prepared to give up privileges and to fit themselves into the ranks of the native church? What is remarkable is how soon it was being said that the time of the foreign missionaries could one day be at an end – and that at a time when the worldwide mission movement was experiencing dynamic growth.

I would also like to invite interest in a question which keeps recurring in the course of this study and which is always important: Who coins and defines certain terms? Is it the representatives of the North, the missionary societies, or is it rather the representatives of the South, the local churches? The conference in Edinburgh showed that the discussion about interchurch relations is always a debate about terminology and appropriate language. This is reflected in the demands made repeatedly at many world mission conferences that certain terms such as "young" and "old" churches or "sending" and "receiving" churches should not be used. The same applies to the term "partnership" and the change in meaning which it underwent in the course of the world mission conferences.

And finally: It is striking and possibly no coincidence that V.S. Azariah spoke of "friendship" when he spoke about the cooperation between missionaries and native Christians. That the term "friendship" played absolutely no part in later developments is also neither coincidence nor logically justifiable. In contrast to the questions being put, which concentrated only on bare working structures, Azariah brought a much broader dimension into the debate. His expectations, as representative of a church of the South, were directed at a comprehensive relationship which embraced working together as equals, living together at a considerate human level, celebrating together and learning from each other. He called it quite simply friendship.

3. Partners as equals: Jerusalem 1928 and Tambaram/Madras 1938
Almost two decades after Edinburgh, missionary representatives met again for a worldwide gathering which has come to be known as a

"world mission conference", although strictly speaking it was not one. The meeting on the Mount of Olives in Jerusalem in Holy Week 1928 was not an extraordinary assembly of mission experts as Edinburgh had been, but a routine meeting of the International Missionary Council (IMC). The IMC, founded in 1921, had proceeded from the work of Edinburgh's continuation committee.

THE NEW SITUATION IN JERUSALEM

This was not the only change compared to Edinburgh. The whole context of missionary work had been transformed, and this influenced both the atmosphere and the choice of subjects at the Jerusalem conference. Between the conferences in Edinburgh and Jerusalem the first world war had taken place. After that, the view of the world as seen in Edinburgh was no longer valid. The world could no longer be divided into a Christian West and a non-Christian East and South. Mission "was in the process of losing its geographical aspect... The borders that the mission had to cross had been transformed into religious, cultural, social and racial areas." Above all it was no longer possible to plan and carry out mission as a matter of course and with no questions asked, as had still been the case in Edinburgh. "The superiority of the white man, the cultural sense of mission especially among the English-speaking peoples, the indisputable absolute claim of Christianity, everything had become questionable." Even the right of mission itself was being called into question.

There were reasons for this uncertainty on both sides. In the West the question was being asked, by what right did Christianity push its way into countries with other religions and claim an absolute superiority to them. The "estrangement from God" in the countries of the North, slave trading, imperialism and human exploitation, as well as the insights of research in comparative religion, dampened the former missionary fervour in Europe and America. Strong resistance also came from the mission fields: Martin Schlunk describes it as follows:

> The question sounds from China, from India to the West: What do you want? Where do you take your right from? We do not want you!... Your Christianity is distortion, contortion, perversion! Let us ourselves seek, research and shape what genuine Christianity should be!

Unlike Edinburgh, where more than 1300 mission experts were gathered, there were only 231 delegates in Jerusalem. Among them were 70 representatives of the so-called "young" churches, of whom 52 – about a quarter of all participants – were indigenous Christians.

A fundamentally new element of the Jerusalem conference may be found in the fact that for the first time delegations of indigenous churches, especially from Asia, greatly influenced the conference. The churches that had come into being in the mission areas were present in a new way, as the opposite numbers of the missionary societies. In this way Jerusalem was "the first really representative global gathering in church history, the first worldwide conference of Protestant Christianity, and so it became a sign and an effective force of the evolving ecumenical movement".

For a whole day, the Jerusalem conference debated the subject of the relations between "the younger and the older churches". As already in Edinburgh, the term "native church" was considered disparaging and was rejected, although a substantial part of the discussion concerned the shape of the indigenous church. Instead it was agreed to use the terms "young churches" and "old churches".

Again and again the reports stress how great an influence the delegates from the South had on the discussions. And yet a remarkable ambivalence in the face of this development can be perceived among the representatives of the Western missions.

PARITY OF THE YOUNGER CHURCHES

It was not long before parity between old and young churches was mentioned in Jerusalem. John Mott, the conference chairman, talked in his opening speech of a 50-50 basis for encounter. Amongst other things, it was because of this "parity of the younger churches" and the position it gave them that the Jerusalem conference would be accorded "lasting significance". It is notable that it was the representatives of the missionary societies of the North who recognized the local churches as churches at all, "in spite of their small size and their weakness" as it was put, and gave them the status of "full parity" or rather "of equal partners". With astonishment the Western mission people noted that the young churches

> had achieved a degree of Christian maturity self-authoritative in its unsponsored claim for equality. Their representatives proved beyond all question that in insight, initiative, and ability to assume responsibility through comprehensive planning, they had come into their own.

They experienced them as "confident, skilful, imposing and eloquent spokesmen for their churches".

The mission representatives felt this gift of parity to be, as it were, a gracious advance concession on their part towards the churches, which they described – as in Edinburgh – as "adolescent". They considered the equality prevailing in the negotiations to be "not completely fulfilled, but given". However, the young churches demanded their independence, and so the days in Jerusalem were not without tension as far as interchurch relations were concerned, "here as there over-sensitivity, here as there insistence on one's rights". Schlunk names the most important questions which had to be discussed in Jerusalem.

> Do the young churches still need the missions to make up their minds for them? Can they exist without missionary leadership, without missionary support? If they need help upon what basis is it to be given? Should the missionaries become members of the indigenous churches? Who should administer the financial subsidies to be given by the old churches? Can the young churches fulfil their missionary duty towards the heathen world in their countries?

In the end, they are the same subjects that were on the agenda in Edinburgh: the independence of the local churches and their liberation from the Western missions making up their minds for them, the decision-making powers over financial and material aid, the role and position of the missionaries and the possibility of the churches themselves setting their own priorities.

THE CONFERENCE NEGOTIATIONS

The world mission conference in Jerusalem looked thoroughly into the questions arising from interchurch relations for the first time, and took far-reaching decisions. For the conference participants what was perhaps the most important question in this context was what an "indigenous church" actually was. The status of churches that had become or were still in the process of becoming independent had to be clarified, both theologically and practically. I shall take a brief look at the negotiations surrounding this set of questions as they show what sort of understanding the new "partners" had of each other, which had consequences for their relationship.

The preparatory material referred back to Henry Venn's definition of an independent church, while at the same time recognizing that the three aspects "self-supporting, self-governing and self-propagating" did not offer a sufficient definition. Above all the financial independence of the churches of the South did not seem possible in the foreseeable future. Therefore the aspect of "becoming rooted in the home country" and "indigenization" gained great importance. In 1925, for example, the American Baptist foreign missionary societies pointed to the spiritual aspects of the question:

> While such a church is commonly described as self-supporting, self-governing and self-propagating, yet the essential characteristics of a truly indigenous church are spiritual.... A church may be small in membership, simple in its organization and activities, and even partially dependent on foreign financial

aid, but if it has real life and is doing its utmost to express such life it may properly be considered indigenous.... It follows that a truly indigenous church will not merely appropriate those values which have been brought to it by others, but will make use of any permanent values in its own heritage.

For John Mott the "becoming at home" was the decisive feature:

Indigenous churches are those in which the natives find themselves at home, and even impress their non-Christian friends as natural, homelike and belonging to the country.... If a church is truly indigenous, the church edifice is planted right in the heart of the people, wherever they are.

At the Jerusalem conference the leader of the Chinese delegation, Dr Cheng, offered a definition of an indigenous church, in which being rooted in Chinese culture and society found expression alongside links to the worldwide church, independence and the will to cooperate.

1) a church that is the natural outgrowth and expression of the corporate religious experience of Chinese Christians;
2) a church that brings out the best in the life, culture and environment of the Chinese people;
3) a church that is self-supporting, self-governing and self-propagating;
4) a church that is an integral part of the church universal;
5) a church that is tolerant towards other religious faiths and rejoices in all things that are beautiful, good and true;
6) a church that is ready to cooperate with the churches in other lands in their common world task;
7) a church in which denominational variety can be merged in a rich and vital unity;
8) a church that clearly recognizes itself as a spiritual and religious institution.

That an indigenous church would and should put forward an indigenous theology, possibly one that was new and foreign to the missionary societies, was made clear by a Japanese contribution in the preparatory materials. The same seed, it stated, can produce different plants in different countries. "A spruce tree in England grows straight, in Japan it grows stunted," said the Japanese representatives. "There the proverb is 'as straight as a spruce tree', here we say, 'as stunted as a spruce tree'." Furthermore the local churches considered the denominational fragmentation of the Western missionary societies to be intolerable and made vehement demands for it to be overcome in one organic united church.

This raised the question of the practical consequences for the relationship of the churches to the missions. The representatives of the mission societies were rather reserved. They feared the local churches could distance themselves from the worldwide church community. They feared the danger of syncretism, if the "young churches" became too rooted in their "heathen" surroundings. It was the German representatives who raised a warning voice. The Berlin Mission director Siegfried Knak, who also wrote about the negotiations in the German report, stressed that experience had shown that it was a long process before the "national genius" of a people was able to grasp the gospel independently for themselves and give it their own expression in their theology and church.

> How long did it take in Germany before a Luther could arrive on the scene! Should the Western influence disappear too quickly, there is a very great danger that the young churches would fall prey to the syncretistic tendencies that are moving through the world, because they are not yet rooted firmly enough in the Bible. For a long time to come, the missionaries will retain the task of making the basic biblical ideas heard within the spiritual movements in the mission fields.

Knak added that subordinating the missionaries to the leadership of the local churches must not "violate" their consciences. The churches had to respect the missionaries' consciences; this was more important than "the question of who controls the use of mission funds". It was necessary, at least as far as the training of preachers was concerned, to make sure that the missionaries "retained a decisive influence for a long time to come".

In contrast, however, many conference participants stressed that all dominance by the missions had to be abolished. Local and foreign colleagues should work "hand in hand and shoulder to shoulder". It was necessary to have "mutual sympathy and understanding on the basis of equality". "Mutual sympathy and understanding was asked for by representatives of the younger churches and was freely offered by them," as it says in the summary of the discussion.

In a challenging contribution Dr James H. Franklin from the American Baptist Mission made very clear what had to change in the relationship:

> The hour has come for passing from paternalism to partnership. It is something more than even cooperation; it is partnership that is required. We want the fullest spiritual fellowship with what we call the younger churches.... We must go on in a fellowship in which there is confidence.

Jerusalem 1928 was thus the first occasion when "partnership" between missions and local churches was demanded, even using the word. Franklin further qualified his concept of partnership by the words "fullest spiritual fellowship" and "confidence". Under the term "partnership" he understood a contrast to "paternalism" and explicitly more than "cooperation" And he made it just as clear that this demanded a change in thinking from the missionary societies, that they should be not only givers but also learners:

> God's Spirit moves no more surely in New York, London and Berlin than it does in Madras and Tokyo and Bombay.... We have been thinking of ourselves as benefactors. Now we think of ourselves as brethren. Soon we shall be thinking of ourselves as beneficiaries.... We speak about sending deputations to the field; let us invite the young churches to come and tell us at home about their spiritual life.

The German delegates could not really endorse this thinking. "Thinking it over in a calm moment", such words "could not be allowed to disguise the very great difficulties and the very serious dangers". While it was true that the Spirit was not tied to London or Berlin, yet the Spirit could not be separated from the biblical revelation. Nor could all enthusiasm for generous trust obliterate the facts of history. In the face of the visibly growing independence of the churches of the South, a hesitant scepticism became apparent among the mission representatives, especially those from Germany.

Apart from these more fundamental considerations, there were many discussions in Jerusalem about the details of interchurch relations. These centred on the questions of the role of the missionaries and the form that financial and material aid should take. With regard to the aid given by the missions, there were many complaints, especially from the representatives of the Indian churches, that the initiative and self-responsibility of the Indian Christians was being crippled by foreign aid. P.O. Philip, of the Indian National Council of Churches, suggested a radical, though brief, cessation of aid:

> The contributions of men and money that have been flowing to the churches in India through the missionary societies all these years have been both a help and a hindrance. After a certain stage I believe they become more of a hindrance than a help. I sometimes think that it will be a good thing for the growth of the indigenous churches in India if by some cataclysm, such as happened in China, this flow of money from the churches of the West may be arrested, even for a short time.

That was certainly only an individual opinion, but there was general support for the demand that the missionary societies should steadily reduce the extent of their aid. The delegates were agreed that the local churches should encourage their members to have a greater sense of responsibility for their own financial support.

THE DECLARATION ON THE RELATIONS BETWEEN THE OLD AND THE YOUNG CHURCHES

The 10-page Declaration on the Relations between the Old and the Young Churches, which was accepted by the conference, took up the points that had arisen in the discussions and made detailed suggestions trying to point the way forward to new relations between the local churches and the missionary societies. At the centre of these suggestions was the concept of partnership.

The declaration takes as its starting point that the proclamation of the gospel throughout the world is the common task of all, and expresses the conviction that the witness of the young churches could be "more natural" if they were more "deeply rooted within their own soil". In five points the declaration attempts to describe the nature of a living, indigenous church. In proclamation of the gospel, and services of worship, in customs, art and architecture, the indigenous church should both absorb the valuable characteristics of the population, and at the same time preserve the heritage of the church at all times and in all places. It should foster and support the abilities and gifts of both men and women. It should take an active part in the life of the nation. It should take a stand on the problems of the times and make courageous and sensitive contributions to their solution. It should retain a missionary spirit.

The introduction to the section on the relations between missions and local churches includes the sentence: "There is possible now a true partnership enabling the older churches to work with, through or in the younger." In Jerusalem the missionary work was very much concentrated on the churches. The setting up of churches became the determining aim of mission work. At the same time the local churches were intended to become the centre from which the mission work of the European and American missions could radiate. Partnership, according to the declaration, enables the older and the younger churches to tackle the incomplete task of evangelizing the world, with greater hope of final success than ever before. Not only is there a continuing need for financial help from the older churches, but missionaries themselves are also urgently required; they must however be filled with the spirit of comradeship. The conference declaration describes how the churches of the South can help the churches of the North:

> The younger churches can serve the older at their home base by giving them a fresh inspiration and new interpretation of the Christian message through such means as deputations.

The declaration makes detailed suggestions concerning financial aid, suggestions which are still under discussion today: it states that in principle the assistance must be such that it enables the local churches to develop and strengthen their own abilities. The aid must neither foster the spirit of dependence nor weaken their capacity to take responsibility for themselves. And first and foremost, the spiritual life of the church must be strengthened. A further decisive factor is training in Christian stewardship. Thirdly, the older churches should steadily reduce their financial aid. Foreign financial aid should be administered by the local churches. Additional suggestions stress that the churches and the missionary societies should reach agreement each time on the procedures and conditions for the aid, and that for areas where the local churches did not or could not bear sole responsibility, agencies mutually agreed upon should be created.

These suggestions are dealt with in detail here because they make it clear that Jerusalem was already demanding a completely new relationship between the local churches and the missionary societies, and was linking these demands to concrete suggestions for their realization. In the English text, the word "partnership" was already being used as the term for this new form of relationship.

The Jerusalem concept of partnership does not primarily mean an association of convenience to fulfil the missionary task. Franklin's contribution had already linked the term "partnership" to the striving for a new spiritual-fraternal relationship. Partnership in Jerusalem is more than a "working cooperative of old and young churches... based on parity between them". The suggestions concerning financial aid point implicitly to a new relationship of the partners to each other. It should be determined by mutual understanding and trust; the relationship should be one which encourages the young churches to grow in independence and self-reliance.

How far the expectations and demands of the young churches were justified was made clear by James Endicott, moderator of the United Church of Canada, in the concluding speech of the debate. He did not want to dispute that there were serious difficulties in the relations between the old and the new churches. But the time was ripe for action. He hoped that the questions raised would be dealt with in such a way that there would be no need to discuss them further at future meetings of the International Missionary Council – a hope which was not to be fulfilled!

> I am convinced that all the essential things that they (the local churches) are requesting should be granted to them. We are afraid, because we have the feeling that the young churches have not yet got enough experience. How should the Christian religion ever have started if the world had always waited for experienced people? They will only gain their experience by action.

Endicott denied that the young churches wished to change Christianity. They really wanted to push forward to its core. What they were resisting was "our theology and our denominations – things which are a burden for them. They want freedom from the incubus which overshadows for them the glorious message of eternal life." And he concluded his speech, and with it the whole debate, with an appeal:

> It would be a profound mistake to wait until these churches become financially independent. Our Lord never gave us that principle.... Are we to withold any right that is implicit in the existence of a church? There is no such thing as an illegitimate church. This situation is urgent; the demand is natural; it is Christian, it is intelligent. We should hesitate no longer to give all that they ask.

THE WORLD MISSION CONFERENCE IN TAMBARAM/MADRAS 1938

When the delegates of the International Missionary Council met again for a world conference ten years after the Jerusalem one, the situation for the missions had yet again suffered a fundamental deterioration. "The dreams of 'an evangelization of the world in our generation' have disappeared," wrote Karl Hartenstein in the German report. "Down-to-earth objectivity with regard to the incredibly difficult situation" determined the negotiations. Even the reserved optimism of the Jerusalem conference had disappeared in face of wars and the deportation of missionaries from several mission fields. The holding of the conference itself was overshadowed by the outbreak of war between China and Japan. Consideration was given to postponing the conference. Finally the invitation of the Indian Christian Council was accepted and the conference took place at the end of 1938 in the Madras Christian College in Tambaram, some 20 kilometres outside the South Indian city of Madras.

The Tambaram conference took up the essential ideas and lines of thought from Jerusalem and went into them more deeply. The question of the church was now right at the heart of the conference. "The strengthening of the younger churches as part of the historic universal Christian fellowship" was the general theme of the conference, and was discussed by 16 sub-groups of participants. Five main subject groupings can be found: the faith by which the church lives (1-2), the witness of the church (3-6), the life of the church (7-11), the church and its environment (12-15), cooperation and unity (16).

In Jerusalem the representatives of the so-called "young churches" had contributed their particular emphasis to the discussions on mission theology for the first time. Now a whole conference was dedicated to these churches. Tambaram did speak of the worldwide church and its mission, and on occasions expressly included the churches of the North; nevertheless the attention of the conference was primarily directed to the life of the churches in the South. This choice of focus allowed the question which interests us, that of the relations between the missions and the churches, to retreat into the background. In essence, Tambaram here did not go beyond what had already been recognized in Jerusalem.

What was new at the conference in Tambaram was that the world mission conference took place for the first time in a country of the South, and that for the first time the representatives of the churches of the South formed the majority among the 471 delegates by a small margin; 77 of the delegates were women. Tambaram was therefore "the first truly worldwide (ecumenical) conference of Christendom", Karl Hartenstein wrote later. Against a background of political tensions and threatening developments in the world, the experience of this worldwide church assembly had a very special meaning for the delegates; it became a "great and wonderful occurrence".

In Tambaram the delegates were able to experience "the whole church of Jesus Christ on earth as a single entity". The title of the German report, "The Miracle of the Church among the Peoples of the Earth", gives expression to this feeling. Hartenstein wrote:

> Since Tambaram we know more clearly than before that the congregation of Jesus Christ really exists in almost all larger nations of the earth, amongst almost all languages, peoples and races. And we know today that this congregation of God really is one congregation.

The sense of encouragement that spread out from this experience to the churches and missions was probably the most important consequence of the conference. The conference had far more effect than any of the resolutions and recommendations made, whose implementation was largely prevented by the outbreak of the second world war less than a year later.

The independence of the churches in many mission areas, especially in Asia, was – even more so than ten years before in Jerusalem – a fact the work of mission could not ignore. This raised a whole series of questions and problems, to a great extent settled in Tambaram from a pragmatic point of view. I would like to look more closely at this part of the conference, for – in similar fashion to the Jerusalem texts – these passages make very clear who the "partners" really were and what sort of an understanding they had of each other; in particular how the churches of the South were seen. It is also relevant in this context to ask how much "foreignness" the partners expected one another to tolerate. In order to clarify their understanding of the nature and task of the church the conference in Tambaram adopted a text formulated by the second world conference on Faith and Order at Edinburgh in 1937:

The church is the body of Christ and the blessed congregation of all believers in heaven and on earth, the communion of saints. At the same time she is the realization of God's gracious plans for creation and salvation, and the constant tool of God's grace in Christ through the Holy Spirit, who fills all aspects of her life and sanctifies her constantly in all her many parts.

The question of the nature of the church was linked with the problem of the so-called indigenization of churches in the South, and so with the question, "which of the ecclesiastical structures brought in from the West are essential and which are merely Western, i.e. inessential and untenable for the East". In order to clarify this question and to encourage the churches of the South to develop their own forms of ecclesiastical structure, the conference returned to an image already used in Jerusalem, that of the seed corn. In each place where the seed flourishes, a form of Christianity particular to that place comes into being, as the fruit that is harvested depends not only on the seed but also on the soil that nurtures it. In the same way the aim of an indigenous church is not to conform to the way of life its members have previously known, but should be to try to "purify the life of the nation through the new life in Christ". It must not become a national church, content to be the church within the borders of that nation, but should rather seek to be part of the life of the church as a whole.

An important and troublesome problem for the churches of the South was the denominational fragmentation of mission work and the churches which had come into being through that work. This could already be seen at Edinburgh. The demand for a unity of the churches realized in organizational structures was to remain – alongside the discussion about "partnership" – the essential concern of the Southern churches at later world mission conferences. The representatives of the South introduced a declaration into the section negotiations on "cooperation and unity", in which they called urgently upon the churches and missions to work towards a real church union overcoming all denominational barriers. They were, however, not able to convince the others. The section report called for more intensive cooperation between the institutions and the churches, cooperation in which the churches of the South should be given decisive influence; the churches of the North were asked to consider very seriously the desire of the Southern churches for organic union.

Tambaram showed far greater regard for the worldwide church than previous mission conferences, in its awareness of the churches in the countries of the South and under the influence of the two other current ecumenical movements (the Life and Work, and the Faith and Order movements, which had both held world conferences in 1937). The title of the official conference report is significant: *The World Mission of the Church*. Nevertheless we must not lose sight of the fact that the counterparts of the representatives of the churches of the South were in the main representatives, not of European and American churches in the narrower sense, but of missionary organizations and societies from the North. In what follows, I would like to pursue the question about the relations between the churches, or rather between the churches of the South and the missions.

A considerable step forward at Tambaram as opposed to Jerusalem was that mission was fully considered and justified by the church, and not, as had so far been the case, by the individual Christian. Tambaram tried to link mission and church closely together with a clearly pragmatic aim: the young churches should be won for the task of mission. This was where the real impetus lay: that the young churches should become the bearers – possibly the main one – of mission in their own countries.

Section III's report ("The Incomplete Task of Proclamation") understood the term mission, or rather missionary proclamation, to be "the task of the whole church in all her branches and through the service of all her members so to represent Jesus Christ in the power of the Holy Spirit that the people put their trust in God through him, accept him as Saviour and serve him as their Lord in the community of his church". This includes proclamation "in the countries of both the old and the new churches". In both cases the task was incomplete. In the countries of the old church there were large parts of the country and areas of life in which renewed missionary proclamation was needed, and even greater areas where the gospel was still unknown. The participants established that in Europe a "deliberate and organized attempt" was being made "to drag millions of Christians into the stream of secularism". This was seen as a "lesson", that the church loses its soul "if the fire of her missionary zeal grows cold".

The moment the mission movement paid more attention to the worldwide church, it was inevitable that attention should also gradually be turned to the situation in the so-called sending churches. That mission was a task not only in the countries of the South but also in the countries of the old churches, can be heard in the Tambaram conference documents, though only in passing. In the German report this aspect was almost totally ignored. The main accent there was placed on the "incomplete task" in the countries of Asia and Africa. There was still a long way to go before the idea of "mission in six continents" could be formulated in 1963 at the world mission conference in Mexico City. In Tambaram, as before and after it, the main focus was still on the situation in the so-called "non-Christian" countries.

As regards the connection between mission and church, the delegates in Tambaram did at least go so far that Hartenstein was later able to write: "Whoever says church says mission. But also the other way round, whoever says mission says church." This insight would have to be "learned and practised in a completely new way". Glossing over it somewhat, he continued:

> We no longer spoke of Western and Eastern churches, of sending and receiving churches, and not at all of missions and churches, but rather we spoke of the church, God's congregation in the world and of its crucial task, the task in which the old and the new, the sending and the developing churches, all participate to the same extent.

Section III's report describes this mutual participation and twice uses the term "partnership" for it, a term which had already been introduced in a similar context in the English language documents from Edinburgh and Jerusalem, but does not appear in the German conference reports. Mission, according to the section III report, is "the task of the whole church for the whole world"; this did not however mean that the Northern churches could reduce their missionary involvement. To quote the report:

> The work that remains to be done is so immeasurably great, so urgent and so important that it requires all the strength of all Christians in all parts of the world. The task must be achieved nowadays in partnership between the old and the new churches by sharing together all aid available and by all Christians cooperating together.

Here partnership is understood as *a partnership of convenience in order to complete a task*; as effective a form of cooperation as possible to achieve a mutual goal. The section report summarizes this in one of eight concluding recommendations:

> We appeal for new forms of cooperation and joint planning of missionary proclamation, in which the various missionary societies and churches take on the responsibility together in each region and combine their personal and financial sources of help, in order effectively both to cope with the missionary needs of the large cities and the sprawling country areas and to meet the urgent opportunities which have arisen through the sudden opening of doors for the churches in India and Africa.

The last, short, recommendation goes beyond this and points the way to a new ecumenical exchange of workers from the South to the North: "We appeal to the younger churches to help the older churches by sending to them missions of witness and fellowship."

Partnership in mission was intended above all to give the churches of the South the right to a greater say and greater participation in the planning, carrying out and financing of missionary activities. The conference in Tambaram went further than the conference in Jerusalem in stating: "The place where this task (mission) is centred is the local church or congregation."

The section III report stresses the unanimous agreement of the young churches that missionaries from the old churches were still necessary, and demands a thorough training in evangelism for these colleagues. Section X was concerned with the role, function and training of future missionaries; it even expected a growing number of missionaries from abroad. The section did, however, say that the selection, training and induction, as well as the supervision, of these workers should increasingly become a shared responsibility of both the sending and the receiving churches. The development of the young churches required a new form of closer cooperation between sending and receiving churches. To bring this about, "possible adjustments" would have to be made to the relations between the missions and the churches.

> As the younger churches develop they should be invited to share responsibility for the assignment and direction of missionaries in their service. Reports of the meeting of the IMC at Jerusalem between the missions on the field and the younger churches may require adjustments to make this possible.

Accordingly, the reports on the financial situation of the young churches reflected the relations between the missions and the churches. The conference discussions revolved round the subject of the "self-sufficiency" of the churches as a necessary sign of their independence. Tambaram retracted somewhat from the demands made by Venn and Anderson in the context of the "three-self" formula and stressed – as had Jerusalem – that on the one hand the financial independence of a church was mainly a spiritual task, while on the other hand pointing out that the work of the missions had often weakened rather than encouraged an awareness of financial stewardship and independence in the churches. Even the German conference report states that the missionaries were "not free from a share of the blame" for the miserable financial situation of the churches of the South. Tambaram declared foreign financial aid still to be a necessity for the churches of the South. Where aid from abroad led to dwindling efforts on the part of the churches to support themselves, the foreign assistance should be slowly reduced but not suddenly cut off. It was suggested that aid payments should be made to the budgets of the church as a whole and not marked for individual projects. Aid payments should not be used "in order to humiliate the young churches or to exercise dominance over them". And finally,

> The idea of the economic common bond between the old and the young churches should be strongly emphasized, making it clear that the help given by the one church to the other should not be viewed as a kind of charitable act but rather as an act of fellowship.

What was new in Tambaram was the idea that the churches and the missions had to concern themselves with improvements in the social situation of the people in the countries of the South, or rather with fighting poverty. This social work had "to become the fourth kind of activity besides evangelization, education and medical mission". Far-reaching suggestions were made in Tambaram stemming from the concept of the kingdom of God. The transformation of the social order was to be seen as a part of the coming of the kingdom of God. The churches should stand up for people's rights without differentiating on account of race, birth, skin colour, class or culture. The congregations had to be made aware of the social consequences of the gospel. But above all the church should dare "to launch an attack on the serious damage caused by the present social order". The members of the German delegation opposed these ideas and contributed a minority opinion in which they pointed to the meaning of eschatology and stressed that it was not for the church to suggest a social programme. Nevertheless this newly extended definition of the task of mission laid the foundation for the later development work of the churches and for ecumenical welfare work.

To summarize, in the development of the world mission conferences from Edinburgh to Tambaram, we can see an ever greater awareness of the churches of the South on the part of the European and American missionary societies, as well as an increasing concentration on the subject of church and the relation between church and mission. While in Edinburgh they referred to the "church in the mission field" and in Jerusalem to "the relations between the churches", in Tambaram they spoke of "the world-wide mission of the church".

The first time the term "partnership" was used for the relationship between the local churches in Asia and Africa and the missions in Europe and America was in Jerusalem – and the second time in Tambaram – but only ever in the English language texts. However, between Jerusalem and Tambaram a significant transformation in the understanding of this "partnership" occurred. The Jerusalem understanding of partnership stressed more the new quality of the relationship as a relationship of confidence and fellowship. In Tambaram everything centred on the aim of partnership: the missionary task – partnership here becomes a synonym for effective cooperation.

The detailed regulations for cooperation in mission (such as the role of the missionary, planning and responsibility, financial aid) negotiated at both conferences were more or less the same. Their basic aim was that the local churches should take over increasing responsibility for mission, while financial and material support from outside should continue to be reduced and at the same time the spiritual consciousness for stewardship and financial independence be strengthened within the local churches.

Both conferences regretted that the availability of financial aid led to the local churches making no efforts to become financially independent. Both conferences also indicated in their declarations that the new partnership relationship and the new form of cooperation in mission also meant that the churches of the South could in future send "missionaries" to the churches of the North. It is worth noting that the term "partnership" is not used at all in the German language reports and declarations. The conference reports in general give the impression that the representatives of German missions had more reservations about the new independence of the churches of the South and placed far more emphasis on the dangers involved. The idea that the missions should also direct their attention to the situation in their own country, and have to rely on help from the churches of the South for this, is not reflected in the German conference reports.

4. Partners in mission: Whitby 1947

The term "Whitby" has become shorthand for the beginning of the concept of partnership. It is usually claimed that the term was introduced into the discussion of mission theology at the Whitby meeting of the extended committee of the International Missionary Council. I have already shown that this is not the case. Nearly twenty years before partnership was already being explicitly talked about in Jerusalem. Nevertheless it is the case that,

> The concept of partnership in obedience will always remain linked with the conference in Whitby. In the years that followed, it became a byword for the cooperation between the "old" churches and the "young" churches, and meant the beginning of a new era in mission history in many places. Mission work has to take place with a willingness to give up responsibility, its chief characteristic is not domination but service.

THE EXPERIENCE OF ECUMENICAL FELLOWSHIP

The conference in Whitby was, in terms of numbers, the smallest world mission conference to date. One hundred and twelve participants from forty countries met in the small isolated town near Toronto in Canada. Again more than half the participants (72) were representatives of the churches of the South. The meeting took place against the background of the disturbing and depressing experiences of the second world war and the developments of the early post-war years. The conference was marked on the one hand by an intensity of an atmosphere of trust and fellowship, and on the other hand by the consciousness of meeting in a time of crisis.

For many participants the experience of church unity and fellowship during the conference became a veritable "Pentecost experience". In Walter Freytag's conference report there is a hint of just how overwhelming this impression must have been against the background of so many years of darkness:

> It was the very composition of this conference that was so special.... What contrasts it embraced!... As well as the extraordinary variety of geographical background, there was the diversity of church background.... And in addition to the geographical and church diversity all the other differences and contrasts.... One could also name other contrasts such as those between old Western missionary leaders, who in long years of devoted service had travelled the whole path of all the changes in mission ideology through recent decades, and the representatives of the young churches, whose youngest members quite apparently thought little of commitment to tradition and pressed forward unimpressed by the deliberation taught by years of experience.

It was not merely contrasts and diversity which made their mark on what occurred, but rather unity and fellowship, a unity and fellowship with a spiritual foundation:

> One cannot forget such pictures: at the altar the archbishop of Sydney, with a Chinese man, a West Indian Negro and a Persian assisting him, and kneeling in a row before them an Indian, an African, a Frenchman, a German and a Batak.... Or the unforgettable evening when, overwhelmingly impressed by the task that lay ahead of us, the whole conference joined together in open prayer, and now voice after voice in many languages laid before the Lord of mission the needs of the nations, the willingness to make total sacrifice, and the plea for many new messengers of his word. Was this the real secret? Certainly, we had none of us experienced before what we experienced in Whitby.

Freytag's words contain a further keyword associated with Whitby and important for understanding this conference's concept of partnership: the "task", the "great commission". The conference delegates saw an abundance of challenges and problems ahead of them; the churches, however, were very weak as a result of the war years. In this situation the conference first took stock of what had happened in the churches, countries and regions during the years they had been separated from each other.

Some missions had not been able to keep their work going. Where it had been necessary and possible, other societies had helped them out. On the other hand, some churches had attained a new independence as a result of wartime events. Pastors and members of congregations had "in true sacrifice for the Lord's cause, battled through to real independence", in Freytag's words. "This was helped by the sudden loss of financial assistance from abroad, but even more by the necessity of standing up for the gospel in front of foreign rulers and their own people."

In Whitby a new spirit of optimism dominated. The delegates were asking "for the revolutionary, prophetic commission of the church and for a proclamation of the gospel which really expressed hope". They undertook, "in humble trust in God, to seek the way for world mission, the way which will lead both younger and older churches forward together with new joy and new trust in their shared task of winning humanity for Christ".

THE EMPHASIS ON THE COMMISSION AND THE IDEA OF PARTNERSHIP

Whitby was moved by a new missionary energy, which was basically the old energy returned. The old idea of the World's Student Christian Federation for the "evangelization of the world in this generation" was filled with new life. "The commission of our Lord Jesus Christ has by no means been carried out yet," wrote Carl Ihmels in the German report. There were still "unoccupied territories", "the vast majority of the population has still not been reached", "in thousands of villages and towns, the name of Jesus is still practically unknown".

Because, as was stated in Whitby, "some countries will perhaps only remain open for the preaching of the gospel of Christ for the next 10 or 15 years", it was "a duty to use this time which God still gives us to the full, with burning enthusiasm and our whole hearts". And finally, "it must be possible, people kept repeating, to enable all people to hear the gospel within our generation". During the conference it was made known that just beforehand 2000 American missionaries had set off for China aboard two steamers.

In order to understand the Whitby concept of partnership it is important to be aware of this atmosphere. For it was quite clear that the missionary societies of the North were unable to cope with this task alone. It was recognized "that this task could only be fulfilled by both partners together as 'partners in obedience'", as Freytag wrote. In this recognition, Ihmels detected an important difference to earlier conferences:

At the mission conference in Jerusalem in 1928, the leading men of Christianity in the East had spoken about the fact that they were now capable of taking over the work which the white missionaries had so far carried out. This raised the almost embarrassing question among the representatives of the missionary societies, "Do they still need us? Are we not a hindrance to Christianity in the mission fields on its way to independence?

In Tambaram the call for missionaries had been "stronger again". In Whitby it had become very clear "that the leading personalities of the young churches have freed themselves from all illusions and see the situation of their home countries very realistically". In the Whitby declaration on "Christian Witness in a Revolutionary World" we read:

In the young churches literally tens of thousands of men and women are needed for countless tasks.... The young churches are asking for men and women with proven spiritual training, whose joy it is to lead through humble service. If that is the case, well trained missionaries of every kind and every background can be of use.

The Whitby delegates were convinced that all divisions had to be overcome in order to carry out the missionary task, not only the divisions between the so-called "young and old churches", but also the divisions in confession and denomination. This feeling was strengthened by the special fellowship experienced during the conference itself. The representatives of the churches of the South pointed out again and again, as at previous conferences, just what a catastrophic effect the fragmentation of the churches had had in their countries. Even the missionary societies had to "allow themselves to be filled more and more with the true ecumenical spirit" and should no longer speak of "our Christians", "our congregations", "our churches". Freytag saw in this "a new perspective on the relationship between mission and church".

Consequences had to be drawn from this, but the process was not without tensions. Spheres of work, authorizations, rights and responsibilities had to be defined. As in earlier years, this gave rise to all kinds of fears. However, it seems that in Whitby the great stress laid on the commission made the difference between the "young" and the "old" churches pale into insignificance.

Alongside the emphasis on the shared commission, there were also political reasons for deciding to do away with the organizational divisions between local churches and missions in the mission fields, in other words, in the countries of the South. The break-up of the great colonial empires was in process, and a growing, strong, national self-confidence gave rise to the fear "that the 'missions', 'mission boards' and their 'presidents' could be seen as organs of a European or American imperialism and therefore as targets for government attack". For that reason, in these states only the churches should be independent bodies, in which native Christians themselves took the lead. This was the idea that finally led to the conference declaration under the title which became so famous, "Partners in Obedience".

THE WHITBY DECLARATION, "PARTNERS IN OBEDIENCE"

We have seen that partnership was already being talked about at mission conferences prior to Whitby, but Whitby stands out by reason of its long conference declaration. In five sections it describes in detail what a partnership relationship really should be and how it should be put into practice. Several of the suggestions made are still relevant today, so the declaration merits detailed examination.

Even the way the declaration came into being was for the participants an experience of "unity of purpose and outlook". It was quite clear that the questions arising would be very difficult to deal with, that they would cause sensitivity and tension. Therefore it was decided that the representatives of the missions and those of the churches of the South should each debate the questions separately with no prior consultation. Both groups wrote reports which were then presented to the forum. To everyone's surprise, according to W. Richey Hogg's report:

> When the two series of recommendations were read before the assembled conference, they proved to be almost identical! The air was charged with expectancy, and in a moment the whole gathering had come to its feet, singing the doxology. Later these two remarkably similar documents were combined and adopted by the conference under the title, "Partners in Obedience".

Stephen Neill remarked later that the conference declaration would possibly be considered a classic expression of the progress of the worldwide Christian church in the 20th century.

The declaration puts the term "partnership" right at its centre. No explanation is given of where the term comes from or what it really means. It is important to note that in the entire report of the German delegation the English word "partnership" is not translated with the German word *Partnerschaft*. *Partnerschaft* does not appear at all in the German translation of the declaration! Instead various different phrases are used: brotherly solidarity, brotherly mutuality, our common interests, our common activities, spiritual fellowship, true unity, model of brotherly fellowship. In his essay on the world mission conferences, Freytag speaks later of *Genossenschaft*, "cooperative". Ihmels offers "brotherly team in obedience" *(Brüderliche Arbeitsgemeinschaft im Gehorsam)* as a direct translation of "partnership in obedience". In another place he uses the

English word "partnership " without translating it. It is therefore quite clear that at that time the German participants did not speak of *Partnerschaft* in any context.

In its first section, the declaration "Partners in Obedience" gives reasons for the need for a new relationship between churches and missions. The participants themselves had sensed how "the power of God's Spirit tears down old walls and welds us together into the great fellowship of his church". They had also "become aware of the power and the passion of the contradicting forces" and had recognized that no divided church could withstand these forces. "Therefore the very force of this challenge drives us to join our union more firmly together and to perfect our partnership."

It is the threat from outside that makes partnership necessary. A further reason given is Christ's command to preach the gospel to every creature; in order to fulfil this command, the churches will have to unite all their powers. Finally, it is pointed out that time is pressing and the situation extremely urgent.

In this way the Whitby delegates arrived at a concept of partnership as something expedient. From this point of view Ihmels's translation "team" *(Arbeitsgemeinschaft)* is entirely appropriate. Such an understanding of partnership is quite different from the strong brotherly (and sisterly) partnership concept of the Jerusalem conference. And it is certainly not what V.S. Azariah had meant by "friendship" in Edinburgh. In view of the shared task, the conference declaration states, the distinction between "young" and "old" churches had become "obsolete"; however the "familiar expressions" would continue to be used "for convenience". The churches of the South and of the North were each allocated certain tasks within the partnership. The churches of the North were to "send the most capable men and women out of their midst to serve overseas". The churches of the South were to

> cast off once and for all the spirit of dependence on the older churches which has so inhibited them, and take their place on the true foundation of full spiritual parity. They should exercise their rights and administer their own affairs, lay down directions for their own work themselves, and under the guidance of God the Holy Spirit witness to the world in their own special way.

Mission boards were reminded of "their responsibility as connecting links by which the fellowship between the older and the younger churches could be made closer and more effective". The missionary societies, which had so far been the counterpart of the local churches even when the "old churches" were named as such, were now given a role as mediators. The actual partnership relations should in future develop between the churches of the South and North.

The declaration dealt with questions of detail in four problem areas: staff cooperation, financial aid, responsibility for decision-making, and administration. The aim of evangelistic work, as stated in the section on staff cooperation, must be to ensure that local personnel take over responsibility as quickly as possible. Absolute priority must therefore be given to the training of church leaders. On the role of the foreign missionaries, it states that they should understand themselves as "called by God to the special service of preaching the Word – invited by the church in a country to which they belong neither by birth nor by citizenship, in order to help the church fulfil her special task". They should integrate themselves fully into the local church and yet at the same time maintain close contact to their home churches. The local churches should have the right to a say in the choice of missionaries.

At the very beginning of the section on financial aid, reference is made to the difference in income between the foreign and the indigenous workers, and it is pointed out that this could become a "source of friction and of weakening of fellowship". The declaration insists that financial matters must "be looked at from a Christian point of view". Within the partnership there were no reasons why economically weak churches should hesitate to accept aid from economically strong churches, though the giving of aid must not be misused to exercise domination or to create dependence. In the case of money donated for a specific purpose, however, it was agreed that the donor had some right to know how the money had been used. Nevertheless the clear decision of the conference states: "The final responsibility for the way such money is used must rest with the church where the money is spent."

All these rules aimed at strengthening the financial independence and self-reliance of the local churches in relation to the missionary societies. The conference participants were well aware that the local churches would need to rely on foreign help for a long time to come. They therefore drew frequent attention to the need for "education in Christian stewardship".

The next section deals with the authority to make decisions and plans. First of all, the partners were all bound by the fundamental call to mission. Each particular question had to be considered and decided upon in the light of its relationship to this one all-embracing principle. The "all-embracing task of evangelism" is described in remarkable breadth, to the extent that here mission loses its traditional geographical North-South or East-West aspect:

> This includes the proclamation of the gospel in our time to those who have never heard it, as well as the conversion of those who are Christian in name

only, the reconquest of those huge areas in the older churches which have fallen away from the church, and the thorough Christianization of all areas of human life that have not yet recognized the rule of Christ.

Churches in the South and North were called upon to work closely together in their planning. To this end delegations from the Northern churches should travel to the countries of the South. But also the other way round, "the leaders of the younger churches should be given the opportunity to visit the older churches". The suggestion is even made that Christians from the South should live and work for a period of time in Europe and America as pastors in local congregation or as missionary society workers. Important suggestions were already being made for the ecumenical exchange of personnel and for ecumenical visits, suggestions which were eventually put into practice much later.

STEPHEN NEILL'S INTERPRETATION OF THE CONCEPT OF PARTNERSHIP

Stephen Neill and Max Warren, two of the men who did much to shape the conference in Whitby, published comprehensive studies on the concept of partnership in the years that followed. As far as I know, they are the only fundamental accounts of "partnership" available.

Stephen Neill reminds us of the atmosphere at the Whitby conference, the experience of spiritual fellowship and the appearance of the young churches "for the first time with fully equal rights". Looking back to earlier world mission conferences, he says that it was in Jerusalem that the younger churches first became visible, while in Tambaram the representatives of the young churches appeared still as "learners".

Neill portrays substantial developments and changes in the young churches. They had grown in size and numbers; they also had trained a class of church leaders who spoke with an authentic and original voice and who were in the process of developing their own theology. The churches had established themselves as organizations and developed instruments for witness and evangelization.

However, a few pages later, after a short description of the Whitby declaration, Neill warns against the creation of a "myth of the younger churches". Their church leaders tended to paint a much too positive picture of their situation:

> When they visit the countries of the West, younger church leaders tend to give a favourable picture of the church from which they come, of its capacities and achievements,... The Western churchman, meeting for the first time outstanding leaders of the younger churches, tends to be so astonished by their intellectual and spiritual grasp as to imagine that all the leadership of those churches is of equal calibre and so to misunderstand their real situation.

Neill claims that the independence of the young churches was not yet that advanced. They were still small in comparison to the task they had to face; they had only a very small class of trained leaders; and most of their members were poor, uneducated and "outcasts". In general the level of spiritual life was relatively low and the church leaders were far from being in a position to carry the burdens that were being laid upon them.

Neill thus puts the positive developments he had described before-hand into perspective. The consequences of his analysis are clear. He himself names them, using as an example something which occurred at the Whitby conference. The "friends from the West" had challenged the young church leaders:

> We fully recognize the right of the young churches to independence and the responsibility for their future. But how should five million non-Roman Christians in India, who are also mainly concentrated in the South, be able to bring about the evangelization of their 350 million compatriots in the foreseeable future?

"On some of the younger church leaders this direct challenge had a sobering effect," Neill reports. They had been speaking in general terms about their own responsibility. However, they had not really given a thought to what it would cost them to take over full responsibility. "And when they began to work it out, they found that the answer could only be in terms of continuing partnership, in a new form, between older and younger churches in obedience to the command of God." In this way Neill refers back to the crucial concepts of Whitby and makes the following explicit statement: "It is in the light of the evangelistic task that this new concept of partnership is to be understood."

This episode is a classic example of the interest of the Western missions and churches at that time. They had in this way made themselves and their work irreplaceable. The question arises whether under "partnership" they really expected anything new in the relationship between the local churches and the missions, or whether they were only looking for a form of words to bridge or indeed to conceal the tensions and conflicts between themselves and the churches of the South.

What becomes quite clear is how expedient the Whitby concept of partnership was. It is a pragmatic concept with the aim of bringing as many forces as possible together in order to carry out the task awaiting them in the shortest possible time. The crucial question is, who actually defines what the "urgent challenges" are and who determines what task is awaiting a church in their situation? Whitby had once again taken up the slogan of the "evangelization of the world in one generation", a thoroughly Western project, whose roots go back to the time of Western expansionism.

Were the Western churches and missionary societies really ready for a new chapter in the relations between North and South? Neill's further explanations of the detailed division of work between churches and missions gives a different impression. For Neill the new partnership demanded alterations and adjustments on both sides, though the position of the missionary, his freedom, his influence and certain privileges had to remain secure. Here the dominant interest is in protecting vested rights, which is why Neill takes great pains to put the young churches' wish for independence into perspective.

MAX WARREN'S UNDERSTANDING OF PARTNERSHIP

Some years later, in his small volume *Partnership*, Max Warren takes an approach different from Stephen Neill's. Warren's observations are particularly important because he tries fundamentally to establish and anchor the concept of partnership both theologically and ecclesiologically. As far as I know this has remained the only comprehensive study on the concept. In contrast to Whitby or to Neill, Warren understands "partnership" not primarily as a matter of expedience, but as something more extensive at the level of relationships between churches and individuals. Ultimately Warren's thinking comes much more from the idea of ecumenical unity, *koinonia*, and in his observations he makes several references to the results of the second assembly of the World Council of Churches in Evanston in 1954.

Warren starts out from a general colloquial definition of partnership: "Sharing with another or with others in action." This definition includes his two essential keywords: sharing and action. Three factors go into making up this concept of partnership: involvement, responsibility and liability. Without these three there is no partnership. These three aspects appear again and again in Warren's deliberations. A further mark of partnership – freedom – is then added: "The essence of partnership is that it is a relationship entered upon in freedom by free persons who remain free." And finally, he writes that the relationship of partnership is dynamic. "By dynamic, of course, I mean a living relationship which is continually growing and developing, the very opposite of 'static'."

Warren understands partnership as the opposite of the dominant patterns of relationships in society, or more precisely as the opposite of the "ethics of dominating power". The adjective "dominating" should give rise to negative associations, whereas partnership is seen as something positive. Warren believes a fundamental change in the relations between people to be necessary, a change which he can call "the new creation", "revolution", or "conversion". He summarizes the necessary change in perspective and location thus:

> The converted man must not only no longer think of himself, a negative change, but positively must think of and for his neighbour, who has hitherto been the victim of his egotism, and is now the object of his concern. Victimization makes way for partnership.

Warren's theological exposition, his "theology of partnership", is crucial. His thesis is:

> First, that partnership is an idea congenial to the very nature of God. Second, that partnership speaks of God's relationship with man. Third, that partnership indicates the true relationship between man and his fellow-men.

In God's revelation of himself to humankind, Warren sees his three named aspects of partnership: God becomes involved with humans (*involvement*); God is responsible for the redemption of all people (*responsibility*); and finally, by giving himself up on the cross, God's Son accepts liability (*liability*) for the creation of human beings in such a way that people can cooperate in freedom with God or can refuse this cooperation. Warren writes: "It is at least a striking fact that in his supreme self-revelation we can distinguish so clearly those elements which, in our human experience, go to make up the concept of partnership."

Going even further, Warren gives a trinitarian basis to his understanding of partnership. When the church confesses its faith in the Holy Trinity, it expresses its conviction that God himself is the "archetype" of every relationship between people. God's relationship to humankind corresponds to this archetype of relationship contained in God himself, and the relationships of people with each other should correspond to this archetype too. He understands human actions as actions that correspond to the divine reality that has gone before.

However, it remains an open question what, apart from the three named principle aspects, determines such a relationship of partnership in concrete and material terms. Warren names only freedom and love as elements. People are free to answer God or to refuse to answer. Every answer, however, means a willingness to get involved on the part of the person answering – *involvement*. Accordingly, the person must also take on *responsibility* and accept the *liability* that goes with discipleship. In this context Warren can speak of discipleship as partnership.

Warren summarizes the theological basis underpinning partnership from which corresponding human action in relationships may then grow:

If, so far, we have established that the concept of partnership is at least congenial to the nature of God as he has revealed himself to us: and if we have seen that there is a proper, though of course by no means exclusive, sense in which God's relationship with man "in history" can be said to find its fulfilment in a partnership of redemptive service; it is both possible and right that we should see what bearing all this has upon the relationship of man with his fellow-men, and discover in that relationship a theological justification for the concept of partnership.

Warren takes up the concept of *koinonia* again in order to describe the essence of interpersonal partnership. Following A.R. George, he is able to translate koinonia with "partnership", "fellowship" or "having a share". The crucial factor, according to Warren, is that the reason for the fellowship be found beyond the fellowship itself. The inner bond which holds the fellowship together is found "in Christ".

> It is then "in him", as an objective reality, that Christians have their fellowship.... It was "in the participation" in the sacrament that the early Christians were most conscious of their oneness with their Lord and with one another.

It is by returning to the idea of *koinonia* that Warren can link "partnership" to the nature of the church at a fundamental level: "The Christian church as the New Testament presents it is intended to be an adventure in partnership." In this way partnership is no longer just one of many possible forms of interchurch cooperation for the joining of forces – as at Whitby – but belongs to the nature of the church and its theologically grounded way of existence. If the church wants to bear witness to God, the only way in which it can do this is by living a relationship of partnership in relations between people and between churches, and that means a relationship of involvement, responsibility and liability in freedom and love.

Warren develops the consequences of such a concept of partnership in two directions: with regard to the ecumenical unity of the churches and with regard to the mission of the church. What is of particular interest here is the consequence for mission.

Warren sees the necessity of a relationship of partnership between Christians in Asia and Africa and in the West. The starting point for any consideration has to be the observation that in Africa and Asia a fundamental revolt against the West is taking place. Warren finds three factors responsible for this: first, the discovery of a new self-respect among the peoples of Asia and Africa; second, the spread of communist ideas especially in Asia; and third, the growth in population. And what does partnership mean in this context? Warren aims primarily at a better human understanding. A first step is therefore a change of perspective:

Perhaps our first task is to see ourselves as others see us. We who come out of a culture which has been profoundly influenced by the Christian faith... are apt to be quite unaware of the degree to which this inner core of Christian conviction is mediated to other peoples of other cultures with the tacit assumption that all the trimmings which go with these convictions are equally part of the gospel.

Warren wants Christians in the West to develop an appreciation of the problems of "spiritual imperialism", which are accompanied by a non-awareness of the values of other cultures and which are now being rejected by Asians and Africans – as are other forms of imperialism. Closely connected to this, Warren points to a certain "impatient, aggressive charity of the West", and refers here to the problem of financial aid and particularly to the injustice which all too often arises from such aid:

It does not make for the flowering of the finer virtues, let alone of partnership, when material resources are poured in from America to one area while an area immediately adjacent, thanks to its historical links with, say, Britain or Germany, has to be content with plain living.

A source of confusion in the churches of the South is the difference in concept and approach adopted by Americans and by Europeans – the Americans geared to rapid success, the Europeans acting rather with deliberation. Warren quotes a Pakistani church leader: "We churches in Asia cannot afford any divisions. But we have to accept divisions, because we cannot afford to lose the support of the divided churches of the West."

Once again Warren looks at difficulties of understanding between the cultures. Christians in Africa or Asia could often not understand the inner spiritual dimension of missionary work or interchurch aid. And on the other side: "There is still on the part of the great majority of European and American Christians an almost complete failure to understand the position of their fellow-Christians in Asia and Africa." Here lies one of the most important challenges for partnership, to enable and encourage each side to understand the other, and so to overcome and remove misunderstandings and conflicts.

What was special in Warren's concept was without a doubt the fact that he managed to supply a fundamentally theological basis for the term "partnership", a term frequently criticized for being neither biblical nor theological. It is for Warren imperative that people, Christians from different continents and cultural contexts, should treat one another as partners because God himself has entered into this type of relationship with human beings. Furthermore, Warren describes the terms of relationship within the Trinity between God – Father, Son and Spirit – as ones of "partnership", a relationship of involvement, responsibility and liability in freedom and love. The relationship between God and humans and the relationships of people with each other should correspond to these terms, and therefore interpersonal and interchurch relations should take the form of partnership.

I have already pointed out that Warren's understanding of partnership goes beyond a pure purpose or task orientation, which was the understanding of partnership held by the world mission conference in Whitby or by Stephen Neill. Warren's concept of partnership contains a further dimension. Partnership for him goes beyond the description of formal structures for relationships, and gains a function as regards content. Warren goes back to ideas put forward at the Evanston assembly of the World Council of Churches. Two aspects must be mentioned as regards content.

First, the experience of Christian unity makes the separation and division of the church increasingly unbearable. For this reason churches must make concrete efforts at all levels to achieve a stronger Christian community.

Second, Christians may not seek peace for themselves alone, but must also work for justice for others. The striving for church unity and involvement for worldwide justice are for Warren the content of partnership. He asks two concrete questions:

> Is your church seriously considering its relations to other churches in the light of our Lord's prayer that we may be sanctified in the truth and that we may all be one? Is your congregation in fellowship with sister congregations around you, doing all it can to ensure that your neighbours shall hear the voice of the one Shepherd calling all men into the one flock?... Does your church speak and act against... injustice?

Warren addresses the local congregation with these questions. The congregation is the ecclesiastical social form which is challenged to exist in partnership. Congregations are called to partnership.

5. The participation of the partners in the *missio Dei*: Willingen 1952, Achimota 1958, Mexico City 1963

I have described in detail the negotiations and achievements of the individual world mission conferences. This served to trace the development from dependent congregations on the mission fields of European and American missionary societies into independent and autonomous churches recognized as partners by the missions. While on the one hand these churches increasingly took over the mission work in their own countries, at the same time they insisted more and more on coming into contact with the churches of the North and no longer having dealings only with the representatives of the missionary societies. This was the first step on the way to the realization of worldwide ecumenical relations between the churches. The 1947 world mission conference in Whitby and the partnership in mission agreement reached there formed the conclusion to the first stage of this development. At this conference the basis was laid for further ecumenical relations in mission.

Around the same time – 1948 – the World Council of Churches was founded in Amsterdam. Here was a new ecumenical forum for worldwide interchurch relations, which had often been demanded by the churches of the South and was welcomed by them. The coming into existence of the WCC had an effect on mission relations. Very soon discussions began about the integration of the World Council of Churches and the International Missionary Council (IMC), discussions whose beginnings went back to the time of the world mission conference in Tambaram.

The theological debate on mission was led to think in greater depth about the relations between mission and church, a process which left its mark on the world mission conferences following Whitby in Willingen, Achimota and Mexico City. At the end of these conferences a new, ecumenical understanding of mission and a clearer view of the meaning of mission for the essence of the church had been reached.

With regard to the "Partnership of the Churches in Mission", no substantial new insights arose immediately at this period. What is important in the context of this study is what new understanding of mission was worked out by the ecumenical church community and what the consequences of this were for the idea of "Partnership in Mission".

THE WORLD MISSION CONFERENCE IN WILLINGEN 1952

When, in July 1952, the 181 delegates of the International Missionary Council came together for an extended meeting at Willingen in Germany, they were under the impression that it was a time of far-reaching crisis for the mission movement, a time of fundamental questioning, of change and of a possible fresh start. Walter Freytag wrote that mission "as our fathers knew it" was nearing its end. While mission in the old sense still took place, it could however have the effect of "a weakening in the fulfilment of the commission of Christianity" and was at best "untamed growth". Among the elements of this "change in era" was the approaching end of the colonial age. In many countries in Asia and Africa national movements for self-reliance and independence were gaining strength.

For the missions this meant some restrictions for their work. Directly before the Willingen conference, the missionary societies discovered that China had closed its borders to missionaries. The shock of this cast a cloud over the conference. Furthermore, the missions and the churches of the South frequently felt challenged by a reawakening of the great religions, particularly in Asia, and by the spread of communism. As far as Europe was concerned the mission representatives saw secularism as a great danger for the churches. The hoped-for revival of the post-war years failed to appear.

The delegates to Willingen found themselves in a changed world. The age of the great pioneers of mission had come to an end. This also meant a crisis in the current understanding of mission. Max Warren, who gave a lecture in Willingen with the revealing title "The Christian Mission and the Cross", spoke of an "orgy of self-criticism" in mission thinking. The time had come for the mission and the churches to consider fundamentally what the nature of mission was, its justification and its aim. In this way Willingen became the world mission conference that theologically speaking achieved the most.

Within the bounds of this study it is not possible to describe the manifold aspects and lines of discussion in Willingen's theological debates. I shall therefore neither consider the evening lectures, which had a great influence on the conference, nor the comprehensive preparatory material.

The theme of the conference was "The Missionary Obligation of the Churches". It took up a line of thought from former conferences, that of winning the whole church over to a missionary orientation. At the same time the question of the church and ecclesiological considerations also became more central. The conference worked on the subject in five groups: (1) the missionary obligation of the church, (2) the indigenous church, (3) the role of the missionary society, (4) missionary vocation and training, (5) reviewing the pattern of missionary activity.

The report from the first group anchors the "mission movement of which we are a part" in the triune God. This points the way programmatically for the new ecumenical understanding of mission, an understanding of mission which differs from the founding of mission at the "time of the fathers". Mission and church, as the report put it, are both derived from the actions of God in the Trinity:

> God created all things and all people, in order that in them the glow of his love might be reflected; therefore nothing is excluded from the realm of his saving love.
>
> All people are entangled in a general alienation from God, from which no one can escape without help.
>
> God sent a Saviour, a Shepherd, to seek and to save all those who are lost, a Redeemer, who through his death, his resurrection and his ascension into

heaven broke down the barrier between God and mankind, who has made a perfect and sufficient sacrifice, and who in himself has created a new humanity, the body whose exalted and reigning head is Christ.

When this work was completed and the foundation laid, God sent his Spirit, the Spirit of Jesus, who gathers us together as one body in him;... who gives us strength to continue his mission as his witnesses and messengers....

In Christ we are chosen, reconciled with God through him, as members of his body, sharing in his Spirit and inheritors of his kingdom through hope, and through just these facts we are called to full participation in his saving mission. We cannot be part of Christ without being part of his mission to the world. The same acts of God which brought the church into existence also place her under an obligation to mission in the world.

Mission and church are "placed in the widest possible frame within the history of redemption and God's redemptive plan". God himself begins with mission by sending his son. The mission of the church is participation in the *missio Dei*, God's mission, from which both church and mission have their origin. This is the crucial new insight from Willingen. Mission is no longer a task or duty which the church sets itself, but rather, as the church originates from God's mission, mission is an essential characteristic of the church. Hartenstein wrote in the German conference report that this was the reason for "the absolute and complete" unity of mission and church:

The nature of the church is to be found in her participation in God's redemptive plan, in his mission for the salvation of the world. Mission reveals the church in its most profound sense to be God's mission, the new humanity, the first fruits of salvation. To speak correctly of the church means to speak of her ministry to the world. The church exists in her mission.

With the Willingen conference, missionary work gained both a new justification and a new goal. That Christ himself "is always moving through the world, going into the nations to call people to follow him and to serve him" was the new insight concerning the reason for mission. Mission is "nothing other than witness to the God who comes, the God who came, comes and will come to reconcile us and to establish his kingdom in a new world". According to the new understanding, it is not the church which is the final goal of mission, but rather, taking the Dutch theology of apostolate, the kingdom of God, "which means, the dominion of Christ over the world and the whole cosmos".

Hartenstein confessed "with deep joy" that this conference declaration blazed the trail for a new theology of the kingdom of God and a view of God's plan as the history of salvation. However, what he criticized about the influence of the Dutch theologians was that the concept of the kingdom of God was restricted to "the vertical", that the church no longer appeared as body, but only as event. The question of the relationship between the church and the kingdom of God as well as between the church and the world needed even further clarification. Nevertheless Hartenstein stressed that mission was "on the right road":

> For too long we have seen the church only as the goal of God's ways. With the recognition of the kingdom, the horizon of God's plan of salvation is torn open and we behold his eternal thoughts and his cosmic miraculous ways, whose end is truly the "physical reality", the real new creation of heaven and earth.

Based on its new understanding of mission, the Willingen conference spoke of the "whole missionary task" and thereby opposed an understanding of mission which was geographically understood and limited. The church was to be sent "into every inhabited area of the world". Mission would always cross borders, but these could no longer be equated with national borders, and certainly not "with some assumed line between the "Christian West" and the "non-Christian East". Hartenstein wrote that every congregation was called to preach the gospel in its own area, and every congregation shared the responsibility for preaching the gospel to the ends of the earth. Much more strongly than at previous world mission conferences, Willingen took up the idea that it was no longer permissible to understand mission as a geographical crossing of borders from North to South. The churches of the North were challenged to missionary activity in their own societies more intensely than before, and the local congregations were reminded of their missionary obligation in their own context. The conference pointed out that not only the terms "young" and "old" churches were factually incorrect and had already been rejected in principle at earlier conferences, but also the terms "sending" and "receiving" churches. This was the consequence of the new theological understanding of mission. Nevertheless the terms were still used, even on this occasion, described by C. Ihmels as a "legitimate abbreviation".

The conference papers and German reports continue to be dominated by the North-South orientation of mission. They do point out, however, that in Europe many people have lost contact with the church. It is therefore the churches' task to evangelize the masses. The missionary societies have a different task: they must arouse enthusiasm for the missionary vocation in their home countries. Congregations need to make intercession for mission. Beyond that the churches of the North should work towards finding more missionaries prepared to serve. A distinction was made in Willingen between the "total missionary responsibility of the churches" and service in "foreign mission". This meant that the existing arrangement of missionary societies' work could continue. The question remains whether the radicalism of the new theological understanding of mission had really been incorporated into mission practice at all.

If one wishes to trace the consequences of Willingen's insights in mission theology, it is necessary to examine the role of the missionary societies. In a contribution to one of the Willingen working groups, Walter Freytag describes a fundamental calling into question of the missionary societies. While mission work had become impossible in certain countries, and other churches in the South expected more interchurch aid than missionary work, the missionary societies faced the actual or threatened loss of their function. According to Freytag, there was an external challenge to the missionary societies' continued right to exist, and the societies were being torn apart by internal tensions. Some congregations were prepared to support only traditional pioneering mission and denominational tensions were making the work more difficult. The missionary societies, Freytag says, were not allowed to be the church; neither were they allowed even to "take on the functions of church leadership" in the churches of the South. Instead they should be a tool and support the "preaching of the gospel by the young churches". This posed the "serious question" to the missionary societies, whether they were prepared, "should the situation arise, to obediently sacrifice their own existence". The more the churches – now including the churches of the North – were being motivated towards responsibility for mission, the more the continued existence of the missionary societies was being called into question. However, it remained unclear whether a greater integration of mission and church would bring about the hoped-for congregational renewal. Many people feared it would just mean more bureaucracy.

The report of group III on the role of the missionary societies rejected a monopoly of these organizations and called upon the churches not to withdraw from their responsibility for mission. Nevertheless, it was agreed that some sort of missionary organization would still be necessary in the future. The most important task for the missionary organizations in the churches of the North was to remind the Christians in local congregations of their obligation to mission. Beyond that they should "explain the significance of the young churches and of new forms of missionary service". The churches of the South would continue to need support from the missionary societies, both with finances and personnel, "as a sign of partnership". The conference document resolutely opposed the demand for financial "self-sufficiency" as the mark and aim of an independent indigenous church. Missionary societies and churches should work towards transferring responsibility to the young churches as quickly as possible. The aim should be the integration of mission into the church.

As a continuation of the theological thinking at Willingen, it would have been a good idea to examine traditional mission structures more closely. And yet in Willingen they still spoke emphatically of the special task of "foreign mission", even though the churches of the South rejected this term. The questions remain, whether in the end the special role given to "foreign mission" prevented the true theological and structural integration of mission and church, and whether this was responsible for the fact that the idea of worldwide, not geographically determined, mission never really reached the congregations at all. The idea of integration threatened the *opus proprium* of the missionary societies. On the other hand, some pleaded to maintain the current position. "The question about the essential nature of foreign mission became louder the more intensively the question of integration was considered."

The principle of partnership is again paramount as far as relations between the churches, or rather between the churches and the missionary societies, are concerned. Group V at the Willingen conference concerned themselves with "reformulating the structures and patterns of missionary cooperation". The comprehensive report begins with the statement that the young churches now appear "as free partners in the Christian enterprise". Real "partnership in obedience between the younger and older churches" is becoming more and more manifest.

With these words Willingen explicitly adopts the formulations of Whitby 1947. The German report also points this out: C. Ihmels writes that the mission boards must be prepared "to work together with the young churches in a truly brotherly fashion". The use of the English term "enterprise" in conjunction with the concept of partnership (translated as "cooperation" in the German version) makes it clear how, even at this world mission conference, partnership was understood in a functional way, as a means of achieving a goal and completing a task.

In themselves the conference demands do not go beyond what had been said in Whitby and earlier on the principle of working together in partnership. According to the Willingen documents the decision-taking competence and responsibility for missionary work should lie with the churches of the South and particularly with the local congregations.

The report from group IV was critical: "Partnership is not enough, for it presupposes both the existence of independent groups and the freedom to work together, or not. In the fellowship of the body of Christ, we are called to serve in unity." Throughout the years the real concern of the churches of the South had been to overcome the denominational fragmentation imported from the West. The idea of partnership was not enough for them or – we may suppose – the emphasis on the principle of partnership had so far had no effect on the problem of the lack of unity, although since Jerusalem it had been linked to the call for missionary societies to cooperate more closely in the mission areas of the South.

To summarize, at a time of crisis in mission thinking the conference opened the door for an entirely new theological understanding of mission and theological integration of mission and church. A new development was set in motion but was a long way from completion. In comparison, the practical clarification of the relations between the missionary societies and the churches of the South was pushed into the background. Using the Whitby slogan, "partnership in obedience", the concept of partnership was adopted and raised to a principle as far as practical questions were concerned, without defining more clearly what it really meant. Only at the following world mission conference in Ghana was a more thorough understanding of the term partnership achieved.

This was the shortest world mission conference so far, and the one with the smallest number of delegates. Assessments of its proceedings and the results of its negotiations are for the most part very restrained. Georg Friedrich Vicedom wrote that it "would perhaps not be counted among the significant" conferences. The English conference report is extremely critical of the proceedings and results. The delegates faced internal and external tensions, and there is mention of a mood of resignation and paralysis, especially among the participants from continental Europe.

The conference declaration was for the first time not addressed to a larger, non-church public, not to "the world", nor even to the churches, but "only" to the member councils of the International Missionary Council. It bears witness to the delegates' great perplexity in dealing with crucial questions which arose during the debates. Questions of organization – particularly the proposed integration of the International Missionary Council and the World Council of Churches – took up most of the time in the conference discussions, not entirely according to plan.

In the context of this study, though, the conference is of special significance. For the first time since Whitby in 1947, the term "partnership in obedience" was a specific topic of the discussions. However, tensions broke out between the churches of the South and the missionary societies which throw light on the problems of interchurch relations and the conflicts arising from the understanding of partnership that prevailed.

Around 180 conference participants, including 68 delegates from the member councils of the International Missionary Council, came together over the New Year as 1957 turned to 1958 on the campus of the new university being built in Achimota close to the Ghanaian capital Accra. The choice of conference venue in the newly independent country was intended by the missions to signal support for independence movements and "to demonstrate the missions' freedom from Western colonialism". The idea was to show how important Africa was for the missions and the church, and at the same time to put in writing "that today mission is no longer the business of Western Christianity alone". The subject of the conference was "The Christian Mission at this Hour". For the first time a procedure was adopted by which the delegates were divided into committees where they discussed the International Missionary Council's various fields of work, and then divided up again into five groups discussing various subjects: (1) the Christian witness in society and nation, (2) the Christian church facing its calling to mission, (3) the Christian church and non-Christian religions, (4) the place and function of the missionary, (5) what does "partnership in obedience" mean?

However, although the subject was nowhere to be found on the agenda, the conference debates were dominated by the question of the integration of the International Missionary Council and the World Council of Churches. The pros and cons were weighed on the basis of a draft plan for integration in special additional plenary sessions. The plan suggested that the IMC should be established as an independent commission of the World Council of Churches, although its members did not necessarily need to be members of the World Council of Churches. After tough negotiations the delegates agreed in principle to the integration plan (with 58 votes for and 7 votes against). As the resolution on integration has nothing to do with interchurch relations, I mention it here only to complete the picture, and will not be discussing it further.

The negotiations and results of the Achimota conference reflect the strained relations between the churches of the South and the Northern missionary societies. Both sides were clearly disappointed and dissatisfied with what had so far been achieved!

Walter Freytag's speech on "Changes in the Patterns of Western Missions" analyzes the problem very acutely. He names three "facts" or "new realities" that characterize the changed situation for the work of the missionary societies. Firstly, "there is the fact of new independent states creating new political and cultural situations". A new national self-consciousness, yearning for equal rights and self-realization, is particularly sensitive to all influences from outside. The second new reality are the independent churches in Asia and Africa who are "striving... to a status of equality, and to find their own way of expressing their faith; and they, too, are sensitive as is all young life". Thirdly, Freytag names the "ecumenical era": the world is drawing closer together, the religions are "transgressing their traditional boundaries". Parallel to this, "new forms of Christian unions "are coming into being, which want to make their members aware of a worldwide fellowship and global responsibility.

These developments influence the structure of Western missionary societies in three ways: first as limitation and constriction of their opportunities to work; secondly, as what Freytag calls "the lost directness"; and thirdly, as the "loss of the model of what mission is". These new developments and demands for cooperation limited the freedom of the missionary societies considerably and often led to a "levelling downwards". The "direct, permanent participation of the giver" was becoming less and less possible within the framework of interchurch aid. The societies had lost their "monopoly of service".

Freytag is the first representative of the missionary organizations to describe with such clarity how far-reaching the consequences of the "partnership" relationship now claimed between churches and missions were, especially for the structures and working methods of the mission organizations themselves. The new partnership relationship (echoing Whitby, Freytag speaks of "partnership in obedience") meant a loss of initiative, influence and power on the part of the missionary organizations. It is equally apparent, both from Freytag's speech and from the conference proceedings in general, that the missionary organizations had not so far drawn these necessary structural conclusions and basically were still not prepared to do so.

Freytag called upon his listeners to consider "the central task" of mission. He started with the theological insights of Willingen, that "mission is sharing in God's action". However, he then demanded special rights for foreign mission and the organizations entrusted with it: "missions in their empirical form... are one essential link in the great variety of services offered by the churches". The task of mission – and here he means the missionary societies – consists in "being sent to proclaim the gospel outside the churches, and to gather the scattered children of God together".

Partnership in mission which had been invoked since the Jerusalem conference called into question the special role of the missionary societies. Partnership required that they give up power. In Achimota it now became clear that the missionary organizations found this very difficult. The traditional structures of the missionary societies proved themselves to be "in many cases almost immune to that which theological insight and the analysis of the situation urgently demanded".

Freytag's much quoted sentence comparing the situations of the Jerusalem and the Achimota conferences makes clear that it really was a question of power: "Then missions had problems, but today they have become the problem themselves." This statement has often been taken to mean that the theological justification of mission had become a problem. However, Freytag's remarks show that, at least in part, the problem was one of the missionary societies' lost claim to leadership:

> There was no question that the initiative in witness and action was with Western missions as they stood. Today we do not speak of the initiative of Western missions but only of their contribution. But more than this: we are uncertain about the form they take, even the historic, basic conceptions of mission are being questioned.

Missionary societies had lost their claim to leadership, and the very basis of missionary activity was being called into question. This led to uncertainty in the organizations, particularly with regard to the role of the missionaries, and to great perplexity about structures for future cooperation. James K. Mathews prepared a paper for the group considering the meaning of the Whitby phrase "partnership in obedience", which included a review of the changes that had actually taken place in the relations between the churches. All in all it was a very disappointing summary. Although a general shift of responsibility from the missions to the churches had taken place, Mathews pointed out that the very talk of young and old churches, or of sending and receiving churches, was a sign that partnership has not yet been realized. Furthermore he pointed to the economic dependence of the churches of the South and finally to the fact that the missionary societies were incapable of giving up their "heritage". He described the prevailing situation thus:

> We have outlived a period in which the older church was expected to say "No" and the younger church "Yes"; and are in a period in which the older church says "Yes" and the younger church "No". But have we reached that stage of maturity where "Yes" and "No" may be used freely by both parties, so that true Christian conversation and true Christian community may be realized because all have heard the "Yes" of God through Jesus Christ?

Mathews stressed that the churches needed one another, because only a brother could speak the word of acceptance. His observations on what that meant were also incorporated into the group work report:

> Can the younger church accept the older church, with all its pride, its shortcomings, its heritage, its guilt by association? Can the older church accept the younger church in spite of its smallness, its weakness, its spirit of independence? By "accept" conformity is not implied, but mutual respect for selfhood.

For Mathews, however, it was a fact "that we do not fully accept ourselves nor our brothers and so partnership in the gospel is inadequately realized".

The report on the group discussions states that the recognition that mission and church belong together "is not a basic principle in much of our thinking and speaking or in our practice". The assembly should "mark the end of the usage of those terms" which distinguish between sending and receiving or older and younger churches. The report saw the real problems in the practical questions, "how are decisions to be made about the sending and receiving of missionaries?" The point was made that the partners had to "decide together", and at the same time that that had very great practical difficulties.

It is no coincidence that the tensions of the Achimota conference centred on interchurch relations. In Jerusalem, the mission representatives of the North had awarded the churches of the South the status of equal partnership as "a gracious advance concession", although they did not seriously regard this parity as already attained. In Whitby, when the missionary societies themselves were in a weaker position, the term partnership served to link the churches of the South to the mission aims of the missionary societies. Even Willingen served – in spite of all the necessary theological clarification it achieved – to "monopolize the church for mission", primarily the churches of the South. At the same time, counter to theological perception, missionary practice and thinking continued to be oriented to a one-way traffic, from North to South. The missionary societies continued to hold on to the old picture of mission in spite of all new theological findings. They had not given enough thought to the consequences a change would bring for their own actions and dealings. They had not reacted to the legitimate demands of the churches of the South – even if it was only the wish for a careful use of language so as to avoid discriminatory distinctions between young and old or sending and receiving churches, or the demand for real church unity. They frequently stated that mission in the old sense had come to an end, but this statement had still not been put into practice.

The Achimota conference statement on this main theme used very strong words. It began emphatically with the recognition of Willingen that "the Christian world mission is Christ's and not ours". The distinction between young and old churches "obscures the status of churches before God, and so obscures the truth that... they are all equally called to obedience to their one missionary Lord". The statement criticized the lack of cooperation and the attempts being made to protect vested rights.

> To seek first to safeguard the interests, the activities, the spheres of influence of our church, our mission, our confessional body is in the end a denial of mission... any kind of claim to the sole control of any area... seems to us incompatible with a recognition of our common calling...

At the same time the conference statement marked out the general help-lessness with regard to new and adequate forms of cooperation:

> Beyond the complexities of interchurch relationships, beyond the safeguard-ing of organizations, beyond any mistrust of one another, beyond any pride in numbers and size... He is calling us out – out beyond the frontiers of the churches, out beyond the sphere of interchurch relationships, out beyond the traditional patterns of missionary activities, out into a new exposure to him, out into a new and more real commitment to one another, out into the world where He is the Hidden King.

The significance of the Achimota conference is that these inconsis-tencies and embarrassing difficulties were actually expressed there. Achimota showed

> that alongside and independently of the theological understanding of mission that had meanwhile been worked out, people still carried around with them the picture of the fathers of the mission, a picture which no longer corresponded to the current situation.

This also applied to the concept and understanding of partnership. So far the idea of partnership, or of "partnership in obedience", had not been able to reshape the relations between the missions and the churches. Achimota had pointed to the conflicts, but had not been able to resolve them. They were to break out again with new vehemence at later world mission conferences.

The world mission conference in Mexico City 1963

The world mission conference in Mexico City, for which approxi-mately 200 participants gathered in the Mexican capital in December 1963, was the first world mission conference after the integration of the International Missionary Council (IMC) and the World Council of Churches (WCC). It was the second general assembly of the Commis-sion on World Mission and Evangelism of the WCC. The inaugural ses-sion of this commission had taken place immediately following the inte-gration of the IMC and the WCC at the third assembly of the WCC in New Delhi, in December 1961. The integration signified a new age in the structural relations between mission and church. From it arose new insights into the questions of unity and the task of the churches.

1. The integration of the International Missionary Council and the World Council of Churches in New Delhi 1961

The integration of the IMC and the WCC was the "organizational expression of the theological understanding of the relationship between mission and church which had so far been achieved". What was being given structural form here was not only the pressure from the churches in Asia and Africa for a greater unity of the churches, but also the theological insight that neither church nor mission can exist without the other.

The formula that "the whole church must bring the whole world the whole gospel" found its institutional expression in this integration. What is crucial is that the integration was understood as mutual and balanced, not an adding together of two institutions, and certainly not as the subordination of the mission movement to the World Council of Churches. The committee of the Commission on World Mission and Evangelism at the assembly in New Delhi used the following phrasing to make this clear:

> The amalgamation must mean that the World Council of Churches take the missionary task into the real centre of its life and that in just the same way the missionary institutions of the church see their work in an ecumenical perspective.

This was intended to prevent the churches from relinquishing to the Commission their responsibility for mission. But neither should the relevant department of the WCC nor the Commission take sole responsibility. The committee demanded

> that all commissions, departments and sections of the Council have the task of furthering the missionary and evangelistic spirit among the members of all churches, as well as supporting the churches in their worldwide missionary and evangelistic tasks.

In this respect the integration of mission and church must also have an effect on those at grassroots level in the World Council of Churches and give them a strong missionary orientation. "The description as 'a community of churches which recognize our Lord Jesus Christ as God and Saviour' should be sufficient definition of this work of unification." In New Delhi, "recognize" was replaced by the more active "confess". What was also added was that the churches "seek to fulfil together that to which they are called".

As a picture of the unity of the churches, which is also understood as "God's will and his gift to the church", New Delhi took up the concept of fully committed fellowship. This demonstrates the mutual dependency of the missionary task and the search for unity, and the common bond between unity, witness and service. The unity of the church is made visible as all in every place who are baptized into Jesus Christ and confess him as Lord and Saviour are brought by the Holy Spirit into one fully committed fellowship, holding the one apostolic faith, preaching the one gospel, breaking the one bread, joining in common prayer, and having a corporate life reaching out in witness and service to all.

This definition of church and mission-oriented unity in "fully committed fellowship" can be understood as the *ecumenical form of the partnership idea*.

In New Delhi the section on "Witness" looked at the consequences of this integration for the life and missionary task of the congregations. Its report shows how, as a result of the integration, greater attention could be given to the missionary task of the churches and congregations in the North, and how in the process the structures of church and congregation came into the picture. The "Witness" report takes up the idea of the *missio Dei* and puts it like this: "God is his own witness, that means: God was and is at work reaffirming his own message to mankind." The churches and Christians everywhere are called to "communicate the gospel".

Writing about "the missionary structure of the congregation", the report says that the command to bear witness to Christ has been given to every member of his church. The report first tries to describe the missionary task, stressing especially the social and political dimension. Among the "blessings of the gospel of Christ" are "that poverty, sickness and hunger should be relieved and a true community created". To proclaim the whole gospel therefore means to participate in the fight for social justice and the maintenance of peace: "Healing and help in need, attack on social outrages and reconciliation, as well as preaching, Christian fellowship and worship, are linked together in the proclamation of the gospel."

In order to fulfil the task of proclamation and witness, especially in those areas "in which the work of the world proceeds", the section report stresses the importance of the laity. People need suitable training in order to give them a "thorough understanding of the gospel". The local congregation is the place for such training, alongside so-called lay institutes. Here the congregation is understood as a place for Christians to learn about their missionary and ecumenical existence. In the congregation it is possible "for laypeople and pastors more thoroughly to grasp the meaning of the gospel for life in the present-day secular world". For this, the traditional structures of the churches must be examined "in order to see whether they promote or hinder the service of missionary proclamation". The report says:

We must ask ourselves whether we do not all too easily fall into the habit of understanding the church to be the congregation assembled for the Sunday service, rather than the laity scattered out into all areas of everyday life. We must ask ourselves whether our present structures do not preserve our divisions as if they were set in stone, instead of furthering the unity of the missionary congregation.

Finally, the section report demands the development of new forms of Christian fellowship, "cells" or groups that can "penetrate" the population so far untouched by the gospel.

The significance of the section report in the context of this study is that here, for the first time, the missionary task is entirely removed from the North-South orientation which had so far prevailed. Instead the task is developed, comprehensively and under the term "witness", as the missionary presence of Christians in their social contexts. The social and socio-political dimensions of the proclamation of the gospel and people's witness to it are given a central place in the report. This opens our eyes to a comprehensive holistic understanding of mission. We must bear this in mind when discussing the significance of "partnership in mission" in the context of the district and congregational partnerships being studied.

The New Delhi declaration can be criticized for taking a social direction which is too one-sided and deficient in its exclusiveness. Also – in contrast to "church centred" mission – the report says far too much about "scattered" Christians, while neglecting the power of the proclamation of the gospel to create community.

2. The world mission conference in Mexico City

Two years after this integration of mission and church, a world mission conference took place in Latin America for the first time, in order to "draw attention to the growing importance of nominally Roman-Catholic South America for the Protestant world mission". Compared to the previous conference in Achimota, the Mexico City conference was characterized by harmony and a new spirit of optimism. This can be attributed to the fact that, since Achimota and Willingen, the theological basis for mission had been firmly established and the conference could build on this and consider its practical consequences. The main subject of the conference, "God's Mission and Our Commission", is also a signal of this. Accordingly the four sections of the report concentrate on the practical realization of the commission. Besides these four sections, several committees also discussed individual aspects of the work of the Commission on World Mission and Evangelism. The task in Mexico City was to put integration "into practice". On the other hand, the "image crisis" of mission which had emerged in Achimota seemed to have been overcome, primarily by the integration of mission and church which had taken place.

In my opinion, reports tend to ignore the significance of the different composition of the delegate group compared to former conferences. This is particularly noticeable and must be taken into account when talking about interchurch relations. In Mexico City, the representatives of the North were for the first time in the majority again. Ninety-five delegates from Europe, Great Britain and the USA were there, as opposed to 30 Asian and only 10 African representatives. Latin America was geographically close and so relatively strongly represented with 40 delegates. The predominance of the "Northern view of things" can almost be felt in the conference documents. The subjects "modernity" and "secularization" are in the forefront. The conference is marked by a certain euphoria at technological progress, and by hope that through revolutionary radical changes – at least liberation and independence movements in the South are included here – many of humanity's problems can be overcome. The theological question raised in this context was whether we must not acknowledge God's activity in the world in the technical, political and social upheavals.

The discussions on partnership and the relations between the churches of the North and the South did not break down as bitterly as they had in Achimota; this was at least partly a result of the mix of conference delegates. At the world mission conferences which followed Mexico, it became clear that the churches of the South remained dissatisfied with the position reached in interchurch relations even after the integration of mission and church. Nevertheless, we should not underestimate the importance of the integration achieved for the assembly in Mexico City. The conference demonstrated by example that it was possible to break away from geographical North-South thinking in mission, by taking as its main theme "Witness in Six Continents". This expression was used naturally, as though there had never been any discussion previously on the proper characteristics of foreign mission.

Furthermore, the effect of integration was visible in that representatives of the European and American churches and the institutions of so-called inner mission *(Volksmission)* were all present as delegates in Mexico City. As a gesture of good will, according to the reports, nobody asked anything at all about the missionary societies. But this should not conceal the fact that, as before, it was often still the societies who were in charge of (foreign) mission. The integration of church and mission was not yet a reality. The missionary societies had still not stepped down, and "mission field thinking" had still not been overcome. Hans

Thimme explained at length how the integration, as "a reforming event in new ecumenical thinking", was very much something that all the conference participants had in common, but he also pointed out that, "particularly for the German reader", the necessary integral link between foreign mission and inner mission was "quite probably not clear without further explanation", because it had so far not found any organized expression within German Protestantism. The same applied "more or less" to the other European and American churches.

"Partnership" was hardly mentioned in Mexico City. The term itself only appears in a short section of the report from committee 5 on "Structure and Mutual Relations", where essentially there is a reference to the programme "Joint Action for Mission". This programme, which is described in the report from committee 4, can be understood as a further development of the concept of partnership. Thimme supports this by putting the slogan "Joint Action for Mission" on a level with the Whitby slogan as far as its influence and significance are concerned.

Characteristic for this programme is its pragmatic and practical approach. In contrast to earlier conferences, there are no detailed demands for cooperation. Instead the section report describes methodical steps which should enable the churches to develop specific forms of cooperation in their own contexts:

a) In the light of an overview of God's call to mission, the churches in a certain area, together with the missionary societies associated with them, should examine the prevailing needs, the opportunities offered, and the means available. The size and special features of the area and the mutual trust of the local churches should enable successful progress to be made.

b) After this examination, the churches and the missionary societies consult together in order to ensure that in the light of the agreed aims a genuine and effective new distribution of the means available takes place.

c) The churches then actually puts into practice what has been agreed upon.

However, the section report also names the obstacles which prevent an effective cooperation in mission:

a) the theological and ecclesiological factors (which church for example would those converted through joint action in mission actually belong to?);

b) the lack of mutual trust and experience in cooperation;

c) the worry that other powerful factors could force a programme for "Joint Action in Mission";

d) the really radical demands which Joint Action in Mission brings with it, namely that all information must be exchanged, all means pooled, and existing plans and relations be changed in consequence; in the process traditional and well-established rights of congregations, churches and missions are called into question.

Against this background, the paper asks whether Joint Action in Mission is really possible. To clear away any obstacles and fears, it points out that cooperation need not necessarily lead to church union, and that the concept of joint action should be defined in a very flexible and comprehensive way.

Thimme quite rightly points out that "neither the idea nor the individual forms it takes" were new. The conference had done nothing more "than put the same considerations into different words, but essentially unchanged, and refer the whole matter back to the church and the missionary societies again, for them to study it and come to practical conclusions".

Nevertheless, these attempts at a "set of instructions for mission strategy" are significant, because they attempt to put the understanding of partnership that had been formed by the world mission conferences to date into more methodical operation. What is new is the greater flexibility and contextualization of the approach. Partnership, or Joint Action in Mission, now begins in a certain area with the participant partners coming to an understanding as to what aims they wish to follow, what means are available to them, and how they wish to use them. Even if the final report still has an undercurrent of the "mission field in the South" and is influenced by a North-South mission thinking, this methodical approach enables the partners to reach agreement on mutual tasks and aims in the churches and societies of the North. This is an approach which can be of significance for the formation of district and congregational partnerships.

However, it is just this pragmatic and methodical approach which makes the obstacles to such a procedure recognizable, above all a strongly possessive attitude on the part of the missionary societies and the churches, combined with a lack of trust towards the ecumenical partners. Thimme points out that churches and missionary societies have worked for "far too long" next to each other, and have each kept their information sealed against the other. For this reason the relationship between the churches joined together in the ecumenical movement must change dramatically in many ways. The German theologian saw – for the first time in a German conference report – a need for action on the part of the German churches:

In the solidarity of responsibility for world mission, the Protestant church in Germany will not only have to face places in the mission fields of Asia and Africa where it is compelled into "Joint Action in Mission" – there will be enough opportunities for this – but also in particular it will have to face places where opportunities for the appropriate action arise in our own country. Even if the uniformity of our situation as a traditional national church means that we do not face certain problems that others do, nevertheless "Joint Action for Mission" is by no means accepted as a matter of course by all our members.

This link to the situation in Thimme's own country is remarkable, even if the idea of cooperation is restricted here to the common life of various regional churches *(Landeskirchen)* and of various congregations in one locality. What he still did not envisage was the need for cooperation by churches and congregations from North and South in partnership for missionary projects in Germany.

3. The study on the missionary structure of the congregation 1961-65

The third assembly of the World Council of Churches in New Delhi commissioned the Department of Studies on Evangelism to prepare a study on "The Missionary Structure of the Congregation". This study was basically carried out by two working groups, a West European and a North American group, coordinated by the working committee in Geneva. The secretary of this committee until 1965 was the German mission scholar Hans Jochen Margull. From 1965 until the WCC's fourth assembly in Uppsala in 1968, the Swiss ecumenist Walter Hollenweger was secretary. The main papers and results of the study on structures were published in 1965, two years after the world mission conference in Mexico City. Asian and African churches participated in the study process, though only to a modest degree.

The crucial new approach of this study, which otherwise builds on the mission-theological insights of Willingen and New Delhi, is the change in how those hearing missionary proclamation are described. First attention is primarily drawn to the situation in Western Europe and North America, at any rate to the immediate context of one of each of these churches. The study sees people addressed by missionary proclamation as "those with whom no one has tried to speak, or those with whom the dialogue has been broken off, or those who themselves have broken off the dialogue, or those who have got bogged down in the present impassable social structures of the church". The aim is to reach "those who are a long way off" or "those who are very different". Attention is focused on those "who have never come to church and those who no longer come".

With this approach the study fundamentally criticizes the traditional structures of the congregations, namely that they are based on the "principle of coming", especially in the parochial system. Such structures inhibit the presence of Christians in the world. The church is then "out of the public eye" and "beyond the people". Margull therefore speaks of "heretical structures" which "prevent the gospel from achieving its aim". The church becomes a stumbling-block to the people, preventing them from even reaching "the stumbling-block of the gospel, the true stumbling-block".

In contrast to the "come structure", the study presents the need for a "go structure" or a "principle of coming and going" as the structural principle of the missionary congregation. Coming from the *missio Dei*, this is the great challenge of mission to the church. At heart, the goal of church reform is the "presence" of Christians in the world, evangelizing and witnessing "at the crisis-points and meeting places of our complicated societies". Margull, taking up Bonhoeffer's words on the "church for others", presents this eccentric form of church existence (hope in action) absolutely one-sidedly:

> The church exists for the world. And this is why we never simply call anyone to us, but we tell everyone about God. Whether everyone comes to us or not, our task is to speak out, to question, to call people forward. There is no church for us. The church is church for others. There is no congregation for us. The congregation is congregation for others. What there is for us, are the others. What we have is a task. The name of our task is witness.

Accordingly, the report of the department on "Questions of Proclamation" given to the WCC central committee at its meeting in Enugu, Nigeria, in January 1965 states:

> The Word of God forms and demands missionary congregations. Through his congregations Jesus Christ, the Lord of the whole world, wishes to serve all people. Just like a missionary, a missionary congregation fulfils its calling by its serving presence among the people for whom Jesus became obedient (Phil. 2:5-11). A missionary congregation is a congregation for others.

Margull stressed explicitly that the aim of the missionary renewal of the congregations was not to win them over to support foreign mission. Nor was it a question of winning back lost members to the church. The only object of the renewal of the church was to enable the congregations to be a missionary presence in the social realities of daily life.

Here the laity gain very special importance, as they are already "on the spot" in both their work and leisure time. For the churches there is "nothing more important than speaking practically with the people of God (i.e. with the laity) about their commission, and empowering them to carry out this task".

The study on "The Missionary Structure of the Congregation" led to many ideas for church reform at the end of the 1960s, though these have changed the church little. Without doubt the importance of the study, particularly in our context, is that for the first time it radically questioned what consequences the idea of the *missio Dei* must have for the missionary existence of churches and congregations in the countries of the North.

It succeeded in removing the mission of the church from its one-sided fixation on activity in foreign "mission fields", and so won mission back for the churches of the North. At the same time it recognized that the transformation of the idea of mission as participation in the *missio Dei* would lead the churches to a radical new way of existence, to a "shift in the coordinate system" as Hollenweger put it.

The weakness, and with it the far-reaching ineffectiveness, of the study lies partly in the fact that it was only able to speak of the church in negative terms, as the church that exhausted itself in action for others. It does not acknowledge the right of the church itself to gather in fellowship, to develop forms of church life, piety and faith. The study gives no answer to the question of how the church can be there for others without being there for those "who set out to reach others".

And secondly, however necessary it seemed then – and now – to look at those structures which prevent renewal when considering the question of the missionary renewal of the church, the study produced only structural arguments too quickly and too one-sidedly. It neglected to clarify the completely new approach in mission thinking from which all its arguments were taken and to develop it in congregational situations. The world mission conference in Willingen, with its breakthrough to a new theological understanding of mission as participation in the *missio Dei*, had taken place only ten years before and the congregations remained largely untouched by what had occurred there. In this respect demands for a new structural order were very much up in the air, unsupported by a new understanding of mission in the congregations. Many a church reform project remained tangled in the thicket of functional and technocratic concepts.

Now, important aspects of the study are being taken up again in the new programme of the World Council of Churches and the Conference of European Churches (CEC) on "Ecumenical Renewal of Congregations". Important ideas from this approach can also challenge congregation and district partnerships and give them a missionary direction again. However, as far as the study of missionary congregations is concerned, it must be said that it did not pay any attention to partnerships between congregations in the North and the South, nor concern itself with their joint search for missionary challenges.

6. The threat to partnership from the poverty of the South and the wealth of the North: Bangkok 1973, Melbourne 1980

After the theological new orientation in mission achieved at Willingen and reinforced by the world mission conference in Mexico City, there followed a phase of tension and polarization in the 1970s and at the beginning of the 1980s, exactly in that period when the first district partnerships were coming into existence in the Federal Republic of Germany. Old conflicts, which had once seemed to have been resolved, broke out again with new force. The conflict between the so-called ecumenically oriented circles and the groups and missionary societies who classed themselves as evangelical, belongs to the polarization of those years. The conflict culminated in the question of what weight socio-political involvement should have in mission, compared to the efforts for individual conversion and certainty of belief, and what role mission should play in the fight against poverty, injustice and oppression. At the beginning of the 1970s, there were many discussions about the theological insights that could lead to appropriate relations between the churches of the South and the missionary societies of the North. They found their most radical expression in a demand for the missionaries to leave. In Asia, and later in many churches of the third world, the call was heard, "Missionary, go home". This was an expression of the dissatisfaction of the churches of the South with what in the meantime had become accepted under the term "partnership". At the same time the basic question was being raised whether the term partnership was at all suitable for the renewal of relations that was required.

THE WORLD MISSION CONFERENCE IN BANGKOK 1973

The second world mission conference held on the Asian continent, in Bangkok, Thailand, became the decisive crystallization point for the conflicts and polarizations already mentioned. The main subject of the conference, at which including guests and observers 300 people gathered, was "The Salvation of the World Today". After the question of justification for mission (Willingen), and the practical consequences stemming from it (Achimota and Mexico City), the questions now in the foreground were the real issues and methods of mission for the present day. The subject of debate was mission in relationship to politics, economics and culture, in all their forms and with all their problems. "Mission in context" was a slogan programmatically used by Philip Potter in his report to the conference, in which he tried to determine the position of the conference "in relation to what has happened in the world since 1963".

The conference, which had originally been planned for 1969 and had therefore been preceded by an intensive preparation process over many years, aimed at getting the participants themselves to give their opinion on the subject from their own individual situational experience. Bangkok therefore marked a new participatory style of ecumenical conferences. Apart from two reports on the work of the Commission on World Mission and Evangelism (CWME), there was only one main lecture. In place of the theological addresses usual at former conferences, the participants met regularly in small discussion groups for Bible study. This group process was accompanied by so-called "reflectors" who contributed their observations to several plenary sessions for the benefit of the whole conference. The aim of including the participants so intensely was to ensure a greater understanding of what was going on, both in a world-wide context and at a local political level. The mission theological debate of previous years – consider the "structure study", for example – had called upon the churches and the missions to turn much more towards the "world agenda" and to seek out the challenges for missionary presence in the conflicts and at the focal points of society.

The Bangkok conference was described by many participants as "an experience", "a special event" and "a conference in which emotions and passions played an intensely powerful role"; but also as a conference which "enabled the conflicts which people had brought with them to be expressed in breadth and depth" in a "sharp yet open exchange of opinion". The negotiations were marked by differences of opinion on the socio-political and individual understanding of "salvation", by a "feeling of frustration" over crises and divisions in the world, and in many cases the concern that the question of political and economic liberation could gain too much weight. In this process the debate on Western colonialism and the role of the missionary societies became more bitter. In several places the conference texts point to the entanglement of the missionary societies in the old colonial structures, but also in the new structures, the "continued dreadful exploitation of the poor nations by the rich".

The dominant subjects were racism and violence, exploitation and oppression as well as the liberation of the South from the structures of injustice. Philip Potter pointed to the "contradictions in the world" as the context of mission: to the increasing reality of the "one world" thanks to communication technology and mass media, and at the same time to the tensions between the power blocs of the super-powers, the economic and racist divisions between poor and rich, between black and white. Human beings had technical means at their disposal to rule over creation and yet they were incapable and powerless to make society "more just and create a sense of common community".

Section II under the heading "Salvation and Social Justice" was concerned among other things with the relationship of the missionary societies to the fight for social justice. The section report describes "four social dimensions of the work of salvation":

1) salvation works in the fight for economic justice as opposed to the exploitation of people by other people;
2) salvation works in the fight for human dignity as opposed to political oppression through our fellow men;
3) salvation works in the fight for solidarity as opposed to the alienation of people;
4) salvation works in the fight for hope as opposed to despair in the life of each individual.

In this way it should be stressed that for mission, economic justice, human dignity, solidarity and personal hope belong together. To lose sight of the way these dimensions belong together and determine each other is to deny the fullness of salvation. In this way Bangkok stands for the recognition of the problems of worldwide social injustice in the mission movement. And just this emphasis on the social aspects of mission led to the flare up of sharp conflicts with the evangelical mission groups in the following years.

Fully in the tenor of the system criticism usual at that time, the section II report established that the spread of mission was closely linked to the "exploitative character of the capitalist system"; many of the missionary and evangelistic efforts were "not so as to follow up the causes of social injustice". The section came out against the "donor mentality" in the countries of the North, in as far as it consolidated the existing economic and political systems. In its place the section called for information and educational work on world economic connections and interrelations and their consequences for the poor countries, and demanded, "to support new forms of investment which further the political and social liberation of the poor and the oppressed". The concepts were formulated here that have remained the decisive framework for development policies and educational work in this field until today.

Section III concerned itself directly with the subject of interchurch relations. It made a devastating appraisal on the subject of partnership. "Partnership in mission", according to the section report, remains "an empty slogan". Even where "autonomy and equal partnership have been theoretically realized", in practice "through the sheer momentum of events a relationship of dominance and dependence is being maintained". The power relationships between the missionary societies and the churches of the South mirrored the economic North-South divide.

Therefore the missionary societies must regard the battle for worldwide justice "as one of their most urgent tasks at the present time". A relationship is desirable between mature churches on the basis of their mutual commitment to work for Christ's mission in the world. In several places in the Bangkok documentation, reference is made in this context to the model of the Evangelical Community for Apostolic Action (CEVAA), which had come into being after the dissolution of the Paris Mission. In this "extensive community of churches" the joint discussions on theological questions and questions of mission practice led to the churches in Europe being questioned about their own work and their own priorities. The section came to the conclusion that on the whole no successful relations had been developed which did not put one side down. Therefore they took up the suggestion of a "moratorium" and recommended it as a "possible mission strategy in certain areas".

The idea of a moratorium, in other words, a break in sending money and personnel from the churches of the North to the churches of the South, came from the Kenyan theologian John Gatu, the then general secretary of the Presbyterian Church of East Africa. In 1971, two years before Bangkok, he had called for the foreign missionaries to withdraw from many parts of the third world. He considered that the time had come, "that the churches of the third world be allowed to find their own identity". The continuation of the mission at that time represented a hindrance to the independence of the church, according to Gatu.

In the same year the Philippine theologian, Emerito Nacpil, had spoken about the impossibility of a genuine partnership, the partnership in obedience: "Under the present conditions... this partnership can only be a partnership between the weak and the powerful. And this means continued dependence of the weak on the powerful and the continued dominance of the strong over the weak, regardless of our statements to the contrary or our efforts to achieve the opposite. In this kind of partnership the missionary becomes an apostle of wealth not of sacrifice; an apostle of cultural superiority not of Christian humility; an apostle of technological achievements not of human identification with his fellow men; an apostle of white superiority, not of the liberation of mankind and society."

Nacpil concludes, "the most missionary service" a missionary can do, is to go home. "The death of the present system of mission" did not, however, mean the end of mission. As mission is necessary for the existence of the church it can awaken to life in another form. This missionary service must then be supported through the faith and the personnel and financial possibilities of each local church.

The protagonists of the idea of moratorium have again and again pointed out that they were not talking about an isolated breaking off of interchurch relations. It was expected that the moratorium would give the so-far "receiving churches" the opportunity "to discover their identity, their own priorities and to find the necessary means to fulfil their authentic sending mission", it says in the section report from Bangkok. At the same time the "sending churches" could determine their own position anew.

Among other means, Gatu worked out his justification for a moratorium in a dialogue with Stephen Neill, the very mission theologian who had played such an important role in the development of the idea of "partnership in obedience" in Whitby. It becomes clear how very much the African theologians felt themselves belittled and put down by the European theologians speaking for them under the guise of "partnership". According to Gatu a situation had been reached in which "we must say to the white advocates speaking for the Africans: I believe that I can speak for myself and I believe I know my own needs, which of course must not necessarily correspond to those that you consider to be the right ones".

Gatu criticized Neill that while he supported a "mission for the whole world" he only spoke of "missionaries for the third world". Neill could not imagine that an African church could survive without missionaries from the West; he could only imagine the evangelization of the 600,000 Fon in the former French colony Dahomey by missionaries from the West, and he called this "partnership". For Gatu this is proof of the "Vasco da Gama mentality of those who set off to explore the world and to help the heathens and the poor, which still drifts through many of the Western churches". This attitude showed that "the churches continue to live as appendices of the Western churches and remain dependent". The churches in the third world must free themselves from this "servitude".

The call for a moratorium was taken up by a further committee in Bangkok. "In order to develop new forms of relationships", it states in the report, a moratorium in the sending of money and personnel should be set up among the churches. The aim was that the churches that requested such a moratorium should be given the opportunity to work with their own means available to them and so to develop their independence and their own identity. The so-far "sending churches" should on their part be "freed" from traditional institutionalized missionary structures and be able to use the means thereby made available to search for new ways of educating for mission among their own people. This committee also hoped that a moratorium would open up possibilities for new relationships, a mature partnership, which included discussions with each other and time to think things over together.

The third general assembly of the All Africa Conference of Churches (AACC) which met in Lusaka, Zambia, in 1974, made the suggestion for a temporary moratorium their own. However, many African churches very quickly distanced themselves from this demand. The next year, in 1975, at the fifth assembly of the World Council of Churches in Nairobi, the question was also put to debate. There, on the one hand a moratorium for certain churches was seen as an opportunity for them to make their witness in their special context more credible. At the same time the churches of the North and the South were called upon to make greater efforts for joint mission.

The discussions at the world mission conference in Bangkok, and especially the demand for a temporary halt in the transfer of money and personnel from the North to the South, illuminate the dissatisfaction of the representatives of the South with the state of interchurch relations so far reached. Stronger than ever before, the churches of the South complained about existing dependencies and their feeling that the churches of the North had a low opinion of them. They saw themselves far removed from the postulated equality with equal rights for both sides. What is remarkable is that they felt the gap between them most of all in respect of the economic situation. The divide between the poor and the rich, and the dominant role or rule of the churches of the North that went with it, made the longed-for church unity and community impossible. In this situation some church representatives of the South saw the only possibility in a radical breakthrough: at least temporarily stopping all aid contributions. It was not a question of breaking off ecumenical relations but rather of giving the churches of the South the chance to realize their own strengths and means and to find forms of witness and service within their own context which fitted their resources and were therefore credible.

The reality of the worldwide church community is not disputed. Just the opposite, the moratorium should serve to develop new forms of interchurch relations. It is worth noting that there is hardly any mention of partnership any more, at least not in the statements of Gatu and Nacpil. This may have to do with the fact that with the change in the situation, a change in the understanding of the term partnership had also taken place. Whereas at the beginning – in Jerusalem, but above all in Whitby and subsequent conferences – the term was used to win the churches of the South as "partners" for the task of mission, in the circumstances of the Bangkok conference the term was used rather to justify the continued right of missionary societies, or rather of the Northern churches, to missionary activity in the countries of the South. This meant that the thrust of the term had moved completely in the opposite direction. The idea of the moratorium – which basically had no real consequences – was diametrically opposed to this.

THE ECUMENICAL DISCUSSION ON THE UNITY OF THE CHURCH IN A WORLD
DIVIDED BY POVERTY AND WEALTH

Whereas at the earlier world mission conferences the question of the
relations between the missionary societies and the churches of the South
had been discussed from the perspective of the churches' independence
in their responsibility and decision-making competence, in Bangkok the
question of the economic dependence of the churches of the South was
at the centre of the debate. Partnership in mission had often been invoked
but not yet become reality, above all on account of the economic differences between the churches. The gap between the poor and the rich did
not concern only the missionary societies but the whole ecumenical
movement.

At least since the world conference on "Church and Society" in
Geneva 1966, the great differences between the churches had become an
important subject of conflict in the World Council of Churches. Since the
integration of the IMC and the World Council of Churches the number
of member churches from Asia, Africa and Latin America in the World
Council of Churches had grown. Therefore the question of how to deal
with social differences was one that the ecumenical church community
faced within itself. As this question also plays a role in all parish and district North-South partnerships, I shall now look at some essential aspects
of the ecumenical discussion that took place other than at the mission
conferences.

In the 1960s, ecumenical social ethics understood the development
problem above all as a problem of growth. Development was understood as catching up on industrialization. The fourth assembly of the
World Council of Churches in Uppsala in 1968 found itself confronted
with the problem of the intensification of the development conflict.
Gradually a change could be noticed in the understanding of development in the ecumenical movement, away from the idea of development
as striving to catch up to the standard of the industrial nations towards
an objective of social justice and political independence. This enabled
people to see the necessity for structural changes in the industrial
nations themselves.

In Uppsala they succeeded in a small way in understanding the
development problem from an ecclesiological point of view: the gap
between the rich and the poor in the churches posed a threat to church
unity and therefore called in question the credibility of church witness.
"Should it become apparent that the divisions of the world are also the
divisions of the church, which they are just as incapable of overcoming
within their own ranks as the entire world is, this would also ultimately
call the missionary dimension of the church into question."

In the years between the assemblies in Uppsala and Nairobi the ecumenical movement completed a gradual change in its position and perspective concerning its understanding of development and in the question of overcoming the gap between rich and poor. In Nairobi – where the delegates looked back on the first futile development decade and with it the disappointed ambitious hopes from the end of the 1960s – not only "the tone" had become "much more pessimistic and cautious", but also two important and theologically motivated changes in ecumenical development thinking had taken place, for example through the influence of the Latin American theology of liberation. The poor themselves were now actively at the centre of the development process and the aim of development was qualified and more clearly expressed through the use of the terms "social justice" and "liberation". This included the demand for changes within the industrial nations and in the international economic system. And it also meant fundamental criticism of the system of funding projects both within state and private overseas development aid. In 1970 the Latin American theologian Dom Helder Camara expressed it in this way:

> The rich countries make it very easy for themselves when they see their relationship to the poor countries under the aspect of financial and technical aid, which is almost always tantamount to pseudo aid, as in reality they do not give but take.... Let us not delude ourselves: structural change in the developing countries is not possible without a structural change in the developed countries. And I really mean that literally. It is not only a question of a new attitude towards the poor countries, it is a question of a radical change in world trade politics.

The new orientation of ecumenical development thinking found its expression in the founding of the Commission on the Churches' Participation in Development (CCPD). "Development", according to the founding documents, "must be understood as a process, through which individuals and societies can fully bring to fruition the possibilities of human life in social justice and particularly in self-responsibility."

In a CCPD strategy paper from 1973 the change in perspective becomes quite clear, not only in the understanding of development but also in the understanding of who plays the decisive role in development:

> CCPD conceives development as a process by which people participate directly in their own liberation. In this way, development is the action people themselves take to change their situation, rather than the result of an increase of the goods and services available to them.

This change in perspective, in the process of which "development" changed from being a technical question to a human question, and thereby gained relevance theologically, was agreed upon for the whole ecumenical church community at the assembly in Nairobi. Konrad Raiser justified the theological relevance in that the "liberation of the poor" was no longer a question of the transfer of money and personnel. According to Raiser, the challenge to the churches was no longer what they were prepared to do for the poor but rather whether they were prepared to live with the poor and support their battle for social justice.

According to the new conviction of the ecumenical movement, the gulf between the rich and the poor in the church could only be overcome by the identification of the church with the battle of the poor for independence and social justice. The necessary identification with the victims of injustice and oppression was raised to a mark of church; with this "stands and falls the authenticity and credibility of the church". The question of active solidarity with the poor was raised to be the benchmark of the true church.

This idea was further developed following the conference in Nairobi and considered more intensively in a study on the subject "Towards a Church in Solidarity with the Poor". The conclusions of the study point out to the churches that the solidarity of the churches with the poor requires a new way of thinking theologically (the poor as mediators of the kingdom of God). It also necessitates a new way of reading biblical texts and requires the search for new forms of church fellowship in which both spirituality and action are one. In this way a process is described of a change of awareness in the churches. The way towards a church in solidarity with the poor is understood as a learning process.

The central committee of the World Council of Churches officially adopted the conclusions of the study process, though altogether they brought about very little change within the member churches of the World Council of Churches. This may well be because many demands never got beyond being mere assertions and in many cases the suggestions for putting them into practice remained very general and unspecific. Furthermore the tendency for persistence on the part of the established churches – above all, but not only, in the industrialized nations – had been underestimated and at the same time the battle of the poor had been idealized. Philip Potter described this collision of interests in a very pointed way:

> What we face here is an evangelical and pastoral problem (and this does not appear in the document): how can we speak through the document to the ordinary member of the church in Western countries, especially at a time when people in the West feel very insecure? At the same time it is necessary to recognize that people in the so-called third world countries are not as conscien-

tized as the document claims: it is important to be aware that "third-world people" live in a situation of cultural ambiguity: they reject the West, but at the
same time they depend on the West.

The ecumenical debate on the division between rich and poor in the
church as described here had led to long-lasting convictions about necessary changes to be made within the churches and in their witness and
service in the world. In the process, the missionary and ecclesiological
relevance of the problem had become clear. It had been recognized that
the unity of the church and the credibility of its mission could only be
maintained if the churches themselves made the liberation of the poor
their own concern and worked together with the poor for the realization
of social justice. That intended to set off a process of fundamental
change within the churches, similar to the one already described in the
study on the missionary structure of the congregation. However, here
also tendencies for persistence in the churches and an interest in maintaining vested rights prevented these demands from being put into practice, which anyway had not given enough consideration to the spiritual
and pastoral dimensions of the demanded process of change.

THE WORLD MISSION CONFERENCE IN MELBOURNE 1980

The world mission conference in Melbourne in May 1980, at which
around 500 participants gathered on the university campus of the Aus-
tralian city, took place against a background of the ecumenical discussion on the importance and role of the poor in the church and its mission.
It was dominated by the ideas coming from liberation theology and the
new spirit of optimism in the Latin American grassroots communities.
The subject of the conference took up the call from the Lord's Prayer,
"Your Kingdom Come", and dealt, as in Bangkok, with question of the
content of mission and the issues involved. Four sections, each with various sub-sections, worked on the subject; the questions of the significance of "good news to the poor" and the "churches in solidarity with
the poor" dominated the debates.

The conference in Melbourne took up the conclusions from the previous ecumenical discussions and in particular from the study on the
"Church in Solidarity with the Poor". It then took the ideas further, inten-
sified them and made practical suggestions. This led to certain conflicts
during the conference between the representatives who were more
involved in socio-political activities, and the more evangelically oriented
representatives of the mission movement. Many section participants
"found it difficult really to talk to each other". Misunderstandings dominated the conference sessions. The rifts and confrontations can be clearly
seen in the section reports.

Melbourne took a step forward in the question of the role of the poor in church and mission, in as far as the conference recognized the poor as having priority in carrying out God's mission, and justified this christologically. In its statement on "God's special preference for the poor", the conference referred several times to the biblical text of Jesus' so-called "inaugural speech" (Luke 4:18-21: "The Spirit of the Lord is upon me, because he has anointed me to preach good news to the poor." The report of section I states: "In Jesus, God identified himself with the poor and the oppressed." "Jesus' option for the poor challenges everyone and shows how the kingdom of God is to be received. The poor are 'blessed' because of their longing for justice and their hope for liberation."

At the same time the section declares that the coming of the kingdom as hope for the poor will therefore be a "time of judgment for the rich". The section, which refuses to play "material" and "spiritual" poverty off against each other, attempts to give a description of what poverty is:

> To be poor is to have not, to experience lack and deficiency... the poor are "the little ones" (Matt. 11:25), the insignificant people of no consequence. They are powerless, voiceless and at the mercy of the powerful. Poverty means suffering inhumanity and humiliation.

Besides recognizing voluntary poverty, the section also recognizes poverty in the necessities of life and poverty amid material wealth. In order to show in more concrete terms what poverty is and who the poor are, the section contains "stories of the poor".

The churches are called upon to preach the good news to the poor. At the same time the report states: "As we look at the churches in the world today, we find some places where a new era of evangelization is dawning, where the poor are proclaiming the good news." In their fight for liberation the poor themselves are seen as the bearers of evangelization, as the proclaimers of the gospel. The poor are already active in working to change their own situation. A "missionary movement" is demanded of the churches, "that supports what the poor have already begun, and that focuses on building evangelizing and witnessing communities of the poor".

> The churches will have to surrender their attitudes of benevolence and charity by which they have condescended to the poor; in many cases this will mean a radical change in the institutional life of the missionary movement.

They must "respect their leadership in the work of evangelization and mission", the section report demands. "The churches must be ready to listen to the poor, to hear the gospel from the poor, to learn about the ways in which they have helped to make them poor." The report of section IV also stresses the special role of the poor in mission and asks:

Might it not be that they have the clearest vision, the closest fellowship with the crucified Christ who suffers in them and with them? Might it not be that the poor and the powerless have the most significant word for the rich and powerful: that Jesus must be sought on the periphery, and followed "outside the city"? That following him involves a commitment to the poor? Who but the church of the poor can preach with integrity to the poor of the world? In these ways we see the "poor" churches of the world as the bearers of mission: world mission and evangelism may now be primarily in their hands.

In the German report, Gerhard Hoffmann describes the change in perspective that has taken place and the change that it implies in inter-church relations. The poor and therefore the majority of the world population achieved a new status through the conference in Melbourne. They were no longer objects of Western benevolence and development aid: "They are no longer the people who need us. They are now (and were really always) people whom we need if we wish to be saved for the kingdom of God: as Christ is with them, we can only have him if we are also with them."

Heinrich Reiss described three consequences resulting from this for the churches and the Christians of the North: personal material aid as "the putting into practice of the responsible community of the family of God"; the question as to the setting of priorities in the use of church finances; and the necessity for political and economic participation in changing the existing structures both at a national level and internationally. As the wealth of the North rests essentially on economic structures that do not give the South a chance, changing the existing structures, which cause misery, is "an act of justice".

In this way at the beginning of the 1980s the world mission conference in Melbourne had already called upon the churches, especially in the North, not to content themselves with project aid for the needy in the South. The conference encouraged the churches to consider more intensively than had so far been the case the reasons for worldwide poverty, and to invest more in fighting against these causes – also in their own countries. The conference saw this as an act of solidarity of the churches with the poor.

The emphasis on the special role of the poor – and therefore also of the "poor" churches – seems to have pushed the question of interchurch relations into the background. At least in Melbourne it was hardly discussed at all. In the conference reports there is hardly anything about the structure of interchurch relations, nor on the subject of "partnership". In his introductory speech, in which he traced the path of the mission movement from Edinburgh to Melbourne, Philip Potter, the then general secretary of the WCC, had drawn a sobering résumé:

We have made valiant efforts over the years to develop relationships in mission which are consonant with our calling as sharing a common life in the body of Christ. At all the world mission conferences up to Bangkok these issues have been hotly discussed. But we have not got very far in the ecumenical sharing of resources and in our partnership in the gospel. The power of money and of other resources has prevailed.

Contrary to Potter's expectations, the conference did not continue this discussion. Nor did it take up again the conflict, which had broken out in Bangkok, particularly concerning the demand for a moratorium. Only section IV recommended at the end of its report that the Commission for World Mission and Evangelism should once again consider the reasons behind the suggestion for a moratorium. Beyond that they only made the very general recommendation to CWME to call upon the churches:

to take the initiative in challenging churches to implement better structures of cooperation in mission, helping them to come together to study new possibilities for sharing in decision–making, better approaches to mutual support, ecumenical exchanges of personnel and united witness....

The difficulties of the traditional mission structures and the imbalance in the giver and receiver relationships had by no means been solved. However, the integration of mission and church was effective in as far as to a large extent the representatives in Melbourne came from the churches and not from the old missionary societies. In Germany, between the conferences in Bangkok and in Melbourne, the process of integrating the missionary societies and founding regional mission departments within the regional churches had been completed.

The Melbourne conference spoke as a matter of course of "mutual witness" and emphasized both the necessity and the possibility of this. The conference, or rather section III which dealt with these questions, did not, however, consider what structures were available or were to be created for this purpose. In the main they simply listed task areas for common witness. The section pointed out that the joint witness would be overshadowed where dependencies came into being through "interchurch aid", where this aid led to church divisions or where the contextual identity of the local church was ignored.

Nevertheless, compared to previous conferences, the Melbourne conference took an essential step forward in the question of the unity of the churches in mission. They overcame the functional character conjured up by the word "partnership" in the understanding of interchurch relations, and they arrived at an understanding of church community in which missionary action and eucharistic celebration were brought together where they belong. Melbourne, one could say, discovered the importance of celebration for the interchurch community. They described this community with the term koinonia. It is thanks to section III that the indissoluble and necessary common bond between missionary witness and eucharistic celebration was worked out:

> This common witness of the church to the world we celebrate by dancing, singing and eating our food with one another. In celebrating, we witness to the power of the gospel to set us free. We can only celebrate in honesty if the churches realize the damage done to their common witness by the scandal of their comfortable life in division.

The section rejected a differentiation or even separation between Christians who are socially active in the name of Christ and those who offer themselves in prayer, study and liturgy. According to the section report, social action may become impatient with activism supported only by vague ideals. In the same way worship may become a private indulgence with no active concern for others. Both aspects must be held together: "Gathering and dispersing, receiving and giving, praise and work, prayer and struggle – this is the true rhythm of Christian engagement in the world."

Koinonia as a celebrating and witnessing community is at the same time the realization of interchurch relations and the painful hint at the completion of the community which has not yet been achieved, and the remaining inequalities and injustices between the churches. It is the starting point for the witness of the congregation in the world, and at the same time for the search for justice both in the world and in the community of the churches. The section spoke in this sense of the eucharist as the "food of missionaries". It encouraged the churches to open the eucharistic celebration and to let it become transparent for each congregation in its own context:

> Where a people is being harshly oppressed, the eucharist speaks of the exodus or deliverance from bondage.
>
> Where Christians are rejected or imprisoned for their faith, the bread and wine become the life of the Lord who was rejected by men but has become the "chief cornerstone".
>
> Where the church sees a diminishing membership and depressed budgets, the eucharist declares that there are no limits to God's giving and no end to hope in him.
>
> Where discrimination by race, sex or class is a danger for the community, the eucharist enables people of all sorts to partake of the one food and to be made one people.
>
> Where people are affluent and at ease with life, the eucharist says, "As Christ shares his life, share what you have with the hungry."

With this rediscovery of the celebration of the liturgical and eucharistic festival, the mission movement had found a way to overcome a purely functionally determined picture of the church and the worldwide church community. However, in Melbourne the question of the relationship between celebration and daily life, of the relative importance of eucharistic celebration and participation in the liberation struggle of the poor – something which particularly sections I and IV had called for – remained in the end unanswered. By frequent reference to the grassroots communities in Latin America, communities which were both celebrating and struggling, this gap should have been bridged, but this succeeded only to a limited degree. At the same time both these elements which the conference tried to communicate, celebration and participation in the liberation struggle of the poor, are still relevant for the form that partnerships take between districts and congregations in North and South.

7. Koinonia – the eucharistic community of sharing: El Escorial 1987, San Antonio 1989, Canberra 1991

After the tense debates on the form of interchurch relations in mission and the ecumenical movement in the 1970s, during the 1980s these questions lost their central importance, and above all their importance as a source of conflict. This was also the case as far as the problem of the division between poor and rich churches in the ecumenical movement was concerned. In the course of the increasing international debt crisis the financial situation of many churches of the South worsened dramatically and most of them became more and more dependent on financial and material support from the North. In this situation the debate on the suggestion of a moratorium died down without ever really having had any consequences. Even the results of the ecumenical study on the "Church in Solidarity with the Poor" were not translated into any practical action. Instead of that the gap increased between the rich and the poor. In the field of interchurch relations it seemed that it was mainly just a case of trying to limit the damage. There was little room left in interchurch relations for more fundamental considerations and the search for concrete alternatives.

The term partnership had developed into a generally used shorthand for any form of interchurch activity, aid or relationship by the end of the 1970s at the latest. This reflected the very broad use of the term within all fields when referring to North-South contacts and cooperation in development work on the part of both governmental and non-governmental agencies. In the ecumenical movement new visions and concepts crystallized around the question of the unity of the church and the forms of relationships between churches. The term *koinonia* was used increasingly – especially in the documents and at the meetings of Faith and Order. The image of the "eucharistic fellowship" was used to describe the ecumenical unity of the churches, or rather, the eucharist was used to justify the fellowship of the churches. These expressions came into common use in the mission and ecumenical movements, as they had already done in Melbourne.

Considerations about interchurch relations in ecumenism were concentrated in the 1980s in the study process on the ecumenical sharing of resources. The main findings of this study process, which had taken a good ten years, deserve to be presented here. This historical retrospective will then be rounded off by taking a look at the world mission conference in San Antonio 1989 and the further ecumenical discussion associated with the assembly of the World Council of Churches in Canberra in 1991 and beyond.

THE STUDY PROCESS ON THE ECUMENICAL SHARING OF RESOURCES

The impetus for the study on the ecumenical sharing of resources goes back to the World Council of Churches' assembly in Nairobi 1975. The programme guidelines at that time called for the initiation of a process to bring about a just sharing of resources between equal partners. The study was a direct consequence of the fierce debate in Nairobi around the call for a moratorium in mission relations. The aim of the study was to overcome the giver-taker mentality, which so dominated the North-South relations between the churches. Right from the beginning this process went beyond the purely pragmatic quest for new structures, in that overcoming the difference between the churches which gave aid and those which received it was seen as a challenge for the churches of missionary and ecclesiological importance. The credibility of the Christian witness over against a divided world was up for consideration in this respect, as had already been the case in the study on "Churches in Solidarity with the Poor". The unity of the churches in ecumenical sharing of resources should be a sign to the world "that the world may believe".

The first meeting took place in Glion, Switzerland, in 1977. This was followed in 1979 and 1980 by a series of regional and national conferences and the formation of working groups in Africa, Asia, Latin America, Europe and North America. In 1980 the results so far obtained were reappraised by an international working group and published in a small workbook for churches, congregations and church groups. The WCC central committee made these conclusions their own and passed a resolution to be sent to the churches with recommendations for ecumenical sharing.

During the process of the study two essential aspects of ecumenical sharing were formulated. The first one was the call to the churches when talking of sharing resources not only to think of material resources but also to include spiritual, religious and cultural values and possessions in the exchange between churches. The dimension of ecumenical encounters was emphasized frequently. In the introduction to *Empty Hands* Philip Potter got to the heart of the matter when he stated that the churches "had to share with each other what they are and not only what they have".

The second aspect was the clear criticism of the relationships of "dominance and dependence", of "power and powerlessness" not only in international North-South relationships but also in interchurch relations. Beyond simply exposing these relationships of dominance and dependence, the process of ecumenical sharing aimed to "empower the powerless". The necessary initiative for this "empowerment of the powerless", according to Potter, had to come from the poor themselves.

Since 1980 the central starting point for all these considerations of ecumenical sharing has been the ecclesiological description of the church as a "sharing community" founded in the eucharist. Ecumenical sharing is not just the consequence of our faith but is an essential characteristic of the church and "the mark of Christian relationships" both among themselves and also towards their fellow human beings throughout the world.

The workbook *Empty Hands* stated that "one-way streets of giving and receiving" strengthened the existing structures of dominance and dependence between the rich and the poor and prevented a change in the existing structures of power.

The givers were thereby prevented from "true giving – from the unlimited sacrifice that Christ demands of us". The recipients, on the other hand, were not able to achieve "independence, partnership among equals or real reciprocity of relationships". The suggestion of a moratorium is explicitly pointed out as an attempt to "break through the vicious circle of dominance and dependence". The workbook makes the point, which is well worth considering, that in many places it seems "that the decisive work in development or in mission occurs there where little or no support from outside is available. It occurs as a rule where people are the subject and not the object of their own development, where their activities are rooted in the cultural and social heritage of their society and have developed with little or no impulse from outside."

It is not enough, according to the report, for churches to be satisfied with just strengthening their unity; they must also actively fight against injustice. They should help people to become aware of who they are;

above all they themselves must "become to a greater extent participatory communities". It is a question of practising a responsible use of power: "Sharing together presumes that the 'haves' and the 'have-nots' have the freedom to share their expectations and their needs with each other and that they are prepared to patiently work out criteria and rules for a partnership together."

To do this requires practical solidarity in dependence and interdependence on each other. This means helping and supporting each other, being accountable to each other, standing up for each other and taking action. Exchange of information, prayer for each other, visits to each other and exchange of experience should have priority. Such practical solidarity demands changes in the attitudes and patterns of behaviour on both sides, "it requires us to question our existence and our actions, our life-style and our set of values". The churches are committed to changing structures that allow oppression, dominance and exploitation. However, the churches are called upon primarily to concern themselves with the problems in their own societies.

In this context the report suggests that models of ecumenical sharing should first be tried out between equally strong churches within one region. The South-South exchange is particularly emphasized. Financial and material support between the churches should be determined by the principles of stewardship, transparency and openness as well as the duty to be accountable to each other. Here the basic fundamentals of ecumenical sharing between the churches were described, which six years later were also taken over by the consultation in El Escorial. The most decisive aim was to try out new models of sharing in order to overcome the giver-taker divide, by "empowering" the poor, strengthening their own initiative and together overcoming the structures of injustice.

In October 1987, the 229 participants who gathered in the Spanish pilgrimage town of El Escorial, under the title "Koinonia: Sharing Life in the Worldwide Community", passed so-called "guidelines for sharing", which in their basic theological statements were based on the work already done in *Empty Hands*. Entirely in this direction, the conference criticized the relationships of dependency and dominance which still existed between the churches, which could lead to a "begging mentality" on the part of the poor churches and take the responsibility for fighting for human justice away from the churches in the rich countries. The first aim of "sharing together" had to be to strengthen the weak and to further their independence. This included getting rid of the causes of injustice. Sithembiso Nyoni, a campaigner for women's rights in Zimbabwe, stressed that the goods that were to be shared were the people themselves. The Christians of the South had human and spiritual gifts to share: "Information, communal traditions, wisdom, organizations and a technology of survival." Compared to these, material goods were of much less importance.

In his presentation to the conference Konrad Raiser spoke of the ecclesiological aspect of ecumenical sharing. The destiny of the church as a sharing community, as *koinonia*, was a biblically justified conviction and a theological statement, which was not to be confused with an empirical description. The realization of *koinonia* remained in itself a gift of God. The church as *koinonia* was called upon to live "as a parable of a successful community of sharing together, as an advance depiction of the community in the kingdom of God".

However, it is subject to the conditions of human life and requires structures and rules and regulations. Every attempt to make an ideal system out of the *koinonia* as revealed in Christ can only fail:

> We can and we must seek to turn relations between the churches into just relations in their structures and their rules and regulations, and to assert an effective and transparent control over the exercising of power and dominance within church structures and between them, especially where money is concerned.

From the theological differentiation between belief in the church and experience of it, Raiser gained a more pragmatic access to the question of sharing in ecumenical relationships. This limited itself to the identification of injustice and differences in the exercise of power, and searched for feasible model solutions. He pleaded for realism in the use of language and warned against too high expectations when making moral appeals. The church as *koinonia* was "the origin and aim" of the church and as such "the power behind all renewal processes in the church". Primarily on account of this ecclesiological exposition, the meeting in El Escorial became a place where practical questions of the development crisis and ecclesiological concepts were brought in relationship to each other more clearly "than ever before in the World Council".

When setting up their "guidelines for sharing" the meeting unfortunately did not heed his call for realism in the use of language and his warning against too high moral expectations. The first of 13 guidelines, which in a final act of self-commitment the participants recognized and promised to see put into practice in their own churches, demanded orientation towards a "totally new set of values which are based on justice, peace and the integrity of creation". The second basic commitment aimed at a "new understanding of sharing", in which those who have been pushed to the edges of society "take their place as equal partners at the centre of all decision-making processes and activities". Thirdly, the participants committed themselves to identify with the poor and the oppressed and their organizations in the struggle for justice and human dignity, as well as exposing, condemning and fighting against the causes and structures of injustice "at all levels". Furthermore, they agreed to openness, the duty to be accountable to each other and to correct each other, as well as to create relationships "in which no one is absolute giver or absolute taker any more". In order to realize this "the institutions of the North" had to "make the structural changes necessary".

The El Escorial guidelines had practically no effect in the churches. Just a few years after the assembly, "the spirit of El Escorial" had disappeared. There were several reasons for this. They include the tendency towards inertia on the part of the Northern churches and institutions, mentioned several times already. It was on them that the assembly had put the main burden of structural changes; trying to implement these in their home churches was too great a challenge for the Northern participants – or once the conference was over, they did not want to try.

At the conference itself, Raiser had pointed out that everything had essentially already been said. It was not necessary to make any new fundamental declaration, as the ones made so far had hardly inspired any change in practice. He mentioned several contradictions in the practice of the churches, for example the division between mission and development work that still existed and the imprisonment in the power of money and the hunt for projects. "Our practice does not keep up with our insights," Raiser said. The basic conflict behind this was the one between power and powerlessness.

However, in the formulation of the guidelines for sharing, the conference itself contributed greatly to their ineffectiveness. The guidelines reflect a globalism exaggerated to the extreme, which so blurs the aims of justifiable demands that they are no longer recognizable. The necessary concretization is in no way achieved by indiscriminately introducing problem situations into the text, to a great extent dependent on the signs of the times. The result is that the guidelines for sharing are not easy to put into practice in churches and institutions. From this point of view, El Escorial fell behind what the workbook *Empty Hands* had achieved.

With his consequential pragmatic approach to the problems, Raiser gave the meeting advice for formulating their guidelines, advice the participants did not take, but which nevertheless is of importance for working out more just structures between the churches in district and congregational partnerships as well.

With reference to the formulation of the Ten Commandments, Raiser pointed out that the decisive commandments relevant for the life of society are formulated as *negative* commandments. They are commitments to refrain from doing things, rather than to act positively. In consequence, the formulation of a "joint discipline of sharing together" would be in the commitment "to refrain from everything that could stand in the way of the realization of *koinonia*". The aim of just a few basic rules must be to protect the rights of the weaker members of the community and to temper the use of power. According to Raiser these "boundary markers" are:

– respect for the self-reliance of the partner: self-reliance and equality are basic prerequisites for sharing everything together;
– equal participation of all partners in the decisions concerning the relationship;
– rules for giving and receiving, especially in the question of conditions attached to the use of resources being offered;
– the scope of the accountability to each other;
– one-sided or joint establishment of mandates and criteria for review.

Finally, Raiser stated, such a commitment to share could not only limit itself to sharing among Christians. The Christian community would only become a parable of life shared together when they shared the goodness of God's creation with all people. The community in solidarity between Christians and the solidarity with the poor in their struggle for justice and human rights belonged together.

It was above all on account of these ideas expressed by Raiser that the consultation in El Escorial contributed decisive insights towards more just relations between churches, which are still relevant today. It strengthened the ecumenical vision of the church as a sharing community, as *koinonia*, and in this way called upon the churches not to accept just giver-receiver relationships and the power divide as it is, either within the ecumenical church community or outside of it.

THE ECUMENICAL AFFIRMATION ON "MISSION AND EVANGELISM"

In July 1982 the central committee of the WCC passed an "affirmation" on mission and evangelism that had been prepared in the previous years by the Commission on World Mission and Evangelism. This was a further milestone in the extensive relations between mission and church since the integration of the International Missionary Council and the WCC in 1961.

In the declaration the fruits of the theological work of both the IMC, the CWME and the world mission conferences were bundled together and presented in concentrated form. With their adoption by the central committee, the statements on the mission of the church gained binding character for the WCC beyond the circle of the mission movement; they were also to represent the obligatory framework for the joint mission understanding of the member churches.

The ecumenical affirmation justified mission entirely in the sense of what had been recognized at the world mission conferences described above, and tried to avoid being one-sided, so that the affirmation was welcomed by both the "ecumenical" and the "evangelical" representatives of mission as a comprehensive representation of the understanding of mission. The mission of the church is founded on the *missio Dei* and described as a characteristic of the church as the body of Christ. The kingdom of God is at the heart of that to which the church is called. The proclamation of the gospel calls the people to "look at this Jesus and to give their lives to him, to enter into the kingdom, whose King has come to us in the powerless child in Bethlehem and in the one who was put to death on the cross".

The declaration contains several concise statements on the unity of the church as well as on the relations between the churches in mission. Here the eucharist as starting point is the central idea: it is the "place of the renewal of missionary conviction at the heart of every congregation" and "food for the missionaries". At the same time it is the place where the still existing divisions and separations in the body of Christ are felt most painfully.

Under the heading, "Mission in and to Six Continents", the subject of the world mission conference in Mexico City, the affirmation looks at interchurch relations. More insistently than in previous documents it stresses the absolute correlation between worldwide missionary involvement and "mission at the parish doorstep". The affirmation sees the latter as having priority: without a serious missionary involvement at home, Christian declarations on the worldwide missionary responsibility of the church were not credible.

The ecumenical affirmation of 1982 brings up again the idea of a moratorium – as an "at least temporary cessation in sending and receiving of missionaries and material support across national borders": "to regain and strengthen the identity of each church, and to encourage concentration on mission at home and a new reflection of traditional relations" was the aim of this suggestion from the 1970s. A moratorium did not mean the end of missionary calling; however, it did mean "the freedom to rethink existing involvement" and to test whether they were still "the right sort of mission for the present day". The moratorium had to be understood as "an element in the concern for world mission". The affirmation links these very cautious reminders of the suggestion of a moratorium to the demand that the churches should in future work better together at a regional level and bring about a change in the direction of mission in this way.

While not in any way denying the continuing significance and necessity of a mutuality between the churches in the Northern and the Southern hemispheres, we believe that we can discern a development whereby mission in the eighties may increasingly take place within these zones.... This development, we expect, will take the form of ever stronger initiatives from the churches of the poor and oppressed at the peripheries.... While resources may still flow from financially richer to poorer churches, and while it is not our intention to encourage isolationism, we feel that a benefit of this new reality could well be the loosening of the bond of domination and dependence that still so scandalously characterizes the relationship between many churches of the northern and southern hemispheres respectively.

It is remarkable that the declaration takes up the demand for a moratorium and combines it with a positive structural suggestion. Missionary relations across national borders should rather be made and built up between churches within a region that is between "equally strong churches", although here too the rich churches should give to the poorer churches to create a better balance. The adoption of this suggestion and the identification of the aim – to dissolve the "dominance" which continues to exist between churches – point to the continuing deficiencies in the relations between the churches of the North and those of the South.

THE WORLD MISSION CONFERENCE IN SAN ANTONIO 1989

The world mission conference in San Antonio, Texas, did not make any great progress in the ecumenical discussions that interest us here as regards interchurch relations. The delegates referred mainly to the results of former world mission conferences, they took up the findings of ecumenical and mission theology study processes and made them their own. As far as the question of the ecumenical understanding of mission was concerned the conference referred consistently to the ecumenical affirmation on "Mission and Evangelism" from 1982. On the question of forms of interchurch community it quoted to a large extent the results of the study process on ecumenical sharing and the consultation in El Escorial. The delegates in San Antonio also described the worldwide church community as a sharing community founded on the eucharist *(koinonia)*.

Of the 275 delegates, 178 were from countries of the so-called second and third worlds. The theme of the conference was once again a petition from the Lord's Prayer: "Your Will Be Done – Mission in Christ's Way". Those who planned the conference in San Antonio wanted to offer a forum in which the many-sided experiences of mission work could be shared together and made vocal. The proceedings offered the delegates, many of whom were actively involved in mission work in congregations and action groups, plenty of room for discussion in small groups. In its diversity and vitality the conference is described as extremely communicative, quite in contrast to the previous one in Melbourne. At the same time, however, regret is expressed that it did not succeed in bundling together the many different insights and differing experiences.

In my opinion, the conference, as many other ecumenical gatherings between the two assemblies of the World Council of Churches in Vancouver 1983 and Canberra 1991, could not resist the temptation of making almost all world problems the subject of their discussions. As a result the delegates' statements did not get beyond certain catch phrases and expressions of good intent. What would have been necessary was a more thorough analysis of the situation, an evaluation of how far former resolutions had actually become missionary practice and an intensive search for the obstacles that had consistently blocked the realization of former conference decisions. This analysis did not take place. At the same time old demands were made in answer to the same old questions, therefore in many ways the conference fell short of the progress made at previous conferences. This is especially the case as far as the search for new structures in mission was concerned.

The report of section I, "Turning to the Living God", calls upon the churches "wherever possible" to undertake joint missionary enterprises. As a sign of the growth of unity in mission the report names joint mission projects, church amalgamations and negotiations for union. However, it also states that differences in doctrine prevent joint eucharistic celebration in many places. The eucharist, the central place of the church community had become the place where the divisions had become most painfully visible. The section report complains bitterly about "proselytism" and "unhealthy competition" in mission and takes the position that old demands for closer cooperation and joint efforts for mission had not been followed. Denominationalism of the churches had even in some cases increased.

Section IV, "Towards Renewed Communities in Mission", deals with several themes of missionary practice, strengthens the right and necessity for mission, both "at our own doorsteps" as well as across national and continental boundaries "to the ends of the earth". Here is reference to the former discussion about a moratorium in mission. According to section IV, mission is "the essential task of every local community".

In its statements on interchurch relations in mission the section essentially limits itself to cautiously formulated appeals to deal with each other in a respectful and considerate way. What is required is "profound sensitivity and openness rooted in spirituality, respect for the cultures and values of other people"; in relations between churches, mutual acceptance of one another as partners and respect must be the dominant features; discussion and cooperation are "essential prerequisites for mission"; the "denominational heritage" must be respected and also the local culture and heritage. The existing "exchange of personnel in mission in many directions" must be strengthened, the possibilities for South-North and South-South exchanges should be made easier. "Those concerned should share all their resources justly with each other."

In this and other passages the glaring deficiencies of the conference declarations are apparent: nowhere is there a description of the existing relations between the churches in mission; the problems facing them are not named anywhere; in certain formulations they are even veiled over.

Peter Sandner attests to a "clear change of climate" in the discussions on interchurch relations in San Antonio. In Bangkok the Western churches and missions had often felt themselves to be sitting "in the dock"; in Melbourne the relations between the churches of the North and the South were considered very much under the concept of power; San Antonio however had presented "concrete models of partnership"; Sandner writes, "in place of making accusations and demands now encouragement is being given".

However the question is whether the problems and conflicts that had arisen in Bangkok and Melbourne had really been overcome. Theo Ahrens points out in his report that the moratorium debate of the 1960s and the 1970s had had "no recognizable effect", at least not in Germany.

The integration debate, while having led to organizational restructuring in the field of mission, had not led to the hoped-for "new practice of mission in the traditional sending churches". Ahrens recognized "internalized dependency relationships in the historical mission churches" and at the same time in sharp contrast an "insubordination" of these churches towards the churches in the North, "an insubordination to which these reacted with the conciliatory statement 'today we are partners!'". In this way the term "partnership" was used at the present time as a "term of exoneration".

Section IV of the San Antonio conference states:

If these new and renewed structures are to be a sign of the reign of God as we perceive it, they should have among their characteristics the following:

- recognition that all God's gifts are common property;
- mutual acceptance of one another as partners;
- recognition of cultural diversity as an enrichment of sharing
- equal access to sources of information;
- transparency;
- joint planning and implementation of policies;

- openness to sharing of non-material resources such as theological reflections, liturgies, hymnologies, new forms of spirituality, life-styles, etc., as well as financial resources; and
- acceptance of mutual accountability and correction of anything that proves ineffective or inadequate.

As a model for such renewed missionary relations the section suggests: "transformation of a missionary society through the transfer of power and funds to a common governing body in which all the partners – in both North and South – can share on a footing of real equality". The churches were called upon to undertake "a great variety of experiments attempting to put these principles into practice".

As far as the question of renewed missionary relations between the churches is concerned, the world mission conference in San Antonio did not get beyond formulating good intentions. This is to a large extent the result of the conference documents, which sought to even out conflicts and either ignored them or sought to cover them up. The term "partnership", which was hardly used anyway, experienced yet again a shift in emphasis. It had been used at the beginning, as already described, to bind the churches of the South into the missionary work (Whitby), and later to justify the continuing right of Western missionary activity in the South in spite of the demand for a moratorium (Bangkok). Now in San Antonio it served to cover up conflicts, which had arisen out of the still existing imbalance in relations. The increasing desolate financial situation of many churches in the South deepened their dependency on the churches of the North dramatically. The term "partnership" now suggested a relationship between the churches based on equality and mutual sharing, which however did not actually exist.

The term and the concept of "partnership in mission" had not led to the intended new orientation of missionary practice in the churches of the North. Theo Ahrens points to this when he questions how far, in newer missionary strategies for a nationwide church in the Federal Republic of Germany, "a reflection of that which we have become accustomed to call ecumenical learning" was to be found. The question was, which "serious expectations" the Christians and churches in Europe had "of the churches in the third world". The "authentic Christian as the twin of the noble savage compensating for the missing utopian drive of his or her own church" was not enough base for a practice of sharing together as equals. Churches in Europe and America had to formulate their expectations clearly and practically "and in this way give the Christians and the churches in the third world the chance to share". It seems to me that the really forward-looking perspective for the new structuring of the relations between the churches of the North and the South might lie in this invitation.

THE ECUMENICAL DISCUSSION AROUND THE WCC ASSEMBLIES IN
VANCOUVER 1983 AND CANBERRA 1991

To conclude this historical review, I should like to take a short look at further ecumenical discussion on the structures of missionary relations between churches. The aim is not to describe the two assemblies of the WCC in Vancouver and Canberra, but rather to pick out certain passages from the conference documents which are relevant for this study.

It can be said of both conferences that they brought no essentially new findings as far as missionary relations between churches are concerned. Instead they worked their way through the results of the study processes already mentioned. In Vancouver the delegates of group I, "Witness in a Divided World", referred mainly to the ecumenical affirmation on "Mission and Evangelism"; at Canberra the churches were once again recommended to follow the "Guidelines for Sharing" from the consultation in El Escorial. The celebration of the eucharist was central, as in previous ecumenical discussions for the unity of the church, which was to be strived for and realized. The picture of the "sharing community" of the churches, as koinonia, became the central concept and the decisive guiding principle for the work of the WCC and for the churches in the ecumenical movement, even if there is no doubt that in practice the churches were "a long way removed" from forming such a "community of healing and sharing", as the moderator of the central committee, Heinz Joachim Held, expressed it in Canberra.

I now want to consider two aspects of this: (1) in Vancouver, how the relevant working group looked more closely at the question of witness among the poor, using the findings of the world mission conference in Melbourne in 1981; and (2) how Canberra took up the recommendations for ecumenical sharing.

The assembly in Vancouver, in accepting the results of the study process on the "Churches in Solidarity with the Poor" and the world mission conference in Melbourne, had taken over the idea of God's special option for the poor, but not the critical statements of this conference about the wealth of the churches and societies in the North. The Christian gospel of salvation was "good news for *all* people, particularly for the poor" – the formulation from Vancouver. The "message of the prophets" was that God did not take a neutral stance between rich and poor. "God is on the side of the poor and fights for their right to justice and fullness of life."

The calling of the churches to witness in the life of the poor was a call to the people of God to set their priorities in his mission and to rethink their programmes and call their life-styles into question both as a community and at a personal level. A "life in greater simplicity or even in poverty" was laid upon the church as witness to Christ's poverty. The calling to "share the good news with the poor" had priority and was to become a special task.

In its witness to the poor and the oppressed the church was able to and had to become the voice of those who often had no voice. This formulation makes it clear that the ecumenical movement had moved away again from the idea of the "church with the poor" and the ecclesiological consequences that it implied. The church here is clearly seen rather as standing over against the poor in a caring role as their advocates. Compared to the demand for the identification of the church with the poor, this is a step backwards.

At the assembly in Canberra in 1991 section III concerned itself with questions of mission and ecumenical sharing under the theme: "Spirit of Unity – Reconcile Your People!". In the section report the sub-section on "The Wholeness of Mission" begins: "We affirm that we are called to share the gospel among all peoples locally and globally." The problems involved with talking about "sending churches" are taken up, at least in cases where this sending occurs in an aggressive form from West to South. Structural changes were necessary, "where 'sending' perpetuates denominational engagement in mission and separated churches". The Christians from "prosperous areas" are called upon to learn in humility from their oppressed sisters and brothers in the South. In this way it would be possible "in the midst of economic injustice and political hostility" to achieve "real sharing and a partnership in mission". "Sharing with each other", the section states, taking up the findings of El Escorial, means giving and receiving on both sides in order to effect reconciliation and to grow together. "In response to the cries of the poor and the marginalized in the world, sharing means committing ourselves as churches to the sharing of power and resources so that all may fully participate in mission."

Even in this point the ecumenical text does not go beyond previous insights. There is no critical discussion about why the declaration from El Escorial had not been put into practice. Instead, the WCC is called upon to recommend again to the churches to put the "Guidelines for Sharing" into practice. In order to achieve this, various models and experiments should be financially supported – an approach to the development of new structures which the world mission conference in San Antonio had brought into the discussion.

8. Partnership – the transformation of a concept: the yield of the historical review

To conclude the first part of this study I shall review the historical changes the term "partnership in mission" has undergone; which subjects and problems were dealt with in the discussions about partnership; and which consequences arise from these when talking about partnerships between churches today. At the beginning, however, I shall make a short digression to consider British colonial policy and its terminology, and to use this to explain important connotations of the term partnership. In the section on the use of the term during and after the world mission conference in Whitby, I already noted that it was representatives of British missions who brought the term into the mission theological debate and predominantly used it. This leads me to the question whether there are links between the terminology of British colonial policy and the terms used in particular by British mission academics.

DIGRESSION: THE TERM "PARTNERSHIP" IN BRITISH COLONIAL POLICY IN THE 20TH CENTURY

British colonial policy proved to be very flexible and adaptable with regard to the special regional situations of the colonies and new challenges of the times. What is most interesting here is which main political terms were dominant and what they were understood to mean. My assumption is confirmed that the term partnership, in its specific usage in the context of North-South relations, came in no small degree from British colonial policy. It is also possible to demonstrate, from the experience of various individuals, that the British colonial debate and the British mission theological debate influenced each other. My provisional hypothesis is therefore that the term partnership, which was introduced into the mission theological debate in Whitby, had its origins to an important degree in the discussions about British colonial policy.

As late as after the first world war the British government was still facing the question of what status of independence and self-reliance should be accorded to the various colonies. Of course the debate was not new. It had been of concern since the North American wars of independence and the United States's break from the British empire in 1776. This date marks the beginning of a process in which the empire receded step by step and a multiracial commonwealth took its place. The unusual feature of British colonial policy is that it did not understand the transition from empire to commonwealth only as a loss of ruling power, but rather tried to bring the transition about as a deliberate and planned reorganization in response to the challenges of the times. According to Rudolf von Albertini, leading British colonial politicians saw in this transition from empire to commonwealth the fulfilment of a concept and an idea,

> which originally after the loss of the American colonies... had led to a partnership of equal rights with nations of British origin, who were sovereign

states and independent, yet under the same crown and with the same ideals and institutions formed a unit – a unit in freedom and an example for the world!

1. "Dominions" of the whites

First of all, a fundamental distinction must be made between the white settler colonies (in Canada, Australia, New Zealand and South Africa, for example) and the dependent crown colonies in Africa and Asia. The white settler colonies had already been allowed relative independence quite early. They were first allowed representative government and later responsible government. They were granted the so-called "dominion status". The British empire conference in 1917 limited the "imperial commonwealth" to the autonomous dominions. India was refused dominion status.

2. "Trusteeship"

At the beginning of the 20th century and increasingly after the first world war – as a result among other things of the emancipation movements of the Middle East and the Far East – the discussion arose about the right to self-determination for the so-called colonial nations. As early as 1905, the term "partnership" was first used in this context. However, the more dominant term at first was that of "trusteeship". It signalled a certain willingness to allow the colonies self-responsibility (for example in economic questions), while at the same time marking a clear limit as far as self-government was concerned, i.e. dominion status.

After 1919 the term "trusteeship" became the real slogan of British colonial policy. This included both retention of a certain British governmental power (particularly in foreign and security policy) and the protective function of Great Britain towards its colonies, as well as promise of a kind of "development aid". British trusteeship over the colonies was seen as being for a limited period. London began to take on a more liberal attitude. A willingness to make concessions grew, especially where demands for emancipation were accompanied by threatened political unrest. It seems reasonable that soon after the end of the first world war it became necessary to discuss whether the non-white colonies should also be granted dominion status. This question became particularly acute in the case of India. Here an essential difference can be seen between British colonial policy and the colonial policy of, say, France or Holland. France set up a mainly direct administration in its mandate areas. Great Britain in contrast "showed herself to be more flexible and tolerated various forms of government, which could develop even as far as formal independence".

However, the intended self-government in the colonies had its share of protests. There was a lack of administrative experience in the colonies; there was a lack of national unity; besides which London could not hand over power to the educated minority, for it understood itself as trustee for the uneducated and politically not yet organized masses. It is remarkable that even at this time J.H. Oldham, secretary of the International Missionary Council, a leading mission man, was already actively involved in the British colonial debate.

3. "Indirect rule", "paramountcy" and "dual policy"

As a first step on the way to independence of the colonies in Africa and Asia, London introduced – in West Africa first – the policy of indirect rule: traditional leaders were given a certain amount of governmental power. At the same time this was to open up the way for the development of autonomous African systems of government. The native administration was to be given real government competence in the areas handed over to them; there was no demand that it had necessarily to be similar in form to that of the mother country. At the same time in the context of the disputes concerning the status of British settlers in Kenya another important term was coined: "paramountcy". The Devonshire declaration of 1926 stated that the interests of the African inhabitants of the country were higher than those of the white minority. This central political concept was also largely developed by mission secretary Oldham.

In contrast, the concept of the so-called "dual policy", carried through on the basis of settlers' objections, was a step backwards. This concept understood the interests of whites and blacks in Kenya to be complementary, and white settlers were conceded certain rights to self-government to protect their interests.

4. "Partnership"

During the second world war the discussion went a step further. The term "trusteeship" no longer seemed to be in keeping with the times. British colonial politicians demanded as early as 1942 that instead of "trusteeship", one should speak of "partnership". With this term, responsible self-government for the colonies seemed to have moved within reach. A new reciprocal relationship between the United Kingdom and the colonies should now be described, in the light of which the idea of "trusteeship" seemed too passive and paternalistic. At the same time local government should also replace the principle of indirect rule.

In June 1942, five years before the world mission conference in Whitby, the British government declared the principle of partnership to be the "governing principle of the colonial empire".

The government wanted to present itself as a reforming government. However, this term also remained very vague. Above all they continued to differentiate between "partnership", the dominion status and the status of full independence. The aim of development was intentionally left open. In this way the government thought "to be able to bring the will for reform into line with the imperial tradition". In the end the British government did not intend independence but rather, according to Albertini, "self-government within the empire".

The different ways in which the term "partnership" could be understood became apparent during the conflict around the Federation of Rhodesia. Albertini made out three different ways of understanding the term: Conservatives, starting from the "dual policy" and the dominance of the whites, intended a slow integration of blacks and the step-by-step handover of certain limited rights. Liberal forces understood "partnership" to mean the equal representation of black and white interests in the legislative assembly and the executive. The London government and the Labour party did not define the term more specifically at all. In the conflict on Rhodesia it was the missionaries and church leaders who, among others, stood up for African emancipation and demanded that the Africans should share in political power much sooner.

During the 1960s and 1970s the process of decolonization came to an end and independence and self-government were fought for and achieved. The commonwealth developed into a "multiracial commonwealth of free and equal members". In political discussions the term "partnership" got yet another meaning: it was now used to describe the demands for equal rights of the white minorities in the colonies.

5. Summary: British colonial policy and mission theology

This short discourse on the main terms of British colonial policy shows very clear parallels to the discussions on the question of North-South relations during the world mission conferences. Even if mission experts took part in the political discussions in England, nevertheless it must be said that British colonial policy was several years in advance of the discussions at the world mission conferences. Conversely it can be said that the term partnership with reference to North-South relations found its way into the mission theological debate through its usage in British colonial policy. To be quite clear about this: the term partnership is a term of the colonial era.

Parallel in both lines of discussion, concerning colonial policy and mission theology, are external events and global aims. Both of them were concerned with gradually granting greater independence and autonomy. Both of them took their impetus separately from the emancipation movements and independence movements in the colonies. The line of conflict is also similar in both cases: while the European side saw the necessity, supported by factual information, to release the Asian or African "partner" into independence and self-administration, at the same time they did not want to give up their power and influence entirely. Against the process of looming independence both of them argued that the overseas partners were not yet "mature" enough, that they had not yet enough education, capabilities or personalities with leadership qualities. Finally, it is striking that in both cases the term "partnership" was introduced and raised to a guiding principle without any further qualification as to its meaning. In both cases the new formula had a veiling, disguising function. The intention was more to signal a willingness for change rather than to actually constitute a qualitatively new relationship.

British colonial policy reflects this specific tension in the term partnership extremely clearly: it is a formula of the former "rulers", who with it wished both to signal a relinquishment of power and also to secure their influence in the future. Therefore the term can also serve both in colonial policy and mission practice to justify continuing rights of the white minority.

In Whitby, the linking of the term partnership with obedience to God's call marked a specific difference from its usage in British colonial policy. In this way the term gained its specially defined form influenced by the insights of mission theology with regard to the North-South relations of the churches. However, if we consider once more the way the British idea of partnership was fitted into the entire context of the coming into being of the commonwealth ("a unity with joint ideals, a unity of freedom, as an example for the world") structural parallels are also apparent here. In the mission theological debate after the second world war the term partnership also served to join together and to consolidate the greater unity of the ecumenical mission community.

THE DEVELOPMENT OF THE TERM "PARTNERSHIP" AND ITS SIGNIFICANCE

The following section does not set out to summarize the results of the historical review. Instead, four thematic strands will be used to develop ways of looking at problems and some of the questions arising out of them for the analysis of case studies in partnership.

Our attention first must be directed to the term "partnership" itself. I have shown that it was already used at the Jerusalem world mission conference, that in Whitby and Achimota it served in a prominent way to describe the relations between the churches of the South and the missionary societies. In the following years the significance of the term decreases as other leading terms become important in ecumenical discussions.

The meaning of the term "partnership" and how it was understood underwent specific changes over a period of time. The striving for partnership in interchurch relations aimed most of all at overcoming one-sided dependencies, and the division of power and rule. Positively used, partnership meant the recognition of the autonomy of the other, respect for their independence and their difference. The partners were to be allowed to go their own way and to be enabled to realize their own individual development. Reciprocity was the decisive thing – reciprocal relations.

Historically this demanded of the Northern missionary societies that they were willing to give up their leadership role and their authority. This breaking of the "dominance of the whites" proved to be very difficult to put into practice. It was opposed by interests wanting to maintain living standards, interests which also used the term "partnership" to assert their own rights. To this extent "partnership" alone cannot really describe the relations sought for between the churches in a positive and clearly defined way. All too often the term was used quite consciously to disguise conflicts.

Essential when examining district and congregational partnerships is the critical question of a continuing difference in the relationship, the question of one-sided dependency. It must be asked whether the ruling dominance of the West, which continues to be the norm worldwide, is overcome in the partnership.

The ecumenical term "partnership" gains its specific form through being tied into the participation of the churches in God's mission. This is therefore the second aspect. In contrast to the beginning of the century, mission can no longer be understood only in the sense of conversion of the heathen and founding of churches. As a result of the efforts made in mission theology since the second world war, the justification for mission is in God's own action and the nature of the church. This implies overcoming the former one-way street of mission from North to South. But in the North too, missionary activity does not consist only of winning back church members. Mission participates in God's mission in his movement towards the world. It is not the task of specialists or specialist agencies but rather belongs to the living expression of every local congregation. Ecumenical study programmes have tried to work out what this can actually mean in practical terms.

It must therefore be asked how far partnerships which have come into being thanks to the historic context of mission contribute to the ecumenical missionary direction and ability of their congregations. Do district and congregation partnerships exhaust themselves in maintaining a bilateral overseas relationship, or do they change congregational life in the sense of an opening up of the congregation and its missionary presence with the poor and those on the fringes of society in social crisis points?

A third aspect: the ecumenical discussion on interchurch relations was from the beginning directed towards the search for greater and organizational unity of the churches. In the context of mission relations it was mostly the churches of the South who complained frequently about the annoyance of denominational fragmentation. The unity of the church, in which they all believed, should be expressed both in joint action and in the joint celebration of the eucharist.

This raises the question for the district and congregational partnerships, in how far they have contributed, as a special form of ecumenical relationship beyond the bilateral relations, to the renewal of the local ecumenical community.

Finally, the division between poor and rich has proved to be a grave and constantly recurring strain on interchurch relations. Again and again the ecumenical movement has made attempts to make clear that this is both a fundamental problem of social and political orientation as well as a fundamental calling into question of the ecumenical church community, and therefore both a socio-political and an ecclesiological problem at the same time.

The search for worldwide justice is both ecumenical declaration and ecumenical task. The churches have repeatedly pointed out that the problems of poverty and injustice cannot be overcome by the transfer of money and material aid, because these lead to new forms of dependence and a new lack of freedom. The experience of a remaining imbalance in interchurch relations led to some of the churches of the South calling for a moratorium in the transfer of money and personnel from the North to the South. The ecumenical commitment is to work for structures that contribute to a sustainable triumph over poverty and injustice. Congregational and district partnerships are to be questioned as to how far they allow themselves to be shaped by this challenge.

II. Experiencing Ecumenism
Partnerships and Their Importance for Congregations and Dioceses, Regional Churches and Their Mission Departments

We have looked at interchurch relations, with the following questions in mind: the North-South divide or rather the poor-rich divide and its effect on partnership relations, and the meaning of mission for churches and congregations. Case studies will look at joint efforts of the partners for unity of the church and for peace, justice and the integrity of creation and question their importance for district and congregation partnerships.

These issues are at the centre of both the second and the third parts of this study. I shall first look at the congregational and district level, and examine the beginnings of four partnerships, assuming that the necessity to justify a partnership is strongest at the beginning. From there it will become clear what reasons led to the partnership and what aims it was intended to fulfil. A second round of questions will be directed towards the institutional level, the regional churches and their mission departments: What are the institutional expectations and concepts of partnership work, and how are the activities of the districts and congregations regarded? Thirdly, I shall consider individual persons, those involved in partnership work, be it as participants on visits, as hosts to visitors or as members of partnership committees: What brought them into partnership work? What interests, motives and expectations play a role for them? The concluding section deals with the importance of mission in partnership work: it refers to the presentation in the first part of the book, and enquires to what extent people involved in partnership work at an individual, congregational or district level are actually aware of aspects of the ecumenical debate.

Visits of delegations from both sides may be the most important part of partnership work. However, I have not included the programmes of the visits in this part of the study. This has to do with the fact that the partners' direct encounters are seen as the essential place for joint learning, and the success of the learning process depends to a large extent on the programme of the visit. Therefore my observations concerning partnership visits will mainly be presented in the next chapter. However, I shall point out where overlapping and repetition were unavoidable.

1. The formation of partnerships

The following are some typical factors that appear to play a role in the formation of a partnership.

First, the strong relationship between individuals right from the beginning of such interchurch partnerships. This is the same for many more partnership relations than the four particularly studied. Partnerships are formed usually because of personal relations or contacts. The idea of seeking a partnership relationship with Christians overseas – in this case in African countries – stems almost always from the fact that members of a congregation have some personal connection to the partner country or partner church.

Very different contacts can start the process off. It can perhaps be a link to a German worker in the partner country concerned, perhaps someone working for the mission department of a regional church or for a German development agency. It is often people who have returned from such a period of service who suggest a partnership in their new place of work. This was the way that earlier partnerships at least came into being (e.g., Marienwerder and Lünen). A second possibility is that visitors from the partner country, possibly during a purely chance visit to a congregation, set off the wish for a long-term relationship. A third factor can be a journey undertaken by members of the congregation, even a holiday trip, to an overseas country.

Only much later did the regional churches and their mission departments try to win almost "blanket coverage" for partnership relations within the districts. The concept of "partnership" was rarely the triggering factor and, if at all, is a much more recent phenomenon only really relevant in the overseas partner churches. There the "partnership movement" has developed its own momentum in the meantime so that many congregations now have first an interest in partnership and only later seek contact with a partner country and partner church.

The second characteristic for beginning a partnership is that it is a very small group – frequently just one person – who gets the partnership going. This was the case in all the partnerships examined here. The individuals could be named who had been mainly responsible for the partnership being established. Here also the very personal nature of individual relationships in district and congregational partnerships is apparent.

Individual partnerships are therefore very much formed according to the personal interests of these persons or groups of persons. In most cases the initiators do not only determine the beginning of a partnership but also work actively in an outstanding position in it over many years and influence it decisively. The face of a partnership – whether its main focus is a church one or a development-oriented one, whether spiritual-theological questions or social questions play a role, or whether it is primarily concerned with financial and project aid – depends not exclusively but essentially on the initiator(s) and is determined right at the beginning of the partnership for the long-term.

The personalized nature of partnerships is the basis for building up long-term permanent relationships and is therefore an opportunity. At the same time one of the fundamental difficulties is that partnerships remain limited to a small circle of activists who do not succeed in establishing them more firmly in the congregation and the district. Here too the decisive course is set right at the beginning. It is very important that the congregational council is involved in discussions and considerations from the beginning and that a large number of members of the congregation support the decision. Only then is there a chance that the partnership can survive when there is a change of pastor or decisive persons leave the congregation.

Where the partnership depended from the beginning on the initiative of a single superintendent or pastor and was limited to a small group of people, it usually remained difficult even many years later to establish it on a wider basis in the congregation. In such cases partnership was often seen as the hobby or the "play area of a few ecumenical freaks".

A further characteristic of the way partnerships began seems to be that the initiative usually came from the German side. Apart from a possibly different development in the last few years, one can clearly state that at first it was the German partners who wanted partnership. They undertook first organizational steps; they directed a suitable request to the African church. The authorities concerned reacted and sought a possible partner district or congregation. This was also the case where German missionaries working in an African country gave the impetus for a partnership. This does not mean that African churches had no interest of their own in partnership. However, it can be proved that at the beginning the movement was one from the German churches to the African ones. The decisive question, which will have to be clarified in the process of this study, is how far this structure at the beginning led to the development of a structure of "dominance" on the part of the German partners.

Here I should like to point to the terminology used in the early years. At the beginning of the 1970s and partly still at the end, the term *Patenschaft* (sponsorship or God-parenthood) was used within the partnerships *(Partnerschaft)* without anyone considering it to be problematic. The changeover to *Partnerschaft* happened gradually. One gets the impression that it was more to conform to social patterns of language than anything else. Amazingly, I have found no indications of serious attempts to find a different term. This is surprising because there were many complaints that the term "partnership" did not have sufficient theological, biblical quality.

But what are the most basic reasons for forming a partnership? The interest aroused by a personal contact is rather too diffuse. The attitude of the congregational council in Marienwerder (one of the partnership congregations examined) is typical of many others: open and interested and at the same time rather distanced. The members of the congregation could "not yet really imagine what it might mean", the instigator wrote.

It seems as though this diffuse interest in partnership consists of two different motives: one is the wish to get to know people in a partner country, the partner church, as directly and as closely as possible. A key motive may be summed up this way: "For once to be able to see it yourself, feel it yourself and taste it yourself and not only to hear about it." And yet the wish to help people out of poverty, misery and oppression through direct financial, material and spiritual help also plays a role. This element should not be underestimated for mobilizing people. It seems no coincidence that – particularly in Marienwerder – the partnership movement often comes into real contact with the congregation for the first time when they make a call for donations. It seems that without a call for donations or aid the partnership does not really get going.

What both motives have in common – direct encounter and direct aid – is their direct access to the partners. Partnerships are interesting because they offer a unique opportunity for close encounters with foreign people and faraway countries. This is reflected clearly in the dissatisfaction with the opportunities offered by Bread for the World projects expressed frequently by those who wish to get involved with the third world. The motives for partnership work are, however, sufficient for a chapter of their own.

2. The aims of partnership

How far were the partnership groups or the district partnership committees able to agree on certain aims with regard to the form the partnership should take? Why is a partnership begun and established? Is there a special intention behind it and, if so, what is it? What does a district or a congregation expect from a partnership with a district or congregation in Africa? Previously we concentrated on the ideas of the initiators. Now we look at how far these ideas were taken over by members of the partnership groups, the congregations and the districts and how far they are still in practice today. This is followed by the question of how far these formulated aims were part of discussions between the partners and whether they managed to formulate anything together.

The most important aims formulated by the initiators at the beginning of the partnerships are, first, that "the worldwide church should be experienced". In other words, the ecumenical church community should become concrete at congregational level. Through interchurch partnerships it should become possible for congregation members to get accustomed to the "ecumenical horizon". Secondly, a "missionary impetus" should extend from the partnerships to the congregations in Germany. It was expected that these congregations would become more open towards outsiders and foreigners through their encounters with Christians in the partner churches, and that through partnership work people would find a new approach to the congregation and the church.

A third aim was raising an awareness of the problems of North-South relations and development education. This was linked to the idea of being able to practise concrete solidarity with disadvantaged and oppressed peoples within the framework of the partnership. Fourthly and finally, it was hoped that partnerships would "reawaken" and renew the traditional involvement for mission in the congregations.

If one looks at the further development of the four partnerships studied, it becomes apparent that there was no further fundamental clarification of possible aims as far as the partnership was concerned. The initiators had probably formulated their ideas and informed others about them and that they therefore had some effect even if only under the surface. Nevertheless, I considered it to be indicative that in none of the four partnerships could I discover a further description of aims which had been worked out as a commitment between the active members of the partnership group or even between the two partners, either from the beginning of the partnership or later on. In none of the four cases did a partnership contract exist, at least not from the early years. The partnerships between Germany and Namibia supported by the United Evangelical Mission (VEM) at least took over the agreements of the consultations from Gut Holmecke (1985) and Swakopmund (1990) and made them their own. Model contracts as since developed by the regional church mission departments, containing a short list of reasons for the partnership, did not exist at the beginning of the 1980s. However, they are still not very often used by the partnership groups. In the interviews conducted during this study I always had a negative answer to the question whether within the partnership there was a joint understanding of what partnership was, which had been worked out together. It is rather the case that the members of the partnership groups each have their own personal understanding of what partnership is.

This does not mean that there have been no statements made about the meaning and aims of a partnership. In words of greeting, in sermons and on other such occasions, especially during delegation visits, statements are made on the meaning and aim of partnership. However these are usually individual statements and as a rule are not taken up in such a way as to get the partners talking together about what their partnership is really about.

An example is the words of greeting given by the acting dean of the diocese of Polkwane, J.M. Senona, on the occasion of his delegation visit to Osterholz-Scharmbeck in May and June 1993. Senona referred to Ephesians 4:7-12, which speaks of the various gifts and offices, and he commented:

> We, who have been called into one of the five leading ministries, have an important three-part duty to perform. We are to teach our church members to: minister to the Lord; minister to one another; minister to the world. The partnership programme should be seen by us all as an instrument to facilitate this threefold ministry both in South Africa and in Germany.

These few sentences do not go beyond general implications. As usual with words of greeting there was no reaction given to them. Nevertheless, two aspects are named here that hint at an understanding of the ideas and aims behind partnership: it is concerned with ministry to the Lord of the church, to the partners and to the world; and this service must occur both in South Africa and in Germany. What that means then for each of the partners in their situation and how this can result in responsible action both jointly and separately, is something that partners could and should try to talk about together.

The fact that partnerships generally do not have clearly defined descriptions corresponds to the rather diffuse interests at the beginning of a partnership mentioned in the previous section. Consequently, those involved often have very different and sometimes vague ideas about what partnership involves. Even the ideas of the initiator are primarily only personal ideas. In spite of this, one aspect has priority – just as in the question of motives at the beginning: the direct personal encounter between persons. That is the answer to the question of the meaning and the aim of ecumenical partnerships between congregations or districts: to enable direct encounters between people from different churches, places, countries and continents. Here partnerships have both their justification and their aim. It is often out of direct encounters that direct immediate project support develops. The financing and running of such projects then often becomes in itself a motivating and meaningful element of partnership work.

However, such elements – against the background of the mission theological debate on interchurch relations – do not strictly count as justifiable aims for partnership. The aim "to make encounters possible" leaves a great deal of freedom and is very unspecific. The encounter is the aim; there is no greater thematic or theoretical interest behind it. In ecumenical partnerships as a rule the partners do not work together at a joint task. As personal encounters are so at the heart of the matter, delegation visits are of central importance. On the other hand, it is difficult to keep the partnership alive across such great distances between such visits.

Seeking a thematic justification or aim for partnership work does not mean that no great value is placed on the aspect of personal encounter. There is no doubt that the level of personal encounter determines the fundamental value of partnership relations. Through these encounters the hoped-for "acquisition of ecumenism" takes place. Through such encounters and only through them is there a collective experience, which can change people and make them capable of acting in a different way in church and society.

However, I must point out that the ecumenical declarations on interchurch relations formulated another aim of partnership, which goes beyond encouraging encounters and financing projects. It was most clearly expressed at the world mission conference in Whitby with the slogan "Partnership in Obedience". This slogan, which today district and congregational partnership groups are happy to use, was originally directed towards the "task of evangelizing the world", a goal the representatives of the missionary societies had at that time. All other ecumenical slogans, which speak of "Partnership in Mission" or "Partnership in Joint Ecumenical Responsibility" stress the ecumenical missionary character of partnership relations between the churches. It is remarkable that partnership relationships between German and African districts and congregations do not take this up. Yet the slogan "Partnership in Obedience" is hardly to be found in any congregation or district partnership. Many of those who are deeply involved in the work are not aware of it or have not heard of it.

It is apparent that existing partnerships are not oriented towards a certain aim, for only very occasionally do they talk about special subjects or discuss certain topics together, whether of a theological, sociopolitical or cultural nature, and this certainly does not play a dominant role in the partnerships. This is the case both for discussions within partnership groups and between the partners. Only a few of those involved expressed their dissatisfaction that partnership work concerned itself so little with relevant topics. This is a crucial deficit in most partnerships.

I would like to offer a provisional hypothesis on the relationship structure in partnerships based upon the review of how the partnerships came into being and their aims, given their specific context. Basically they all stem from an optimistic movement in the 1970s and 1980s, which against the background of mission and colonial history tried to build up new, more just relations between the North and South, based on equality and equal rights. My provisional hypothesis, which takes up information from the coming chapters, is this: many partnerships are still influenced and shaped by structural inequality and a structural divide to the disadvantage of the African partners.

I draw this conclusion first of all from the observation of typical characteristics at the start of many partnerships. First, I must acknowledge the primary initiative of the German partners. It was they who first had an interest in partnership. The German side put forward the leading ideas as well as the forms and structures of partnership contacts. Second, the wish for opportunities to give direct financial and project aid led to an active involvement of the German partners, which forced the African partners into a recipient role. It is furthermore undisputed that the real work in a partnership is done on the German side. It is here that committees meet, seminars are held, and planning and organization take place. Here also the money is raised. While this has to do with the fact that the infrastructure and the possibilities for organization are incomparably better in Germany than in African countries, nevertheless this inevitably leads to a dominant role of the German side in the partnerships. The problematic nature of this difference within the relationship is made worse by the lack of orientation in the partnerships towards thematic discussions or joint tasks. A mutual orientation towards a task where the partners stand "shoulder to shoulder" could overcome the unequal status of the partners in their relationship. The concentration, on the one hand, upon visits to each other without any thematic programme (the motive of direct encounter) and the support of financial and material aid projects by the German partners (motive of direct aid) tend to reinforce the global North-South divide, with its structures of dependency.

One must ask whether, by searching for an aim meaningful to both partners, the two sides can reach a new level on which steps can be taken to overcome inequalities. My hypothesis, which will be developed later, is that only through working together at meaningful aims in a partnership can the structures of inequality and the dependency that results from them be overcome. This does not mean lessening the importance of direct personal encounters. On the contrary, in most cases a deepening of meaningful content would also deepen personal relationships.

Such an aim would need to be an individual task, one in which those on both sides could work at together but which would also concern each side separately in their daily life and work. Such a situation would express the fundamental ecumenical experience that the churches of the worldwide church community are called to joint witness and service. It is a question of joint responsibility for the expression of this witness and yet in each case also a local expression in the district or congregation of each of the partners. These could be church tasks, socio-political tasks, tasks related to the suburb or the village, but which have been identified and agreed upon by both partners. This would also raise the partnership out of its niche as a limited church or congregational field of work. Partnership work would then no longer consist only in preparing delegation visits, coordinating projects and raising funds; partnership could far more be the starting point for the congregations to identify ecumenical missionary challenges in their daily lives, in their congregation and in their society.

3. The partnership work of the regional churches and their mission departments

The German regional church mission departments gave the impetus for establishing church partnerships and supported them at a time when the work of mission was under sharp criticism, both by society and within church and theology. Traditional congregational mission circles also were losing their support. At the same time many churches of the South were complaining about the imbalance and lack of partnership in mission relations.

On the one hand the fostering of district partnerships was an opportunity for the regional churches and their mission departments to further the integration of church and mission at a congregational level. Mission should not remain the affair of the missionary societies or mission departments of the churches, their experts, officials and church leaders. Congregations should have their own opinions on mission and make their own experience with ecumenical contacts. The fostering of district partnerships was on the other hand an opportunity to counter the criticism of mission by propagating new forms of interchurch relations in mission. The dominance of Western missionary institutions in relations with the churches of the South was to be overcome with interchurch relations based on equality and equal rights, giving the congregation members both in the overseas churches and the German churches the opportunity to participate in mission work. Finally the mission departments were able to win new support groups through the partnership work, as the old support structures through their "circles of friends" were breaking down. It was also necessary from a financial point of view to win new groups of interested people who were then also potential donors.

For the mission departments and the churches in the North and the South, partnerships meant a balancing act. On the one hand, such an arrangement would allow participating groups and congregations the greatest possible freedom for the development of their partnership. On the other hand, it would integrate them into institutional links and already existing agreements between the leaders of the two churches. The mission departments concentrated on making certain agreements mainly of an organizational nature. No rules were made concerning the content of the partnership and the form it took.

The most important model for partnership work for both mission departments and churches is without question Paul's picture of the body of Christ and the members of the body (1 Cor. 12:12ff.). The regional churches hoped for a spiritual renewal of their congregations from the partnerships. However, if one compares the statements of representatives of the institutions with observations in the congregations during this study, it becomes apparent that the meaningful formative and renewing effect of partnerships on congregational life was to a great extent over-estimated. Often that which position papers from the churches and mission departments warned against did occur: old thought-patterns in North-South relations were reinforced; new dependencies arose; and partnership groups remained caught up in the provinciality of their bilateral relations.

For the African churches there have been two main motives for partnerships. On the one hand, partnership contacts are connected with recognition as an independent church. On the other hand, partnerships mean a not-to-be underestimated financial and material support for church work. It is often considered problematic that direct relations between congregations and districts disturb the hierarchical structures of the church and create unrest in the churches and between the districts and congregations. The new dependencies, which have developed from the aid activities of the partnerships, also call forth criticism.

The United Evangelical Mission (VEM) took up the idea of partnership much sooner and presented it much more aggressively in the beginning of their work than the Evangelical Lutheran Mission (ELM), where the initiative to establish district partnerships came much more from the regional church and the synod. In various publications the VEM had tried to get support for a new understanding of mission in the congregations by using the term "partnership" and stressing the necessity for missionary activity in their own country. In contrast, the ELM was on the whole more directed to mission work overseas as a result of its mission seminary where missionaries were trained for service abroad. In spite of these differences between the mission departments of the regional churches, no basic differences are recognizable between the partnerships supported by them, either in their structures or their content.

Both mission departments stress "missionary cooperation" as the task of partnerships. However, they soon found fault with the lack of such missionary direction in the partnership groups' practice and criticized the fact that the partners concentrated too much on encounters and project aid and spent little or no energy on the search for mutual missionary challenges. This point of criticism, which is supported by the results of this study, poses the question of how far the integration of church and mission has taken place in Germany at congregational level. The mission departments have frequently emphasized that mission is an essential characteristic and integral part of the church and that participation in the *missio Dei* must be realized in the life of the local congregations, yet in the partnerships there is hardly any reflection of this at all.

The mission departments themselves have, however, remained directed towards their work overseas and have only very hesitantly begun to understand it as their task to identify missionary challenges in their own society. The regional churches for their part have delegated their missionary ecumenical competence to their specialized agencies. And here is one of the main reasons why the partnership groups also almost exclusively concentrate on work in the overseas partner circles and hardly concern themselves at all with ecumenical and missionary challenges in their own context.

4. Motives and experience in partnership work

Observations there show that the motive of direct encounter in partnership work is of outstanding importance. In contrast, those involved have no clear concept of the aim of partnership, and no motivation can be found that sees it as a means of coping with a task. Also, it is apparent that the active members of a partnership group, to a very large extent, come from the circle of those who are already involved in congregational (or district) work or already hold some form of office. The sociological make-up of the partnership groups reflects to a great extent the make-up of the active "core congregation".

For the German partners the decisive motivation for participating is to be found primarily in the experiences of human warmth and warmheartedness and of a vibrant infectious spirituality. Here experience and motivation are mutually dependent. Many of those who are involved in partnerships express the feeling that it is especially in these areas – human warmth and living spirituality – that their own society and church are lacking. In the encounters with the partners something is sought for and found which has been longed for in their own context, sometimes even a kind of "flight from civilization". There is the experience of having little compared to the modernization and mechanization of their own society. However, in the encounter with the foreign world they do not seem to question how the two worlds actually relate to each other. The experience of human warmth and living spirituality cannot be transferred to their own context in order to change this context. Both worlds remain unconnected, side by side.

In contrast to these positive experiences, there is also an element which causes some reluctance: the confrontation with poverty, suffering and misery. These are impressive and negative experiences, not only because for most travellers it is the first time they have encountered such poverty and many are not prepared. It also contributes to the negative feeling that efforts to overcome poverty have little effect in the long run. These experiences could lead to deeper consideration: they could set them thinking about the connection between the human and spiritual vivacity they have experienced at the same time as the presence of overwhelming poverty; the connection between their own European context and the African context; the relationship between their own world and the world of their partners. German partner groups react almost without exception to the experience of poverty with offers of financial and material aid in projects. In further partnership work this area generally gains paramount importance, with the German partners frequently applying their own models and standards to the African partners.

Seen in this way the German partners have two motives next to each other, often totally unconnected, certainly with no conscious thought behind them: the motive of flight from civilization and a "sense of mission in terms of civilization".

On the African side some aspects are similar: there is no specific interest in concerning themselves with meaningful topics in the partnership; those who are active in the church also get involved in the partnership and already have an openness and interest in meeting Christians from overseas. The real motivation is often only aroused through the encounters themselves.

The interest in contact with Christians overseas is at the same time an interest in contact with representatives from Europe or rather Germany. The travellers are seen as representatives of a Western way of life, which is a desirable model for many Africans. In their desire for encounter they express a longing to share the wealth and achievements of the Western way of life. Another motivation for getting involved in the partnership is also that it offers, at least potentially, the possibility of once travelling to Germany. Seen in this way I can at least systematically describe one group of motives – and possibly the most important one here – as the yearning to share in the Western way of life (a desire for civilization).

How do the motives of the German and the African partners relate to each other? The motive of "flight from civilization" associated with the German partners is in direct contrast to the "yearning for civilization" seen in the African partners. Many of the things the German partners consider extremely negative in their own context appear extremely desirable to their African partners.

On the other hand, the motive of "desire for civilization" corresponds to the motive of "a sense of mission in terms of civilization". There where the German partners transfer elements of their context in project aid – be it material goods, know-how, or financial contributions – they experience great willingness and acceptance from the African partners.

Between these two sets of motives, a network of interests begins to exist in which both sides complement and strengthen each other. This network of interests finds its expression in the project aid of the partnerships. It is here especially that both sides find a large number of their expectations fulfilled. It is here the reason can be found why project work and financial and material aid are so at the forefront of partnerships in spite of all declarations to the contrary, although they represent traffic only in one direction and reinforce an almost insurmountable structure of givers and receivers. This network of interests, which is reinforced from both sides, is also basically the reason why it is so difficult really to consider seriously the Northern way of life and its possible or actual effects on the South.

On the other hand, it must be realized that as far as the really active people in the partnerships are concerned, fundamental ecumenical principles – such as, "the church can only be church with others", or ecumenical relations between churches should serve to proclaim the presence of God in the needs of this world and to witness to it symbolically – are by no means self-evident. In fact, they are practically unknown at this level. Thus they are generally *not* the motivation for getting involved in partnership work. In order to discover these ideas as the reasons behind ecumenical partnerships and as their task, and thereby to put "ecumenical existence" into practice in the congregations, a great deal of hard work and learning processes must first take place within the partnerships themselves.

5. The importance and meaning of partnership for the life of the congregations and the dioceses

When considering what ecumenical partnerships mean for the life of the congregations and the districts and whether through them processes of ecumenical congregational renewal can be set in motion and supported, the conclusions are on the whole very sobering. The weakness of direct encounters without meaningful aims or thematic content becomes apparent here. Where everything is geared to individual encounters, with no other specific intentions, much remains at an individual level. The partnership becomes meaningful for individuals and even leads to changes, but it requires great effort to transfer this to a congregational level. Often this does not succeed at all.

Therefore the conclusion is: partnerships can be the starting point and the reason behind ecumenical congregational renewal, but it is certainly not necessarily the case nor a matter of course. Furthermore it is apparent that learning processes and processes of change do occur especially at congregational level, but much less frequently and with much greater difficulty at district level.

Although positive examples should not be ignored, nevertheless on the whole it is clear that ecumenical (district) partnerships hardly develop any strong influence on the work in the district or in the congregations. Partnerships fill a niche, in most cases, intensely worked at with great *élan* by very few people, but hardly noticed at all by the majority. This has much to do with the diffuse nature of the aims and interests in partnership work mentioned in previous chapters. Where a meaningful directive is lacking, it is very difficult to explain to others, beyond the circle of those already interested in meeting with foreign people, what relevance the partnership work has for the work of the church, and to make clear to them why it is meaningful and necessary.

The meaning that partnership has for the life of a church district and its congregations can best be described by a model of concentric circles. The partnership is begun and carried forward by a small group of activists, often only four or five – even throughout the whole district – and rarely more than ten people, even if the committees concerned have more members. Positive, fulfilling encounters and learning experiences that bring about change are most likely to be found here, but also frustration and great disappointment at the difficulties in communication, misunderstandings, annoyance at failed projects and the feeling of being overburdened and suffering too much strain. In this circle, learning processes are most likely to occur and bring about changes in attitudes and actions; however they often occur rather under the surface, often not intentionally and often not consciously noticed. In negative cases, however, clichés and prejudices may be confirmed and strengthened.

Around this small circle there is a larger circle of congregation members and interested people who come into contact with the partnership work at irregular intervals. These are, for instance, those who receive the partnership newsletter; people who give money for the partnership work, whether of their own accord or as a result of a call for donations; those who have taken visiting delegates into their homes as hosts; helpers at special events or just interested people who visit partnership activities. They are positively inclined towards the cause and allow themselves to be motivated to spontaneous involvement, but they do not continually keep up with the work. They allow themselves to be drawn into the encounters with people from a different culture, but there is no intention of setting off a process of change for themselves.

The outer circle is made up of those who have little or nothing to do with the partnership. Some probably do not know it exists.

An extension of the partnership in a district and its congregations and thereby the impetus for ecumenical congregational renewal could only succeed through a much stronger and more meaningful thematic content. In addition, this brings in a further aspect, that of crossing inner-church borders. It is noticeable in the programmes drawn up for the delegation visits – basically for partners on both sides, perhaps even more so in African countries – that the programme, and the topics related to it, are mainly to be found within the field of inner-church concerns or even inner-congregational ones. The visitors and the hosts remain to a large extent within parochial borders. This means that exactly what is demanded for ecumenical congregational renewal does not happen, that is, the crossing of these borders and movement towards "the world".

It is indicative how subordinate if not even marginal the role of social and socio-political questions and conflicts are in the individual partnerships. Even in the case of such a pressing concern as the overcoming of apartheid in South Africa and Namibia, this issue can be evaded, at least when more is demanded than just information about the situation in each case. The special forms of Lutheran theology and piety and its own special relationship to politics and the sphere of the power of the state play a decisive role in this situation. But against the background of many years of intensive controversial debate in the worldwide ecumenical movement on the condemnation of apartheid and the struggle against it, this means that even in the North-South partnerships denominational characteristics have more influence than ecumenical debates and declarations.

Another observation is that the partnership visitors to African churches are treated with much more importance than visitors from African churches to Germany. This is in inverse proportion to the amount of work and organizational achievements of the German partners. In African churches, organizational proceedings, committees, seminars, and so on are unimportant. From their point of view everything depends on the actual fellowship with the partners themselves. To achieve this everything conceivable is made possible. In German churches it is the other way round. Here events, fund-raising activities and projects are organized; however, when the African visitors are there it is often only a few people who take time for intensive encounters.

As an example, a short exchange during the evaluation session at the end of the visit of four South Africans to the Osterholz-Scharmbeck district in May 1993 makes quite clear that the phenomenon described above has its roots in a different understanding of partnership. During the visit it had become clear that it was not possible to extend the direct congregational partnerships beyond the three partnerships already in existence, as no other congregation was willing or in a position to take up such a relationship. The chairperson of the partnership committee wanted to explain to the African visitors how difficult it was to get enough active workers for a partnership in the congregations. He used his own congregation as an example, where two or three persons would be interested, but that was not enough. A member of the South African delegation replied that partnership was not a question of few or many interested people. If two people were interested then one could begin with them. The German pastor disagreed with him, and explained that they were not enough to cope with all the work involved. During a short exchange backwards and forwards the South African guest pointed out repeatedly that it was not the work that was decisive but rather the interest of the persons involved. Neither of them could make themselves understood, the subject was changed, the South African pastor shook his head and buried his face in his hands. Questioned on this later he confirmed that the most important thing in partnership is not the work involved but the existential link to people in another continent, in a church that is linked in partnership.

This brings us to the fourth conclusion: congregational partnerships showed that they were more likely to have an influential effect for change beyond the circle of those directly involved. The probability of a partnership setting off learning and renewal processes lessens the larger and less clearly structured a place is, and the less a congregation considers itself as "a place of learning". A district is in general not a suitable "place of learning". And this poses the question whether the attempts of the regional churches and their mission departments to consolidate partnerships at a district level is a good idea. The reasons for this are primarily of an administrative and technical nature. A district is more in a position to make the necessary financial efforts; a continuous and correct development of the work can be more easily guaranteed, it is claimed. Furthermore there is a greater continuity of personnel at a district level.

With the present form of partnerships, where the planning and carrying out of projects often takes more time than the initiation of learning processes, these are certainly fitting arguments. Another important argument is that the initiation of further direct congregation partnerships would lead to proliferation in the African churches and possibly to greater injustice. This is the reason why particularly African church leaders press for the necessity of linking partnerships at least at an administrative level to the districts. Behind this approach is a functional understanding of partnership and church. Persons in official office should guarantee continuity and correct administration. The structures should serve for functional processing. However, the vision of an ecumenical renewal of congregation and church, for which the interchurch relations can and should serve as an ecumenical congregation of learning, is absolutely secondary, if it is considered at all.

6. Mission and partnership

Historically the idea of partnership is linked very closely to the task of mission. But a look at the partnership groups shows that this connection has to a great extent been lost, because a traditional understanding of mission still dominates in the congregations. The groups themselves do not speak of "Partnership in Mission" as it was called at the world mission conferences. Mission is generally not an important subject in the partnerships, and the question as to whether there is a new understanding of mission and what importance it could have for their own work is simply not considered.

As already shown, partnership is understood as an opportunity to meet with Christians from foreign cultures, and beyond that as a forum where the worldwide unity of the church of Christ can be experienced. An orientation towards more far-reaching tasks or aims – as for example the world mission conference in Whitby saw it – cannot be found, although this is claimed by the institutions, the regional churches and their mission departments.

Partnerships understand themselves as critical alternatives to the mission relationships of the 19th and the beginning of the 20th centuries, which are judged to have been imbalanced, and which stand accused of being involved in colonialism and imperialism.

As we have seen, clear concepts of what mission means today can hardly be found in the partnerships, on account of the fact that the groups do not concern themselves with this question. Rather vague associations predominate. In most partnerships the word "mission" is associated with the churches of the South. There, and not in their own church, they see the necessity for missionary work supported by the churches of the

North. In this context mission means proclamation of the gospel, baptism and founding of new congregations. The opposite perspective – that mission means participation in the *missio Dei*; is also a challenge to the churches of the North; has something to do with the churches' presence at centres of social conflict; and can be the expression of God's special option for the poor and the weak within society – exists as little as the idea that the churches of the North need the help of the churches of the South to fulfil this task.

The new understanding of mission as worked out by the ecumenical (mission) movement is to a great extent unheard of in the partnership groups. The idea of the *missio Dei* – the mission theological insight that the churches participate in "God's mission" in that through their witness and service they proclaim God's nearness and *shalom* for the world and invite people "to enter into the kingdom of God" – has so far had no influence on the partnership groups' understanding of themselves or their work.

Instead of that, "traditional" mission circles, which are rather interested in evangelization and personal "conversion", exist beside the partnership groups, which consider themselves progressive and are interested in encounter and "solidarity". There are few conflicts between the two groups, but also few attempts at understanding each other or cooperating together.

If one looks back at the beginnings of the partnerships examined here, it is apparent that at first they were closely connected to mission work and the initiators hoped for a revival of the mission idea. However, the groups have in the meantime emancipated themselves almost entirely from the subject of mission. People involved in partnership groups often take a distanced stand towards mission. The contacts to mission work are limited on the whole to the services offered by the mission departments of the regional churches.

III. Partnership as a Community of Learning
Learning Processes in Ecumenical Partnerships

1. Learning in the partnership: basic comments

The third part of this study is concerned with opportunities for learning in ecumenical partnerships, and obstacles against them.

THE NEED TO INFLUENCE LEARNING PROCESSES IN PARTNERSHIPS

Within the framework of a study on partnerships it is essential to ask whether learning takes place. On the one hand, opportunities for mutual learning in intercultural encounters have been described in numerous ways and offered as concepts for many years. A number of agencies and institutions offer such opportunities in the form of tours or seminars. On the other hand, partnerships are sometimes against being used as an "education event", fearing possible misuse. While it is frequently claimed that the partners learn from each other, nevertheless in reality very little attention is given to evaluating the outcome of partnership programmes.

There are three reasons why people in partnerships should consciously concern themselves with learning processes in intercultural encounters.

First, only when the partners consciously make the effort to learn from each other and to learn together can the divide in North-South relations be overcome. North-South relations are strongly influenced, as we have seen, by the dominant role of the North on account of its economic strength. Interchurch relations are also affected by this. At first glance, even in interchurch relations the gap between rich and poor makes a partnership encounter of equals sharing equally together impossible. But by consciously initiating joint learning processes, the partners accept each other on an equal footing and thereby both enrich each other and yet can look at each other critically.

Second, learning in intercultural encounters is necessary, because it is only in this way that stereotypical ideas can be examined and prejudices overcome. Mutual understanding does not automatically come about through meeting with others. Meeting with people from a different culture can often be difficult, disturbing and full of conflict and, in the worst cases, can reinforce existing prejudice. The ability to communicate interculturally must be learnt. Intercultural exchanges demand of people that they learn new things and how to think in a different way, but this has to be initiated and developed. As Horst Siebert has pointed out:

> The more closely people with different habits and customs live together, the more likely they are to have clashes of interest. There is also a greater danger of conflict and aggressive discrimination. Encounters do not automatically include educational experiences and explanations of why people do things. As a rule we notice what we already know and what we want to see and hear.

Third, only a few people are actively involved in partnership visits. If the partnership is to have a wider effect, then it is important to make specific provision to disseminate experiences together with their potential implications for the congregation. As encounters occur in a foreign cultural context, it is quite possible that these contrast strongly, or even diametrically oppose, those of the individual or the congregation. It is usually not possible, therefore, simply to adopt what one has experienced. And for this reason it is important to reflect on the experiences and to test their relevance for the context in which one lives.

Using the so-called Breitenbach project on intercultural learning in youth encounter programmes conducted at the end of the 1970s, we may differentiate between three levels of experience and learning:

1) the academic level, in which partners exchange information about their own situations and daily lives and talk about politics, society, religion and culture;
2) the level of experiencing different cultural behaviour: different values and standards, different eating habits and ways of spending free time as well as different forms of behaviour towards each other may be encountered; while they offer opportunities for discussion, they can also lead to conflict;
3) general group experience, which often influences the emotional aspects of the encounter: experience of appealing and not so appealing behaviour on the part of others is important in intercultural encounters as this is usually considered to be representative of the national and cultural way of thinking.

According to Margot Umbach, the communication taking place at these three levels "can be both beneficial and damaging". It can trigger off learning, but can also reinforce prejudices. Experience of other cultures can encourage people to question their own cultural traditions, but it can also lead them to distance themselves from everything foreign. Conflicts with the behaviour of foreign people can be an occasion for making a greater effort to understand the reasons for it, but they can also lead to an ethnocentric interpretation and condemnation of it.

Communication processes in intercultural exchanges should, in principle, be very open. According to Josef Freise it matters crucially whether participants' experiences are accepted and adopted by the group. "Meta-communication" must be put into practice.

In respect of conditions affecting intercultural learning, Siebert points out that not only is the interest in getting to know more about countries and people in the third world waning, but that specific obstacles stand in the way of efforts to learn more. Preoccupation with problems of the third world is "neither professionally useful, nor fun"; "rather it encourages sadness, a feeling of helplessness and discouragement", which has to do with the fact that while there is a lot of information available about the problems, there is a lack of opportunity to do anything to solve them. This "cognitive dissonance" disturbs our need for harmony, and results in "suppression and defence mechanisms". As "third-world education" does not console us, but rather calls into question the interpretation of our existing views of the world, learning only makes us aware of new problems rather than solving existing ones. For this reason, very few people find this form of further education attractive.

Siebert names five motivating elements that make learning possible. Their relevance for partnership work is obvious: (1) learning in a socio-emotional supportive group atmosphere in solidarity; (2) longer-term concern; (3) opportunities for action; (4) personal contacts; and (5) social acceptance of the role of further education and personal involvement. On this basis, interchurch partnerships between congregations and districts should be very suitable, if not ideal places for learning processes in intercultural exchange to take place. How far this is the case and whether the opportunities are realized will be examined in the following section.

Aims and objectives of learning in intercultural encounters

Learning processes in intercultural encounters are informal. In partnership exchanges learning happens incidentally, in the daily life of the culture and without guidance. This is the difference between this kind of learning and courses in schools or institutes of adult education. However, informal learning does not mean that these experiences should not be reflected upon or articulated. Intercultural learning should be positive. "Intercultural learning denotes the process by which an individual changes his or her way of doing things as a result of the experiences gained in direct or indirect encounters with aspects of a foreign culture."

The "learners" themselves not only change as a result of this interaction but, according to Bernd Sandhaas, they also influence this learning themselves.

The formal aim of intercultural exchanges is the "learning of a foreign culture", as stated by D. Breitenbach. Learning should lead to understanding. In his typology of 25 types of intercultural encounters Sandhaas names "international and intercultural understanding" as the primary aim of "group partnerships". By this he means the acquisition and use of both culture-specific and general intercultural communication skills.

Ability in communicating foreign culture means a stage, in which one possesses sufficient knowledge and skills that one can, firstly, communicate effectively and satisfyingly with people from other cultures and, secondly, in principle apply this ability in every situation in which people from different cultural backgrounds are involved.

In summary, Sandhaas defines a "multicultural person" as a person "who has learnt how one learns culture".

METHODOLOGY

It is difficult to define learning processes or to judge their success. During the course of this study it soon became apparent that there would be no direct way of measuring successful learning. Conversation partners almost always gave no answer when asked what lessons they had learnt from partnership encounters and how these had been applied in congregations or districts. This is accordingly the first finding, but it did not go far enough.

I therefore used several other approaches, in addition to the direct questions. First of all I identified three areas of learning in intercultural encounters: intercultural, ecumenical and development-oriented learning. There are overlaps and inseparable links between them. Ecumenical and development-oriented learning are always intercultural learning. Intercultural learning also includes questions relating to development policies, etc. However, the concepts underlying this differentiation offer focal points for more effective analysis of various kinds of learning in interchurch partnerships and allow us to look more closely at the specific strengths and weaknesses of these relationships.

The question of ecumenical learning looks at experiences gained in the field of church and theology. It is intended to reflect experiences of faith and belief encountered during contact with a foreign culture, as well as one's own and the foreign understanding of what the church is and what being church means. The concept of development-oriented learning examines how the economic disparities between rich and poor are handled in partnerships and in North-South relations, as well as the use made of project aid. It assumes that the causes of poverty and the connections between poverty and injustice should be recognized, as well as the responsibility of each individual to become involved in this issue.

Finally, intercultural learning covers experiences of foreignness and cultural difference, of successful and unsuccessful communication, and the concept that people should recognize the limitations of their own culture as well as develop an understanding of that of others. For the analysis and description of these processes in interchurch partnerships I shall adhere to these definitions, which will be summarized at the beginning of every section.

I begin with a more superficial question: Where does reflection on experiences, an unequivocal component of learning, take place within the framework of partnership? To establish this I relied initially on active observation and a study of the minutes and publications of the partnership committees. Then, in conversation with the people concerned, I tried to find out how far it was possible to establish any changes introduced as a result of partnership visits. I was interested in changes in personal attitudes and awareness, as well as changes in behaviour and new forms of activity, and in how far these changes could be translated into action in the congregation. The findings from these conversations were then correlated with the observations I had made. Finally, in observing and researching publications I paid particular attention to attitudes and patterns of thought that became apparent during partnership encounters, in other words, how far they saw themselves as others see them.

These observations and studies were only made possible by frequent meetings with the people actively involved in the partnerships over a period of time. They were therefore almost exclusively limited to the German partnership groups. Visits to the African partnership groups were too short to allow significant observations, but they did provide me with important information enabling me to evaluate the importance of learning processes in interchurch partnerships.

Lastly, I consider some of the criticisms levelled at the learning models and methodological concepts I have used. My observations of the partnerships provide the basis for questioning these concepts on specific points.

The theoretical models of learning in intercultural encounters all adopt an intellectual, rational approach. This assumes that learning normally occurs in the form of rationalization after discussion. This approach is derived entirely from Europe and the forms of learning that are employed there. Some models are aimed primarily at school learning programmes, but also claim to be valid for out-of-school and informal learning processes. However, in this case they pay far too little attention to learning techniques other than rational discourse. Above all they do not even consider the question how learning actually takes place in cultures outside Europe.

Understanding this is the first step towards learning in an intercultural encounter. The partnership groups complain justifiably that the models are too Western and intellectual and thereby ignore entirely whole areas of experience in the encounters between Germans and Africans. While these discourse models have a relative justification in the Western context and accordingly particular relevance for the German partners, their perspective is limited. Therefore I see specific opportunities for partnership exchanges to develop new learning models, suitable for use by both partners.

A further point of criticism relates to whether the intellectual demands made in the models are too great. Recognition of global responsibility, preoccupation with world problems and the search for solutions in the complex context of the world economy, global politics and interchurch relations expect too much, both cognitively and morally, from congregations and partnership groups. The requirement that learning must be consciously initiated and developed is in most cases beyond the groups didactically. It cannot be carried out without qualified assistance.

Finally, it must be asked if the emphasis placed on the need for learning in intercultural encounters does not overlook or ignore the real interests of – in this case – the African partners. How far do they expect such learning from interchurch partnerships? Is the demand for such approaches not again a form of dominance, with Germans speaking for their African partners? The African church representatives endorse the view that partners should learn from each other. The form this learning should take, however, must be decided collectively in the partnership.

2. Intercultural learning in the partnership

Ecumenical partnerships are relationships and encounters that cross borders and cultures. On their journeys and during their stay in partner churches travellers are able to experience directly the daily living conditions of their hosts and so gain intensive insights into the culture of their partners, a culture that is foreign to them. This forces them to consider how they cope with the "difference" of their partners and their own experience of being foreign. Do both accept that they experience cultural differences? Is this seen as an opportunity for learning together? And if so, for learning what? Where are the obstacles, where are the opportunities? The experience of feeling foreign can lead to tension and to conflicts. We need to know how the partners deal with this.

INTERCULTURAL LEARNING: THEORIES AND MODELS

The term "intercultural" has become a fashionable term and has been used extensively in the past twenty or thirty years. There is hardly an area of social life to which it has not been applied. This is not exactly helpful when it comes to giving a clear definition of the term. In more recent years the term "multicultural" has also become frequent and has gained political relevance, but it also needs to be defined more clearly.

In the field of education and teacher training several different theories are associated with the term "intercultural learning", each of them derived from its own historical context. In Germany from the middle of the 1970s, it originally denoted the "education of foreigners" *(Ausländerpädagogik)*. With recruitment of "guest workers" *(Gastarbeiter)* and the arrival of their families, models concerned specifically with the needs of foreign workers first began to be developed. Even today most models of intercultural learning are directed at schools and educational institutions with a high proportion of foreigners. Their aim is to help the foreigners get to know the culture and the way of life in Germany and thereby contribute to the integration of these foreign citizens into society. The underlying intention is that they should adjust and conform to life.

A second area of intercultural learning, which began somewhat later, is the preparation of experts (development volunteers, missionaries, company workers, diplomats) for professional work abroad. Here it is more a case of passing on information and knowledge about a foreign culture and offering advice on "correct behaviour" abroad.

A third is the support of foreign scholarship students studying in Germany. Organizations for educational work and development aid have developed concepts for in-service and further training measures that go beyond teaching essential language competence. They aim to enable students to reflect intelligently on the experiences they make during their study visit to Germany.

Finally, intercultural learning has gained in importance in general (adult) education work on account of the growing number of tourists travelling to distant places. Anyone wishing to discover more about a country to be visited will find a great number of educational opportunities available.

Renate Nestvogel identifies three basic concepts offered in education for intercultural learning. The first concerns the need of German immigrants to learn how to fit into "our" society. In this definition, which is mainly used in the "education of foreigners" and "still constitutes a large percentage of what is today called intercultural learning", foreigners are "considered above all to have linguistic, social, cultural and professional deficits". The aim of educational measures is the assimilation and integration of the foreigners to make them acceptable in German society.

In contrast to the deficit approach, the second emphasizes the peculiar, or different, characteristics of the foreign culture. Intercultural learning is understood as "learning a foreign culture" (Breitenbach). Here the "in-comers" are also treated as learners who are acquiring knowledge and competence in coping with a new culture. However, according to Nestvogel, it is often not clear how this approach differs from that of etymology and regional and cultural studies. Both approaches concentrate entirely on that which is foreign and ignore almost entirely that which is their own.

In contrast, Nestvogel describes, thirdly, "normative" intercultural learning as "a process of looking at foreign cultures on the basis of a critical reflection of one's own historically developed culture(s)". This includes becoming aware of one's own place in ethnocentric models of realizing, thinking and acting. Decisive for understanding this type of intercultural learning is appreciating that it stems from a comprehensive view of culture, such as I use in this study. Culture is not used in the narrow sense as only related to art, literature, music or philosophy. Such a limited understanding, frequently used in Germany, includes only forms of expression that have a high standing in Western society and excludes other aspects of individual and social behaviour. This approach risks reducing intercultural learning to the exchange of folklore and the exotic.

In contrast, a comprehensive understanding of culture includes everything that belongs to the human "secondary environment"; everything that people add to their own biological equipment on the one hand and to their primary environment (nature) on the other.

"The members of a group express through their culture how they see their relationship to nature. On this relationship they base their fundamental beliefs and morals." In 1871, the Englishman E.B. Tylor developed a definition of culture, which has since become the basis for all further considerations of the concept of culture:

> Culture or civilization is that complex whole which includes artefacts, beliefs, art, all the other habits acquired by man as a member of society, and all products of human activity as determined by these habits.

In 1952, the American anthropologists Alfred Louis Kroeber and Clyde Kluckhohn presented a collection of 166 definitions and 109 longer explanations of the term "culture" from the European and Anglo-American field, and concluded as a result:

> Culture consists of patterns, explicit and implicit, of and for behaviour acquired and transmitted by symbols, constituting the distinctive achievement of human groups, including their embodiments in artefacts; the essential core of culture consists of traditional (i.e. historically derived and selected) ideas and especially their attached values; culture systems may on the one hand be considered as products of action, on the other as conditioning elements of further action.

This encompasses two essential characteristics of culture: it cannot be isolated from people and society, and it is acquired. A person learns to behave in a certain way.

> The individual, confronted with a totally new situation, does not react according to any objective reality, but rather according to the values, knowledge and attitudes which he or she has internalized during the process of interculturalization. The interpretation of a situation by an individual follows the basis of understanding of his or her culture. This determines reaction and behaviour within a given field of variation.

The specialization of the form and importance of norms of behaviour, which occur in every culture, make it more difficult for members of different cultures to understand each other. Intercultural learning aims to a certain extent at overcoming these barriers to communication by increasing communicative competence.

Intercultural learning is essentially learning through social experience. Its specific characteristic is that it necessitates interaction between members of different cultures. Through the experience of cultural differences and in the form of cultural comparisons, intercultural learning can both lead to a more exact analysis and qualification of people's own cultural norms and social systems. Also, when meta-communication about cultural norms and differences is achieved, such experience can lead to a reduction in socially conditioned cultural prejudice. It is decisive that intercultural learning does not only aim to acquire knowledge about foreign cultures. Learning of foreign cultures should automatically lead to critical examination of one's own culture and society.

Two elements are therefore indispensable for intercultural learning. Firstly, the acquisition of abilities and practical competence in order to be able to participate actively in dialogue with culturally different partners; secondly, intercultural learning must take the form of "looking into one's own culture". If one bears in mind that intercultural learning should be conceived as the mutual learning of partners from each other, then three steps of intercultural learning can be established. The aim is the acquisition of communicative competence:

1) each learner's growing consciousness about their own culture and its particular importance for their own actions, thinking and life;
2) the acquisition of knowledge about the peculiarities of the other culture (or other cultures) for their actions, thinking and life;
3) the acquisition of competence and abilities in dealing with people from a different culture and acting together in cooperation with each other.

PARTNERSHIP VISITS AS PLACES OF INTERCULTURAL LEARNING

Most opportunities for intercultural learning are offered by regular partnership visits. These offer direct interaction between members of different cultures. The travellers, both when they go from Germany to Africa and vice versa, enter a foreign world. "The first impression of every visitor to equatorial Africa is that of being in a totally different world," wrote a member of a German delegation. Having reached the destination, almost everything seems to be different from "home": climate, landscape, sounds and smells. The foreign surroundings barely resemble anything comparable to living conditions, surroundings or way of life back home. Germans who travel to Africa must adjust to much simpler conditions without their usual comforts. African travellers to Germany are confronted by an unknown wealth and luxury.

In conversations with travellers this experience of "foreignness" occurs frequently. As a particularly striking example I should like to quote from a report by a Tanzanian delegation in 1980. The text, which is signed by the four members of the delegation – Blasio Kasimoto, Regina Ntimba, Gabriel Kasenene and Gideon Lyakugwile – reflects better than almost any other document the "foreignness" that was experienced, and is therefore quoted at length:

> We got into the plane on 14 August and left Dar Es Salaam. We continued our journey via Bujumbura and travelled to Brussels, where we arrived at 12.30 local time. Before we changed our watches they showed 3 a.m.
>
> When we arrived in Brussels we had to cope with many things that were foreign to us. First we had to negotiate with immigration authorities, after they had tried to detain us because we had no Belgian visas. When we had solved the visa problem we were able, with apprehension, to leave the huge building. When we got outside, thanks be to God, we met a man who had a taxi. He was waiting for us to take us to the hotel where we were to spend the night.
>
> We spent the night in the hotel and very early in the morning our benefactor with the taxi was ready to take us to the customs building, where we again began to encounter the problems that we had met with the day before....

Almost at the last minute we boarded the aeroplane that took us to Düsseldorf, which is a town in Germany. As we were now beginning to get used to it, we were able to follow the other passengers and luckily we were met by our benefactors, Pastor Jasper, Pastor Kantz and the driver from the Mission. They welcomed us and showed us the way. They were able to recognize us quite a distance away and waved their arms, but initially it was not easy for us to recognize them because of the colour of their skin which was predominant in the country we had come to. After a short time we met, were able to communicate with each other, and embraced each other as long-lost brothers.

The report describes the confusion caused by the cultural strangeness. The travellers have to cope with various difficulties and obstructions. Adjustment and conformity (not only to time changes) require quite a lot of effort. They get into situations where quite literally words fail them. The foreign surroundings (here the airport building) appear inaccessible. But it is also important that the meeting with their partners inspires trust and a feeling of protection in the midst of the foreignness.

A decisive factor in partnership visits is that the partners meet each other as brothers and sisters. This differentiates them from long-haul tourists and some study tours and at the same time it has, or can have, a positive influence on intercultural learning. The partners are familiar with each other. It is as though they had just not seen each other for a few years – even when visitors and hosts meet for the first time. During partnership visits the foreigners have people around them who can help them to cope with and to understand the things that are strange to them. Partnership visits are marked by trust, great openness and willingness to discover new things. This is their great strength and at the same time a specific weakness. This "assumed" closeness can *prevent* participants from being consciously aware of their foreignness and having to endure it. Foreignness always means potential conflicts, misunderstanding and a disturbance of trust and harmony. If the recognition of foreignness is avoided in order to maintain harmony, the partners cannot learn from each other.

Partnership visits offer a great wealth of opportunities for intercultural learning, especially through encounters in the daily life of the hosts. With reference to the three levels of experience and learning previously mentioned (academic, experience of different cultural behaviour, general group experiences) there are striking differences as far as learning environments are concerned.

Group experiences and experiences of different cultural behaviour are paramount in partnership visits, by comparison with academic experiences. The programme generally consists of visits to congregations and congregational groups, as well as church and social institutions and centres. The visits are usually only of short duration. They are encounters between groups (the delegation and those accompanying them together with, for example, church workers or employees of the institution, congregational groups, and so on). The main focus is on exchanging information. Longer, more analytical discussions are normally precluded on account of the shortness of the time.

There is, initially, little dialogue, and intercultural learning is not stimulated. At the same time certain topics or cultural peculiarities may be raised, and these could well offer starting points for intercultural learning. A visit to a rural hospital in Africa, for example, may be an opportunity for exploring traditions and customs concerned with childbirth. Comparisons could be made; the partners could analyze together their own cultural norms and qualify cultural prejudices. Issues such as how women in each country prepare for birth; the role and importance of a hospital; how men behave in this situation – these and others could offer opportunities for a more intensive exchange about values and the patterns of thinking and acting that lie behind them.

This is only one example. Potentially every encounter during a visit can offer such opportunities, whether it be the tram ride through Hanover, the shopping spree in the main pedestrian shopping centre of a large German town, the visit to a second-hand clothes shop or a meeting in a church youth centre, where young people simply come together for a Saturday afternoon disco. In the same way a walk through the South African township, the visit to a local dispensary or social centre, the journey through the hilly landscape in Western Tanzania where, in spite of government regulations forbidding them, fires for slash-and-burn agriculture are constantly aflame, a visit to the market place in Moshi, and so on, offer similar scope. But observations of the partnership visits both in Africa and in Germany reveal that neither at the time nor in later discussion was there the evaluation necessary for intercultural learning, meta-communication". The questions important for intercultural learning were not posed or explored. On a superficial level time is too short for this. Participants get no further than just passing on information and knowledge. The programme with a number of varied activities means that impressions cannot even be pursued later, because no time is planned for regular evaluation meetings. Analytical reflection and reappraisal does not take place either within the visiting group itself or between the partners.

During a partnership visit to Tanzania, for example, a dance presentation was part of the programme in many congregations. Youth groups beat their drums, sang and danced to the beat, and a little later invited the German youth to dance with them, which created a great deal of laughter among the spectators. On one occasion the German brass band members "got their own back": they played a waltz and two members of the band danced together to the music and then invited the Tanzanian young people to dance with them. It is evident that such presentations reinforce stereotypes, especially the exotic picture that Germans often have of Africans dancing to drumbeats. There would have been an opportunity here to make these impressions the subject of discussion. Such discussion is necessary if prejudices are to be dispelled. The occasion could have been used to consider the importance of music and dancing for the Tanzanian partners and the effect the presentations had on the German youth as they watched them.

A discussion of this kind partially took place during the visit of the youth brass band, when the Tanzanian partners explained and demonstrated to the Germans how drums were made and used. Here the young people learned that drums still have an importance today for local communication, for example to call together a village meeting or to give warning of fire. A lengthy "drum practice session" followed, in which the Tanzanian partners explained the manifold nuances of the beats and rhythms and the special meaning of each one. Both sides declared this evening to have been exciting and instructive.

Similarly on another occasion, when the situation of young people was discussed, especially in relation to the roles of the sexes and mixed gender friendships. Here, however, the German young people, bombarded with questions by the Tanzanians, found the situation too one-sided and unproductive. They did not put many questions to the Tanzanian young people as – some of them admitted later – the Tanzanian circumstances did not seem to them to be so interesting, or relevant.

In these instances, by explaining, demonstrating and sharing information it was possible to make each other far more aware of foreign cultural characteristics and to acquire some basic knowledge. But more far-reaching observations, or feelings and attitudes of the participants were not pursued, either that evening, in later group discussions, or in the final evaluation of the visit. There was no application to their own situation.

It would be conceivable, for example, as a follow-up to such discussions, to look more closely at the symbolism of actions and ways of behaving. It would then be possible to lead into questions about the role of the missionary, the church and the transfer of Christian moral concepts from Europe. Drums and other traditional forms of expression in music and art were often banned as "heathen" and have only been rediscovered by the Tanzanian Christians for use in their services and gatherings in the last few years.

It is not just coincidence that longer discussions on cultural backgrounds and differences only occurred when guests and hosts lived together for longer periods of time, such as in the youth centre in Nkwenda, where German and Tanzanian young people lived, worked and celebrated together for ten days. I got the impression that interest in learning and in posing questions, as well as interest in demonstrating and explaining traditions and ways of living, was stronger among the Tanzanian young people than among the Germans. It seemed as though the physical presence of the Germans was an invaluable source of information for the Tanzanians, who have no access to television and hardly any to radio. The suggestion to hold the discussions came from them on both evenings.

Other examples also prove that intercultural learning processes are most likely to take place where the partners are together for a longer period of time and share daily life with each other. It is often just the banal situations in daily life that offer surprising discoveries, if the hosts are prepared to look at the world through their guests' eyes. Even a walk through the town can offer starting points for such learning. But it is necessary then to take time and to leave space for such learning.

I should like to quote two examples here. During a walk through the town of Lilienthal (Osterholz-Scharmbeck) a South African group visited the local cemetery. The local pastor had mentioned beforehand – more as an aside – that it was possible to learn something about the culture of a society from the form their cemeteries take. When the group entered the small chapel they saw a coffin in the centre aisle, and the church warden making final preparations for the funeral that was to take place in the afternoon. The South Africans were horrified that the deceased had been left alone, with no members of the family or mourners present. That would be unthinkable in South Africa, they said, and shook their heads in sorrow and disbelief. The group continued its walk around the town. The topic was not revived. It would have been fascinating for both sides to consider what patterns of thinking and acting lie behind the different mourning rites in each country. Despite being uppermost in peoples' minds, the issues were not verbalized.

On another occasion, the visitors and a few of the hosts sat together one evening in a small private circle. The conversation turned to the factors determining the naming of a child. The South Africans indicated that in their tradition the name of a child was not a free choice, but decided by rules of family relationships. In Germany there is a similar tradition, at least when the first-born son is given the name of his father, but otherwise such traditions have been relaxed and other factors – even fashions – are important. A heated discussion followed in which the South

Africans indicated the reasons behind their practice of name-giving; that they were determined by the family social relationships or groups. By this means the individual learns his or her place in the family. When the most important information had been exchanged, the discussion on this subject broke up. The Germans discussed among themselves for a short time whether a computer could be used to generate a genealogy; the South Africans – as far as I can judge, for they spoke Sotho among themselves – talked about people they knew and how each of them had got their name.

These observations show it is a big step from sharing information and experience to considering patterns of cultural thinking and behaviour in an empathetic way. Such reflection rarely occurs, at least not in the context. In the partnership groups there does not seem to be sufficient awareness of the importance of joint discussions on what has been experienced. For this the groups need professional support from outside. The necessity of such learning is proved by questioning how far the experiences of individuals in encounters with the foreign guests can be passed on to the congregations. I shall develop this by considering to what extent partnerships enable people to meet foreigners in their own country in a new and different way.

RELATIONS WITH FOREIGNERS IN ONE'S OWN COUNTRY AS OPPORTUNITIES FOR INTERCULTURAL LEARNING

During the period of this study xenophobia increased in Germany, with brutal attacks being made on asylum-seekers and foreign citizens. But how to cope with foreigners and refugees was not solely a question for German society. After abolishing apartheid in Namibia and South Africa both countries had to foster justice and encourage reconciliation between alienated sections of the population. In Tanzania, particularly in the diocese of Karagwe, the population faced the challenge of taking in the enormous streams of refugees from neighbouring Rwanda.

In general the question of "understanding what is foreign" was an issue for churches and social groups in view of ethnic conflicts, not only in Eastern and Southern Africa but also in Europe in former Yugoslavia. Could ecumenical groups contribute to solving the problems – even in a modest, local way?

The insights gained through my study vary greatly. On the German side two positive examples come to mind. In the district of Lünen, concern and care for foreign citizens is part of the partnership work. This was an obvious objective for the churches in Lünen, as in greater Dortmund there is a very high percentage of foreign citizens in the population. On various occasions during the partnership, efforts were made to come into contact with foreigners and their organizations and occasionally to organize joint events, for example during the "Kirchentag" in the Ruhr in 1991.

The other example is the Marienwerder congregation, where in 1991 asylum-seekers were to be housed in an empty school building. This led to protests by some in the population and in the congregation. It was members of the partnership group who vehemently supported the asylum-seekers in public and took action themselves. They welcomed the new residents and accompanied and supported them, setting up homework support groups and offering help when newcomers had to visit an official office.

How far this was the result of partnership activities cannot be ascertained. There were no direct links. Yet individuals will certainly have learned how to associate with foreigners in a different way as a result of experiences gained in the partnership. One of the female staff in Marienwerder put it this way: "If I had not had the experiences that I had with the Masai women in Tanzania, I don't know how I would have behaved."

Similar examples can be found in other partnerships. Nevertheless, helping foreigners to feel at home in a strange society hardly played any role in many partnerships. This is borne out by the views of members and confirmed by the minutes of their meetings. Two main reasons account for this: firstly, most partnerships focus very strongly on relationships between the participants. All efforts concentrate on this bilateral relationship. In many ecumenical partnerships it is very difficult to broaden the horizons beyond this. Secondly, in German-African partnerships there is on the whole only a very weak expectation of political action as a consequence of the partnership relationship.

Those who have participated in partnership encounters are usually aware of the needs and difficulties of foreigners in their own country. Their experiences enable them to face up to intercultural encounter in their own country. But this does not mean that congregations involved in an ecumenical partnership then see the necessity to influence their society to improve the way foreigners and refugees are treated. Individual lessons learnt do not necessarily have any effect at a congregational or district level.

This underlines the need to initiate intercultural learning quite consciously, to stimulate shared reflection in the congregations and also to allow opposing views to be expressed. Only then can partnership work become relevant for the ecumenical work of districts and congregations. To achieve this, members of partnership groups must look more critically at their own society, identify the challenges and areas where they can make a difference and see how they can use their personal experiences to change patterns of thinking and acting.

SYSTEMATIC EVALUATION

Partnerships make it possible to get to know a foreign culture at close quarters. By sharing day-to-day life – either during visits or through letters – partners are able to get to know new ways of living together and different attitudes and patterns of thinking and acting. The particular strength of partnerships that differentiates it from other forms of North-South contacts is that the experiences are embedded in a long-term relationship of trust. The visitors have trusted persons with them, who can help them to interpret what happens to them.

On the other hand, it is just this closeness that can prevent intercultural learning. If closeness and understanding are postulated as the basis of the relationship, then it can also obscure non-understanding, the realization of foreignness and the potential conflicts that go with them. Conflict justified as cultural difference is not seen as a learning opportunity.

Theories of intercultural learning, directed at the analysis and qualification of one's own cultural norms and the reduction of cultural prejudice, neglect this dimension of exchange, which is also insufficiently incorporated into the planning of partnership work. The aims of partnerships are oriented towards demonstrating the unity of the worldwide church and supporting the partners. By contrast, the dimension of cultural exchange is not considered important.

This is reflected in the programmes prepared for the partnership visits where the main focus is on getting to know the various fields of church work. As a rule the partnership programmes do not concern themselves deeply with issues of culture, values, attitudes and patterns of behaviour in either country. To date partnerships have not been used to analyze or qualify the cultural values of each group, to examine stereotypes or to reduce prejudice.

Individuals have experiences in partnerships that change their attitudes and their behaviour. These could be described as intercultural learning, but such outcomes do not occur automatically. The same situation can be shared and evaluated in quite different ways by different people. During partnership visits it would be necessary to ensure joint and separate regular, lengthy communication about shared experiences. Such meta-communication is necessary to analyze existing role patterns and stereotypes in North-South relationships and to overcome prejudice.

In my view, only a conscious initiation of intercultural learning will make it possible to overcome the existing imbalance in the partnerships arising from the division between rich and poor. Only when partners deliberately use their partnership as a community of learning and expect intercultural exchange, with the inevitable conflicts associated with it, can they work together simultaneously to overcome the disproportionately strong emphasis on project aid and to foster a relationship based on equality and reciprocity.

Intercultural communication is in itself a learning process. The ability to use experiences of cultural diversity to lead to understanding in unfamiliar countries cannot be assumed, yet is at the same time the aim and means of intercultural learning. Partnership groups require specialized help from institutions to achieve this.

3. Ecumenical learning in the partnership

Over the past ten years the term "ecumenical learning" has become a fashionable slogan in ecumenical circles, including the partnership movement. Interchurch partnerships are considered particularly suitable fields for this learning. I shall now examine whether that is the case. First, I shall define what I understand by ecumenical learning. This is not the place to describe the various models and concepts of ecumenical learning in great detail. That has been done elsewhere. This introductory section offers a short description of what is understood by ecumenical learning and the ways in which it can be used as a mechanism for examining interchurch partnerships. In so doing, I shall pay particular attention to those aspects of direct relevance to the case studies.

Concepts and models

The term "ecumenical learning" is frequently assumed to derive from the report of Philip Potter, general secretary of the World Council of Churches, to the WCC's assembly in Vancouver in 1983. Thirty-five years after the founding of the WCC, Potter reviewed learning experiences about the nature and calling of the church, taking as his text 1 Peter 2:4-10. He called the churches a "community of learners". Learning was a personal journey on which individuals developed a relationship to God, and his way of truth, justice and peace, so that they could follow this path obediently in their relationships with each other and with all nations and peoples. This did not simply mean acquiring knowledge or skills:

> Far more it means that with our whole being and with all other people we should enter into a relationship with God through his revelation of himself, so that our vision may be opened and our will strengthened to do what is right in word and deed before God and among ourselves.

If the WCC laid great stress on this "ecumenical learning", it did so to enable people "to open themselves to the reality of the word of God in the midst of the rough realities of our world". At the same time Potter criticized the programmes of the WCC and its member churches for not having sufficiently adopted the lessons of ecumenical learning. He stressed the urgency: "The extent to which we do not succeed in putting such forms of learning into practice will be the extent to which we do not succeed in becoming a house of living stones."

Potter's speech was not a lecture on ecumenical learning as such; this must be made clear when people try to use his statements as evidence for the concept of ecumenical learning. On the one hand, his statements are too short. On the other, they extend more widely. What Potter describes are basically characteristics of an ecumenical existence as they have developed in the history of the ecumenical movement since 1945. He was concerned with comprehensive learning: the churches had learnt that they had to become a "community of witness", a "community of learning", a "community of possessors", a "community of sharers", a "healing community", a "community of reconciliation", a "community in unity" and a "community of expectation". From this it is clear that ecumenical learning means, on the one hand, opening oneself as a member of the ecumenical community to the reality of the word of God and his way of truth, justice and peace. At the same time, however, a comprehensive process of change is expected: the practice of an ecumenical existence.

The Chamber for Education and Training of the Protestant Churches of Germany (EKD) adopted these ideas in 1985 and brought out a workbook, which has since gained the status of a fundamental text on ecumenical learning, but which unfortunately has been out of print for many years. It must be considered alongside two further studies by the Chamber for Congregation and Adult Education. The workbook endorses holistic ecumenical learning as "the basic task" of the church, describes how to put it into practice and offers several case studies. It suggests that "ecumenism" should not only refer to the cooperation between Protestant and Roman Catholic Christians but should look more deeply at the way denominations live together and, beyond that, to how all people on the earth live together. The question of church unity has closely to do with issues of justice and the overcoming of racism, war, poverty and oppression. The study emphasizes, in the sense of Potter's speech, the holistic existential character of ecumenical learning. It is not simply a case of introducing a new field of work, "but rather of the 'rediscovery' of this dimension in all existing areas of work and service".

The workbook develops the broadly accepted characteristics of ecumenical learning that have been endorsed in all later publications. Ecumenical learning "transcends barriers"; is "action-oriented"; is "social learning in networks"; includes "intercultural learning"; and is, finally, a "holistic process". It is surprising that with these characteristics no educational methodologies are described for such learning. Nor are they developed in later publications, which is why the understanding of ecumenical learning has remained to a large extent vague and diffuse. This also has to do with the fact that it is very difficult to set limits to this approach.

In its expectations and methods ecumenical learning goes beyond the concepts of learning used in school. It is – and that is the decisive thing – not primarily concerned with the transfer of knowledge. The learning process is fundamentally open, which does not exclude planned methodological steps. It is participatory learning, where all participants are simultaneously learners and teachers. In its theological section the EKD workbook justifies the necessity for such learning on the basis of the existing spiritual reality of the one universal church. Ecumenical learning should enable Christians to discover and celebrate the universal community of the body of Christ, especially in congregational worship. At the same time a congregation with an ecumenical vision must ask itself, "what standing up for justice and peace means to them, what contributions they can make to preserving God's creation and what consequences follow from this for their own life-styles".

Klaus Gossmann describes three approaches to ecumenical learning. One essential element is encounter with the ecumenical movement itself, in other words, direct contact between individuals in the ecumenical movement. The growth of a relationship is the second element; and long-term continuity of such learning, during which it will evolve characteristic phases is the third. No further explanation is needed, other than to say that these three elements are the special characteristics of congregational and district interchurch partnerships.

The EKD study also lays stress on the importance of direct encounters:

> Encounters between Christians with a different piety and theology, different traditions and forms lead us to ask: What determines our lives? Where are our own gifts and our own limitations? How can we make our contribution so that the witness of faith can be credibly proclaimed and lived out?

Ecumenical learning is not only aimed at understanding others, but also at discovering and understanding ourselves anew.

In summary, I would like to cite a number of Gerhard Orth's theories, which describe the precise aim, methods and bias of ecumenical learning. These are restricted to issues with which this study is concerned, and supplemented with some critical comments.

- From the beginning, ecumenical learning is concerned with individual religious education and the educational experiences that make it possible for that person to participate responsibly in shaping his/her environment and that of the wider world.... Issues of the orientation of our entire civilization and questions of a living personal faith are equally important for this work...

- Methodologically there are four key steps for learning in the ecumenical movement: analysis and interpretation of the situation; adopting a stance on recognized challenges; achieving a consensus among Christians and churches with different backgrounds and diverse links; and providing guidance on responsible action...

- The place for ecumenical learning is alongside the oppressed and those deprived of their rights, the poor, the women and children; it is a case of learning from and with these majorities.... The demands and struggle for justice are crucial to ecumenical education. Education should aim to liberate people and nations, not domesticate them. Learning must therefore be practical and aim to foster participation, justice and thus liberation.

What conclusions can we draw from these theories as far as observation and critical evaluation of learning in intercongregational partnerships is concerned?

First, one must always remind oneself that ecumenical learning is concerned with more than just the exchange of information and acquiring knowledge. Ecumenical learning does not occur in the partnerships when the partners only inform themselves about the partner country and its political and economic situation. The acquisition of knowledge about the history and present constitution of the partner church, its spheres of church work and current problems, is also not in itself ecumenical learning. It is part of it, but not the totality.

Second, existential and procedural aspects of ecumenical learning should be stressed. The learning goal of action resulting in change cannot be neglected. In the context of this study we must continually ask how far partnerships enable Christians to influence and shape their environment responsibly. Also, how far, and in what way, are a living personal faith and the living church topics for discussion in partnerships alongside questions about the "fundamental direction of our civilization". Can partnerships act as catalysts for change?

It then follows, thirdly, that a restriction of discussions to interchurch matters must be avoided. Do partnerships really break through "parochial boundaries"? The interconnected historical aims of the ecumenical movement must be incorporated. These are: church unity; missionary witness by Christians in the times and the places where they live;

and the socio-ethical motive, i.e., the liberating involvement of Christians in the fight against injustice, poverty and oppression.

The concept of ecumenical learning began with Ernst Lange, who described the nature of church renewal as "practice in the ecumenical world horizon" and therefore advocated the "liberation of Christian conscience from its parochial limitations". The significant and critical characteristics of ecumenical learning have already been mentioned many times but bear repeating here. When people speak of ecumenical learning they are talking about the ecumenically responsible renewal of the church. With that in mind, I offer some critical comments on conditions and opportunities for ecumenical learning.

This study tries to limit the use of the term "ecumenical learning". Not everything that is so-called – certainly not in partnerships – is really ecumenical learning. Not every ecumenical encounter necessarily offers opportunities for ecumenical learning processes. In many cases this concept, with its aim of a fundamental renewal of all forms of church life, threatens to become "only a didactic method for integrating ecumenical subject matter into church educational programmes". Or, to take up Ernst Lange's point, quoted in the EKD workbook: Is "ecumenism" integrated into congregational life or only superficial so that the potential for change and impulses for action do *not* occur locally, and the "practice of ecumenical existence" is avoided?

Ecumenical learning, as stressed in almost all publications, is above all "learning through conflict". Here we must ask how capable of conflict, both internally and externally, congregations and churches are, especially in their partnership relations. My examination of partnership case studies will look at this closely. Behind this lies a fundamental issue. As Konrad Raiser puts it, "The learning objectives of ecumenical renewal should not inevitably lead to conflict with church strategies of securing existing progress and ensuring continuity." Are congregations in the majority of churches capable of ecumenical learning at all? How is the relationship between the partnership groups and the congregations to be defined?

PARTNERSHIP VISITS AS VEHICLES FOR ECUMENICAL LEARNING

Considering the definition of ecumenical learning given above as "learning through encounter", it is appropriate to look for examples of ecumenical learning in interchurch partnerships and especially in the context of the regular visits made in both directions. The hypothesis to be tested is that the most likely place for attempts at ecumenical learning to take place is during the course of these visits. At the same time, comment is needed on how these are linked into the normal partnership work and the life of the congregation. Ecumenical learning experiences are not just a matter for individuals but must lead to action that can be seen in the activities of the congregation and the church. In this section I shall analyze a typical programme for a partnership visit and show how this offers opportunities and obstacles for ecumenical learning. Observations have shown that visits made by German delegations to Africa differ in many ways from the return visits of the African partners. Therefore I shall first describe some aspects common to both and then consider other special situations.

1. Basic characteristics of partnership journeys with regard to ecumenical learning

Partnership visits normally last four weeks. Only in very few cases is there a deviation from this "norm". Many partnerships have agreed to an annual exchange. Others have a year without a visit after every two visits made. In the partnership between Marienwerder and Arushachini/ Chemchem the visits are concentrated into one year. The return visit of the Arushachini/Chemchem delegation follows immediately after the visit of the Marienwerder delegation. In the following year there is no visit.

As far as ecumenical learning is concerned it is clear that the programmes for the visitors do not have a specific theme. When the time for the next visit has been agreed – often the invitation is made at the end of the previous visit – exact dates and technical details are then also agreed on and all further organizational measures taken. As far as the programme itself is concerned very little detailed discussion takes place between the partners. None of the partnerships I studied had agreed together on special topics to be used as the framework for the visits. Therefore there is no such preparation beforehand among the members of the travel group.

In Marienwerder before each visit the German group prepared a Bible study with which they then – sometimes in the form of a short drama – introduced themselves to the Tanzanian congregations. The Marienwerder members decided on the themes among themselves.

The preparation of the group, at least in German partnership circles, takes place over several months. The main emphasis is on information about the partner congregation and church, about "the country and the people" (economic, political and cultural facts). As there are almost always members of the travel group who are both "experienced" and "new" to partnership work, a large part of the preparation time is also spent on exchanging practical travel tips. The group rarely discusses beforehand, or only superficially, the state of partnership relations or particularly burning questions and problems. Often it is only individuals, who have been involved previously in the partnership, who have possible questions or even a list of topics in their head or on paper, to be discussed with the appropriate contacts.

Not infrequently the travellers have no idea what sort of programme has been planned for them, but sometimes they are informed of some components beforehand. Occasionally the sending-side requests something specific, but there is no feedback about whether this request can be met. The result is that the travellers, particularly those taking part for the first time, set off with very little idea of what to expect. They have a general interest and a few hopes and expectations.

If we look back at the aims of ecumenical learning as defined by Orth, the first observation on learning on partnership journeys is that there are no aims and objectives planned for the visit, irrespective of whether these relate to personal faith or to "influencing and shaping the environment". The "call and struggle for justice" which Orth deems "constitutive", essential to ecumenical learning, is not found in programme planning for partnership visits. The partnership committees, the hosts and the guests leave the topics to chance. Already a decisive pattern has been established which militates against maximizing any potential learning opportunities during the visit.

Orth says that, when over, partnership journeys have to be evaluated and acted upon. As a rule this means that the delegation members present a report to the relevant committees – at district or congregational level such as the partnership or district committee. Particularly in the African churches this is normally the only form of evaluation. The decisive question, however, is how individual or group experiences can be transferred into the life of the congregation. Here there is a difference between the situation in the German and the African churches. In Germany it is a matter of course that members of the delegation report on the journey in congregations and congregational groups, usually in the form of a slide show. In addition they write articles for the congregational newsletter and sometimes even for the local newspaper. Where partnership newsletters exist, a special edition is usually brought out after the visit with extensive reports and photos.

Quite a different situation pertains in the churches in Africa. There they have neither the technical opportunities for slide shows nor facilities for extensive publications. The congregations learn very little about the journey after the return of the delegation. Normally they have to make do with a short word of greeting in the Sunday service. In some cases the idea is that the delegation members inform the pastors at the district conference, and they pass on the information to their congregations. In this way it can happen, as one member of a group told me, that there was no opportunity for her to give a report on her journey even to her own congregation. The pastor had probably done that, she said, but she did not know exactly as she had not attended the service that Sunday. This explains why many congregation members, when asked whether anyone from their congregation had been on a visit to Germany, do not know what to say.

It appears that the reports and information given by travellers after their return from Germany are kept deliberately brief. A pastor explained that it made no sense to report extensively, since the congregation could do nothing with it. A short word of greeting from the partners in Germany was sufficient. A European worker in an African partner church explained that extensive reporting could lead to jealousy and unpopularity in congregations. The implications of this for ecumenical learning and the question of how far experiences from such encounters can be made fruitful for the life of congregations and groups are self-evident. Under these circumstances, partnerships cannot develop into a power for change in the life of the congregations.

2. Typical elements of a partnership visit in an African partner church

The distinctive characteristic of a partnership visit by a German group to their African partner church is that there are visits to many congregations and churches. Partnership visits to Africa are above all visits to the congregations. While German partners sometimes complain about this, it is quite obviously very much desired by the African partners. Depending on the distances to be covered between the individual congregations or churches and the conditions under which they are possible, several congregations are often visited in a single day (I experienced between two and six!) This means an incredibly full programme, a daily schedule under great time pressure, and above all very little time for the congregations during the short visits. Some visits to a congregation do not last longer than half an hour.

The nature of such a congregational visit is repeated in each place, which the visitors often find very tiring. When the car with the white visitors drives up a great crowd of people is already waiting. Singing, clapping and dancing they approach the visitors, receive them into their midst and accompany them to the church or the building in which the congregation meets for worship. Garlands of flowers are hung around their necks, green branches are distributed around. Words of greeting follow, sometimes also short sermons by the visitors interspersed with singing together and (particularly in Tanzania) traditional dances. A representative of the congregation describes its situation in a few words. If the guests have a little more time they are invited to stay for a meal and served a real feast. Something small is always offered: tea, peanuts or biscuits. Longer phases of discussion are rarely possible. Soon the presents are handed over and it is time to go. The guests drive off quickly and the hosts remain behind singing, waving and dancing in a cloud of dust.

In spite of being tiring for the visitors, it is exactly these visits, which are so full of the exuberance, warmth and joyfulness of the congregation members, that are the experiences the German partnership travellers to Africa remember as the happiest moments of their journey. Here the picture of the living spirituality of African Christians develops and is regularly confirmed. Here is the reason why, when talking about how to overcome the difference in giving and receiving in partnerships, you often hear that African Christians can help German Christians with their spirituality.

However, European workers in the African partner churches, who are able to observe the situation over a longer period of time, speak of a "show" which is put on for the visitors; they see that partnership delegations "are treated as kings", that the partners from Germany are shown an exceptional situation, which has little in common with the daily routine of Christians and congregations.

Often on their return delegates try to transfer elements of the spirituality they have experienced into their own congregations, by bringing African songs with them and trying to communicate this living spirituality in their reports and when they talk about their visit. However, these attempts are rarely successful.

It is not my wish here to criticize the joyful exuberance of these moments during the visits. But I must raise some issues, especially some relating to ecumenical learning. What "pictures of the others" are conveyed by such North-South encounters? I believe that they threaten to reinforce and consolidate well-known stereotypes: the African with a joyful, living faith, the European travelling around in a hurry and distributing gifts. During these quick and often hectic visits it is not possible to learn from and with each other in any depth. The encounters remain – as warm and friendly as they are – superficial; they are chance encounters and interchangeable.

Such schedules become problematic when the situation quite obviously demands more time. The fact that many of those who are waiting for the German visitors have walked for many hours from their house to the church, and that many congregations spend several hours waiting together for the arrival of the visitors should be sufficient reason for making more time available. One hears again and again how happy the

African Christians are "that you Germans have undertaken the long and difficult road to come to us", therefore the disappointment that the visitors flash past in such a hurry must be even greater.

A programme put together in this way prevents learning. Examples of this were the meetings with congregations that had been hit by a great drought at the time of the visits. As we drove through the area we could see emaciated cattle out of the car windows. The local pastor explained that some families had already left the area in order to find food elsewhere. During the visits to the congregations the visitors made reference to the great drought. But time was far too short to do more than express their regret at the dire situation and strengthen hope that it would soon rain.

However, if understanding is really to come about, questions must be asked, which – on the part of the German visitors – try to help them to understand what "drought" actually means for the people who are gathered in the church. What are they living on at the moment? Can they still buy lettuce and vegetables? Have they still got seeds available? Have the prices of food increased? And if ecumenical learning is really the aim: What is the church doing in this situation, what is its role? How can it help? Can it help fight the causes of the drought? And also: What does faith mean in times of drought? How is the faith of the Europeans, who themselves experience no droughts, challenged by this encounter? What action will arise from this situation? Mutual ecumenical learning could then begin, if the South Africans were able to see their own situation in a new light through the perspective of the German visitors. In order for that to be possible the visitors would have to articulate and evaluate what they had seen and how they felt about it, which would then enable them to see their own living conditions in Germany with new eyes. But that needs time, so that people can really meet together, learn about each other's situation and begin to understand.

All the evidence showed that this time was not available, Space was not planned for intensive encounter that could facilitate learning. It is interesting that hardly anyone expressed fundamental criticism of this practice. The visitors moaned about the tight schedule that inevitably made them arrive late wherever they were expected. In some travel reports there are complaints about the programme being too full. But no one went as far as to request, or suggest, a fundamentally different programme schedule.

The partnership between the Lünen and Usakos districts is an exception. In 1993 the delegation tried out a new programme structure for the first time: the group was divided up and individual members were placed in different villages where they remained for a whole week, taking part in the normal daily life of their hosts and their surroundings. The idea was to visit fewer places and congregations, and place greater emphasis on more intensive opportunities for meeting together and exchanging ideas over a longer period of time. The changes were evaluated by everyone as a very positive new step in the partnership.

As visits to congregations are at the centre of partnership programmes the most frequent occurrence during visits is the joint celebration of services. In my observation it was especially in these services that the unity of the partners could be experienced. The African partner churches are churches that have developed out of the work of German missionaries, and their administrative framework and forms of service are still influenced by the German missionaries. Often the tunes of the hymns are familiar to the German visitors and they can usually easily follow a service in the local language and recognize its various parts. Apart from their vitality and exuberance the services offer little that is foreign.

By contrast, Bible studies and discussions on questions of faith occupied much less time during the visits. In some partnerships there have been attempts at joint Bible studies, but they were not generally considered very successful. Discussions on questions of faith were particularly difficult in a foreign language. In addition different forms of piety and ways of looking at biblical texts were important, but participants did not manage to speak openly about them. Intensive spiritual exchange is not one of the main focuses of such visits.

Discussions on other important subjects are also very difficult and rarely succeed. The Tanzanian partnerships, arranged through the United Evangelical Mission (VEM), spent several day seminars studying the paper of the Evangelical Lutheran Church of Tanzania on debt relief. The groups travelling in 1992, shortly after the seminars, were advised to try and talk at least once with the Tanzanian partners about the problem of debt and to ask directly about its effect on local medical care. When the group reconvened for a partnership seminar after the summer travelling months, not one of the seven groups had been able to learn anything of any importance. Discussion on the subject with the Tanzanian partners had been impossible, either because of lack of time, or because, according to the groups, the partners were insufficiently informed or were not interested in the subject.

In conclusion, during the partnership visits time allocated to longer discussion between partners was insufficient. Apparently, the partners do not consider this to be a grave shortcoming. This is the only explanation why, after so many years of travelling experience, the structure of the visits has hardly changed at all.

Official meetings and appointments must also be taken into consideration, especially those with congregational committees, district or congregational councils as well as the partnership committees, and the evaluation meetings at the end of a journey. These occasions were mainly concerned with questions of organization. The visitors briefly reported their impressions. Most of the time was spent considering problems to do with projects that had been supported and questions of finance. The progress of existing projects was discussed and ideas for new projects considered.

In contrast, academic questions about interchurch relations or agreement on the basic aims and objectives of partnership were of no importance. For example in a three-hour evaluation meeting with a nine point agenda, only one item, "our theological basis", was discussed for around ten minutes. The main points taking up the majority of the time were a long list of projects and questions of organization. This is a typical example.

Finally, it is remarkable how little the members of the delegation reflect quietly among themselves about what they have experienced. Even when time is planned for talking together within the delegation, this is usually used to talk about the programme for the following days. There is little recapitulation of what has occurred to date and how individual members have felt about particular situations. A wealth of strange impressions washes over the visitors, yet they do not share these with each other. In the end, individuals are left to cope alone. Unless there is more sharing with each other, understanding cannot flourish or only under great difficulties. Negative experiences can easily lead to the strengthening of prejudice and sweeping judgments. My own findings endorse this.

3. Typical elements of a visit to a German partner church

In the German congregations the visitors' programme is, as in Africa, very full and very tightly scheduled, so that the delegates – in spite of all their enthusiasm about what they experience – complain. The German congregations offer their partners a wide range of events. In contrast to Africa, these are not visits to many different congregations, but rather visits to many different church institutions and congregational groups. The visitors take part in meetings of women's groups, old people's afternoons, youth groups and house-circles. Other popular places are kindergartens, hospitals, museums and regional and district church institutions. Visits to the town, shopping excursions, drives in the surrounding area, visits to farms and industrial plants are all part of the programme. Many partnership groups, accompanied by their hosts, also visit the regional church offices and their mission departments.

Compared to Africa, it is noticeable that usually only a few congregational staff and members of the partnership group (perhaps only one or two) accompany the visitors. On occasion, I was the sole person who went with them! There are no meetings when many members of the congregation welcome the visitors with singing and dancing, so typical of the visits to Africa. The element of celebration is not so prevalent. Participation in the congregational groups and circles usually means that the visitors are expected to talk about where they come from and to answer questions. Where institutions or industrial plants or farms are visited, the guests are given information about the field of work, which is usually new to them, and they have the opportunity to ask questions.

Thus there is more opportunity for discussion during the visits to Germany, mainly because of the shorter time required for travelling from one place to another. But is learning more possible as a result? Ecumenical learning is more than just passing on information and knowledge and the aim of the visits and sightseeing trips is mainly just that. What is lacking is any help with absorbing this information, analyzing it, and seeing how it fits into the broader picture.

There is no proper progression in the planning of the various activities on the programme. They cover a broad spectrum especially within the church but also within society. Their choice is fairly accidental and, to a certain extent, quite arbitrary. In addition the guests as a rule arrive without any prior preparation. Often they have only a vague idea about who the people are and what they do. For the people sitting opposite them it is often much the same. This means that only superficial exchanges are possible, covering each side's local situation and answering questions. I could find no example where a central theme linked the activities in the programme and the places visited. The nearest was the vague theme of "getting to know the partner's situation". There was no evidence of a steering of the discussion towards questions of personal faith or how the participants influenced and shaped the environment around them, basic elements required for ecumenical learning. Nor was there any evidence of use of the four learning steps discussed at the start of this chapter: situation analysis, joint statements of positions, finding a consensus and instructions for action.

4. Initial reflections on observations made during partnership visits

Partnership visits offer unique opportunities to travel to a foreign country, to be close to the people who live there and thus to learn from and with them. In contrast to tourists, who travel to countries of the so-called third world, visitors in partnerships do not live in hotels with European standards but rather in the houses of their hosts. They experience directly and at close quarters how people live in South Africa, Namibia or Tanzania. They spend their days together, eat together, and they discover the foreign world accompanied by people who live there and to a certain extent see the country from their perspective. There are very few opportunities for travelling to a foreign country and experiencing it at such close quarters and so intensely as within the framework of church partnership relations.

The opportunities for ecumenical learning arising from such visits, are, however, barely put to use. To reiterate the reasons for this: time plays an important role in the form the programme takes; partnership visits do not usually have a central theme; visits follow one after another in a coincidental and arbitrary fashion, without any recognizable relationship and no obvious value or purpose for the partnership or the individual partners; there are no joint periods of reflection when experiences can be shared regularly together and developed further.

In contrast to the general statement often heard that ecumenical learning takes place – more or less automatically – on such partnership visits, I am of the opinion that learning processes are planned in and worked at far too little and that this should be an essential element in the planning. As it is, the majority of the opportunities for learning are wasted.

In this context it is worth looking a little more closely at informal conversations occurring during a partnership visit, such as those with the hosts at the breakfast table, or in the evenings after the programme is over, or between two or three people in the minibus during a drive somewhere. Here decisive questions are sometimes asked, explanations are given, and there is a certain amount of peace and quiet to pursue an idea and to toss it backwards and forwards between the partners. For some participants their most important experiences derive from such chance conversations. But these are individual experiences, not joint learning, and they are often not shared within the delegation, far less with the partners, and are very difficult to pass on to members of the congregations.

To avoid misunderstandings, I should make clear that it is not a question of turning partnership visits into educational events with the character of a seminar. This would be totally contrary to the position and interests of the partners. Above all it would not accord with the character of partnership relations. However, if learning is to come about in interchurch partnerships it is necessary to plan it consciously, stimulate it and reflect on it methodically. The participants must want to learn. On the basis of my findings, I doubt this is the case.

In order to initiate learning, the form of the programmes must be changed. Reflection must be a part of it and that means looking at things from a distance. Both partners must take time to work through what they have experienced, and to tell each other how they felt. They need to formulate feelings and observations and thereby become aware of them themselves. Regular evaluation sessions are absolutely necessary for joint learning.

Observations confirm that when this happens, partners will very quickly become aware of their differences and just how foreign they appear to each other. This can lead to conflicts, which have to be worked through, sometimes even bitterly. Ecumenical learning is "learning through conflicts".

Here we come across a further, perhaps decisive, reason why this kind of learning is so little sought in partnerships. Partnerships claim closeness. In face of the historical background of colonialism and the inequality in the early mission relations, partnerships claim to institute a new relationship of equality, unity and harmony, summed up in the phrase "today we are partners". This harmony is threatened when the feeling of being foreign to each other creates conflicts. It is this wish for harmony that makes partners avoid looking at things objectively, which is essential if both sides are to learn from each other. Ecumenical learning can become a burden for the partnership. It can also lead to conflicts within individual congregations when lessons learnt during the visit call into question well-loved habits and attitudes or engender other forms of resistance. These are the reasons – at least I presume they are – why progressive learning is so rarely sought after and put into practice. On the other hand, it must be said that ecumenical learning can lead to enrichment and an intensification of the partnership.

5. Opportunities for learning

Learning is possible if it is consciously initiated and stimulated. Two examples may be quoted to refute the claim that conscious stimulation of intellectual learning is something brought into the partnership from outside. A closer look also shows that the supposition that African partners consider it important to visit more congregations and have less interest in thematic work does not hold good either. These positive examples were associated with significant observations of a willingness to make progress in learning together.

Example 1: A different programme for the visit. During the visit of a delegation from Osterholz-Scharmbeck to the district of Polokwane in 1992 the Seshego congregation organized a different programme from those organized by the Lebowakgomo and Eldorado congregations. On this occasion the usual congregational visits did not take place. Various churches were visited, but only to see the buildings and their location.

Members of the congregations had not been alerted to the visit and therefore did not turn up. This irritated some of the German visitors. Just looking at the empty buildings, some of them only half-finished, was not particularly interesting.

But instead of the congregation the local pastor had invited representatives from various congregational groups, social institutions and also from political parties and action groups to meet with the visitors for lengthy rounds of discussion. For example, representatives from all the congregational groups spent a whole morning with the visitors. They talked about the main focus of their work and about possible plans for the future. And they articulated very clearly what they expected from partnership.

These meetings served as the first step in getting to know each other and exchanging information. The South Africans, for example, indicated what opportunities they had for doing social work in their township, and the Germans then talked about social work in Germany. The comparisons served to introduce each country to the other. The exchange of ideas did not go any further, nor did it bring the two sides together. Yet such a discussion could have offered the chance to focus on joint themes and directions for the future work of the district and congregational partnership.

It is interesting that it was the Germans who were disappointed by this form of programme. They had the feeling that the congregations had not been sufficiently informed or did not participate enough in the visit, so that the fledgling partnership had failed to come alive. A second factor that caused uncertainty and confusion for the German visitors was that in the meetings with a more official character they constantly expected to be asked for help in financing projects. But the African partners did not do so. They emphasized several times that they expressly did not want any project support. Their only expectation was the wish to exchange ideas and experience with suitable groups in the congregations in Germany.

Example 2: A seminar on the subject of water. This example is also taken from my observations of the partnership between Osterholz-Scharmbeck and Polokwane. During the visit of the South African delegation in 1993 there was an attempt to hold a seminar on the subject of water. There was a reason for this; parts of the Polokwane district had suffered from severe drought in 1992. Over a period of years several water-pump projects had been supported by the Osterholz-Scharmbeck district, some of which however had not proved successful. A water-engineer from the Stuttgart Centre for Appropriate Technology was invited as an expert to the seminar, but this seminar deemed biblical questions on water as equally important.

The discussions on the importance of water in biblical texts were particularly exciting. The different ideas both groups associated with water soon became apparent. The people from the Weser marshlands had fought hard to wrest their land from the water and had remained threatened by flooding for many years. The people from South Africa suffered from drought and lack of water and longed for water and rain. An exchange followed on how far the constantly decreasing rainfall in Southern Africa could be attributed to interference by Northern nations with the climate. This brought both sides very quickly, through their mutual sadness, to consider how they could cooperate to influence and protect their environments in face of ecological dangers. Here the participants made progress in learning together and recorded this step by step at the end of the seminar. The discussion of the biblical texts was as much part of this as the exchange about their different situations in life. So was their search for ways of solving the problems together: sensible wells and water projects were proposed. All this transpired within the shared fellowship of a community living together for a short time and was rounded off with joint liturgical devotions conducted in such a way that everyone was able to share in them.

This example shows that learning processes are possible in partnerships. Similar opportunities must, however, be created and fostered if they are desired. But at this point I wonder if those involved in partnership work really want to embark on a path of learning together with their partners, which inevitably will lead to change. The example of the water seminar makes the point clearly, as there were hardly any participants from Osterholz-Scharmbeck who did not have to be there on account of their office or function. The guests were also embarrassed by this fact.

An observation made during the evaluation session of a visit to Germany by African guests echoes this. Towards the end of a several-hour session in which mainly organizational questions had been discussed, a participant asked the guests whether they would like to say something about their impressions of life in Germany and the position of its church. Before she had finished her sentence the questioner was shouted down by the other German participants. That was expecting too much of the South Africans, they claimed. Later, when I questioned the guests, they indicated that they would indeed have had something to say. They had even prepared a few points.

THE PARTNERSHIP COMMITTEE AS A PLACE FOR ECUMENICAL LEARNING

Delegation visits are the highlights and focal points of a partnership. But partnership work also goes on apart from these visits, at least in German partner groups. The partnership committees are responsible for continuing the work of the partnership "at home". The following section looks at the work of these committees. First of all I shall show how they are put together and how they work. Then I shall consider the tasks and subjects with which they are mainly concerned from the perspective of the opportunities presented for learning and the actual progress made in the learning process.

1. The structures of the partnership committees

In the district of Osterholz-Scharmbeck the recurring partnership work is done at a district level by the committee for mission and ecumenism. The district administration is directly responsible for the main part of the official regular correspondence, the financial transactions and the administrative work. The committee meets approximately once a month. Visitors are occasionally invited to the meetings, including, for example, the delegation members before and after a delegation visit.

Since direct partnerships have been established in three congregations they each have their own congregation partnership committees that are responsible to a certain extent for the work in their area. This includes correspondence, preparation of visits and preliminary discussions of projects. Small projects (up to an agreed limit of DM 500) can be dealt with independently by these committees.

The Lünen district has adopted a different structure for its committee work. Here there is a partnership committee consisting of delegates from all the congregations in the district. This committee only meets four times a year to discuss and agree on important principles of partnership work and to prepare larger events. A small committee consisting of five people meets approximately once a month to deal with ongoing work. Occasionally the members of all the committees and other interested persons are invited to special Namibia days or weekend seminars in order to generate greater interest for the partnership in the congregations.

In the Lübbecke district there is also a district partnership committee that meets regularly once a month. The members are representatives of the congregations involved in partnership links and all those who have taken part in delegation visits. This means that there is a long list of participants, who at least receive the invitations to the meetings and the minutes, even if they no longer come regularly to the meetings.

In Marienwerder there is a partnership committee called the Tanzania Group. This comprises all those who have been involved in the partnership from the beginning and several members of the congregational council. The congregational council is also heavily involved with the ongoing work of partnership.

The partnership districts and congregations in Tanzania, South Africa and Namibia have also set up committees of similar structure. However these normally only meet before partnership visits. In these partnership committees it is usually the employees of the district and the congregations who have the main say. The pastor or the dean sends out the invitations and is the chairperson of the committee. Voluntary workers (members of the congregational council) are represented as are those who have participated as members of a visiting delegation or as hosts to the partners during previous visits.

2. The most important thematic emphases

When looking for examples of learning in the partnership committees I concentrated on the topics and problems that occupied the committees in the normal course of their work. In order to identify these I studied the minutes and the files of the partnership committees as far as they were available. In none of the case studies in question were the minutes of all the meetings still available. Nevertheless, the material enabled me to get a general picture that was then supplemented by the comments of the members interviewed.

In general it became apparent that the committees mainly occupy themselves with questions of organization. The preparation and organization of the visit from the partner church generates the most work. All available energy is often bound up for several months in working out the programme and in detailed planning. Members of the committee then spend a lot of time in carrying out projects or coping with the problems and difficulties arising from these. A great deal of time and energy also goes on clearing up communication misunderstandings between the partners.

Compared to these much less time is taken considering aspects arising from partnership relationships, be it the ecumenical question of church unity, development-oriented subjects such as apartheid in South Africa, the debts owed by the continent, or the problems of people of different cultures living together. According to the documents available hardly any time was spent on such matters. In general the committees concentrated on the situation in their partner church. They did not concern themselves with the situation of their own congregation and its position in the local society and environment.

Beyond these organizational aspects, the following topics were also dealt with in the partnership committees: in the district of Osterholz-Scharmbeck in the 1980s issues of direct congregation partnerships were frequently on the agenda. This was raised by the South African partners at a very early stage and there was much discussion on the subject in the committees, particularly from 1988 onwards. In 1985 the so-called Kairos document was published in South Africa, a critical statement by South African theologians on apartheid and the role of the churches. The paper is mentioned in the minutes, but no lengthy discussion of it seems to have taken place. The Kairos document analyzes the various positions adopted by the churches towards the oppressive power of the state, and in a unique way challenges the churches worldwide to concern themselves with their own situations. During a visit of the South African partners an attempt was made to discuss the Kairos document with them. The attempt failed as the African partners did not know the document and were also unwilling, given the political situation at the time, to express opinions on the quite dangerous statements made in it.

The minutes also refer to the assembly of the WCC in Vancouver (1983) and the assembly of the Lutheran World Federation in Budapest. It was here that the white Lutheran church in South Africa was suspended from membership of the Lutheran World Federation. There was an interesting occurrence in the context of the preparations for the first-ever visit of a delegation from South Africa. The partnership committee had applied to the committee for development education and publications (ABP) in Stuttgart for financial support. In order to receive funding it was necessary to list aspects of the planned visit that were concerned with particular topics. For the programme the committee drew up a long list of topics and questions which they then assigned to individual programme events. It was not possible to find out how far these topics were actually discussed during the various events. But it is clear that the committee was forced to link the programme to certain topics and questions. Later the committee decided that it was too restrictive to have to give everything a thematic focus and therefore decided to forego ABP financing in future. The programme had been far too intense because of the strong learning element in it. The superintendent at the time reported that they had felt themselves "far too much under orders" from the ABP regulations. The regional church regulations on financial subsidies had been "much more generous". There is no evidence that during later visits so much emphasis was given to thematic issues.

In the Lünen district, besides the various activities and projects of the partnership, they also focused on the theological and political discussion about apartheid in Namibia, which led to preparing political statements and writing letters to German and Namibian politicians, as well as holding public campaigns in Lünen itself. Many Namibia groups were involved in the debate about the Special Fund to Combat Racism of the WCC in the early 1980s. In the Lünen documents there are occasional hints that fundamental discussions took place, for example on the subject of partnership, something that hardly ever occurred in the other groups. But if the time given to this subject is compared to the time taken, for example, talking about a wage-subsidy for church workers in the Usakos district, it remained a very fringe issue. The German-Namibian partnership consultations in Gut Holmecke in 1985 and Swakopmund in 1990 were occasions that elicited a more fundamental discussion on partnership in the committee.

The German-Tanzanian Group in Marienwerder offered the best and most continuously kept minutes book of the four case studies examined. Here it was possible to judge how much importance had been given to each topic. As in the other groups, by far the most time was spent passing on news and information from Tanzania, discussing projects and the transfer of money, and the preparation and planning of delegation visits. Much less time was taken to talk about experiences during the visits and to consider what new findings resulted from the various encounters and their implications for the partnership and the congregation. The most that happened was that the delegation reported and issues concerning the projects were discussed. However in Marienwerder there were frequent complaints that not enough evaluation was done after the visits. In the 1980s an important question was the sub-dividing of the Tanzanian congregations on account of their growth in numbers, and later (occasionally before 1989, but mainly afterwards) the inclusion of the congregation of Leipzig-Stötteritz in the partnership. These issues offered many opportunities to think more fundamentally about the partnership, relations between the churches and the congregations and suitable ways and forms of developing partnership relations.

The subjects discussed in the partnership group in the Lübbecke district were more or less the same as in the other partnership committees. It is apparent from the agendas of the meetings and the incomplete collection of minutes that – at the suggestion of the pastor attending the meetings from the mission department promoting education for mission – lecture evenings were held at regular intervals, for example on the situation of women in Africa.

In the minutes of an evaluation discussion after a visit by a German delegation to Tanzania a number of matters are listed as learning experiences: "piety, willingness to witness to their faith, calling into question the credibility of our faith, questioning our congregational life". The positive experience of the joyfulness, vitality and spontaneity of the African services during the visit, which were experienced as very positive, were felt to be a critical challenge to their own faith and congregational life. However, it proved very difficult to transfer the specific experiences, experienced in a similar way by all groups, to their own situation and to act upon them. I could find no reference in the minutes to what extent the questioning of the African congregations resulted in changes in congregational life. Nor could the people I spoke to give me much information. In one set of minutes it states briefly that: "the critical enquiries (of the partners) can unfortunately not be reported here". In which case their ability for change was taken away from them.

In my opinion this situation is typical of many partnerships, and reflects the twin problem of closeness and distance in partnerships. The German partners are filled with enthusiasm for the lively services in the African congregations. Here they feel very close to their partners. In order to really understand and learn from each other, however, it would be necessary to have a certain detachment. It would be essential first of all to observe what is happening in a neutral way, and then to understand it within its context. After that they need to ask what elements of the services of the African partners were culturally determined. The relationship of the African elements and the influence of the theology and piety of German or other Western missions should also be considered. Only on such a basis can similarities and differences between the cultures be recognized and then transferred into German congregations.

CONGREGATIONAL LIFE AS A PLACE FOR ECUMENICAL LEARNING

To summarize at this point I would like to recall that the aim of ecumenical learning is the renewal of the church. Through ecumenical learning initiatives and encounters with the partners, congregation members should be empowered and liberated to responsibly influence and shape the environment of their congregation and society. Congregations are challenged to influence this process of renewal by taking sides with the oppressed and the poor, the weak and those deprived of their rights. This means opening up the congregations and new considerations about the role of the congregations in society, both at a local and a global level. In the partnership committees these issues are hardly ever raised. The groups are mainly if not entirely occupied with administering the organizational side of the partnership. Nobody denies that the active members of the partnership committees are extremely well informed about the situation in the partnership country, both in relation to its historical and political as well as its social and economic aspects. There is an enormous amount of knowledge available in the partnership committees. There is great interest in any information whatsoever concerning the partnership country, as demonstrated by the collection of articles from newspapers and magazines and the literature available. My question, however, is whether they succeed in using this knowledge and linking it to responsible action in their own society and church.

What importance could ecumenical learning have for the partnership committees? Firstly, the experiences gained from encounters with the partners must be evaluated and analyzed much more deeply. The participants on visits must be given much more time to reflect methodically with members of the congregations on what they have experienced. Consideration should be given how to transfer experience into the home situation; how the experiences of a few individual persons – especially the encouraging experiences and those that strengthened their faith – can be made fruitful first of all for the partnership group and beyond that for the congregation as a whole.

Secondly, the partnership committees could consider the wider role of the church in society more intensively. I pointed out earlier that meetings and visits often remain imprisoned in the "parochial sphere" and do not manage to open up the congregations to the secular world. The encounters during such visits are related to the central areas of congregational life and the diaconal activities of the congregation without considering them in the broader context of society, politics, economy, art and religion. This is reflected in the work of the committees. The internal affairs of the partner church and the partner congregation are followed closely and social activities supported by projects. Yet the broader context in which the work takes place is hardly considered at all.

Thirdly, I investigated ecumenical learning processes and the changes or influences in the life of the congregation arising from partnership work. The people I questioned found it very difficult or even impossible to name specific things that had changed as a result of the partnership (or even where the partnership had played a role). To some extent they listed very general things (openness, broadening of horizons, expansion) and expressed assumptions such as that the services "might" have become more lively. Sometimes they commented that their answers were perhaps wishful thinking on their part and hoped that the congregation had perhaps learned something new.

It proved the exception when a congregation was able to name specific changes. This was the case in Marienwerder where the people I spoke to found it easier to give examples. There were on the one hand attempts to introduce new elements into the services: the services were to be given a much more personal character (for example by welcoming people at the beginning), laypeople were to take much more part in the conduct of services (reading the lessons, lay sermons, spontaneous statements, and so on).

Furthermore, attempts had been made to open the congregation and congregational life more towards people who lived around the church and the congregation. Sometimes at the end of the service the congregation processed outside the church doors for the blessing, as is common in Tanzanian congregations. They had held services regularly outside on a piece of open ground between several blocks of flats, to make it easier for people who had no contact to the church to come into contact. But neither of these things happened any more; on the one hand they had not had the required effect, and on the other hand many people felt these forms of service to be too showy.

The Brambauer congregation in the Lünen district was the only other comparable congregation that could show that it had been influenced by partnership work. But this did not apply to the rest of the Lünen district. There were some congregations for whom the partnership played only a very marginal role. And yet it is quite clear that some congregations in the Lünen district managed to make a successful connection between the partnership and the church's political involvement in overcoming apartheid in Namibia on the one hand and the church's social involvement against unemployment in the area and for integration of foreigners living in Lünen on the other hand. It was exactly this correlation that deeply impressed their African partners.

In contrast, in the conversations for this study, those who were most at a loss to articulate any learning outcome were the people in the districts of Lübbecke and Osterholz-Scharmbeck. My contacts there were quite open about their doubts whether one could speak of lessons learned at all as far as the congregations were concerned. Even when an active group was involved in current partnership work they were unable to introduce long-term learning in the congregations.

The case studies showed clearly that it is most difficult to bring about change when the partnership is primarily based at a district level. When decisive questions concerning the partnership are discussed in committees at district level and decided over the heads of the congregations, it is almost impossible to establish the partnership in the congregations. These observations indicate that the district is not the right place for shaping and reflecting on learning processes in the partnership. In order to make progress it is necessary to pitch learning at the right level, where those concerned can talk about what they have experienced and reflect upon it, where they can work together with others, arrive at an understanding and decide on the steps to be taken that are relevant to their situation.

Finally, I shall look at what those actively involved in the partnership work pass on to the members of the congregations, either in the form of personal reporting or in information brochures. The answers to these questions will help to clarify the understanding of partnership of many of those actively involved, but also what lessons a congregation can possibly learn from the "usual ways of passing on information".

It is striking that certain themes appear again and again. If a delegation group has been on a visit they usually write general travel reports, focusing mainly on church life and especially its worship. These are reports based on personal experience, which recall the main places and events of the programme and give information about the living conditions of the partners. They provide a picture of lively, spontaneous services; they talk about the joyfulness of the congregations, the warmth and friendliness of their welcome. In addition they talk about the poverty and the difficulties of the partners and as a result describe in detail projects that are planned or those projects that have already been financed. They contain a lot of information about the political and economic situation of the country but far less about cultural and religious questions. The search for similarities between Germany and the relevant African country is hardly to be found at all. Besides the wealth of information offered, there is far too little orientation given or connections made.

In contrast to what was often talked about in the partnership committee meetings and that I could learn on the side from the active members of the groups, it is striking that practically nothing is reported about the difficulties and conflicts in a partnership. The problems, whether of communication, disagreement or trouble, are not reported to the congregations.

I observed a particularly striking example of this when a woman who had been actively involved in the partnership for a long time returned after staying several months in the partner congregation. One evening she reported to the congregation, showing pictures and talking about what she had experienced (mainly the good things), and what tasks she had been able to carry out within the women's work there.

But the picture was quite a different one when the following day the members of the partnership committee met in the morning. Here the "internal" difficulties of the partner congregation and their effect on the partnership were paramount. As a number of the pastors in the African partner congregation had been transferred, it was a time of radical change there. This situation had made quite obvious how much the partnership had been dependent on one single pastor over many years and how little was therefore actually rooted in the African congregations. It had become apparent that the partnership committee there had had no real influence. This was at the same time a very crucial question for the German partner congregation who for their part had relied heavily on the one local pastor, as communication with him was so much easier. With the departure of this pastor, however, a new committee had been established and laypeople had taken up the partnership work anew. All the resulting problems and uncertainties were discussed in the partnership committee including conflicts in the past. However, the congregation was told nothing about this situation, or at best a very watered down version.

This pattern was repeated in other partnership case studies. Specifically the problems and conflicts that occurred during visits or in communications were frequently omitted from reports to the congregation. They did not cover questions of distance, foreignness or lack of understanding. To put it more pointedly: the congregations are mainly presented with a picture of inspiring closeness between the partners and the necessity to help with their needs and problems.

Here again two typical characteristics of the partnership movement are apparent: the unity or oneness of the partners implied in the term partnership, which makes it difficult if not impossible to absorb and accept the feeling of foreignness; and the perception of the African partners as mainly rich in spirituality but materially poor and in need of help – a widespread stereotype of North-South relations – is not corrected by the partnership encounters.

The question of how far ecumenical partnerships initiate a process of ecumenical learning in the congregations must unfortunately be answered largely in the negative. The fact that many congregations have become receptive to questions about the relationship between North and South and the issues of justice, peace and the integrity of creation, which go way beyond the field of partnership work, can be considered as ecumenical learning in the widest sense. The partnership visits contribute to this as do the information given in congregation letters, regular reports and the publication of letters or sermons from the partner congregations. While this only leads in extremely rare cases to personal involvement on the part of members of the congregation, nevertheless it is possible that it brings about a change in certain individual attitudes.

There is no real information available, however, to show how far these changes really affect the majority of the congregation. In the current discussions on saving money raging through the church and congregations there are more and more signs that many people see ecumenical involvement as a "luxury" that one could afford (and finance) in good years but which does not deserve particular support in times when finance is short. Many workers in partnership groups are very concerned about this trend.

The coming years will probably demonstrate how far ecumenical awareness is really rooted in the congregations and what part the partnerships play in it. Beyond that, there are only some exceptions where the effects of a partnership are visible in the life of the congregation. As a rule learning experiences in partnerships are confined to individuals.

I do not need to repeat here that partnership relationships offer enough opportunities for learning. Congregations could also be places where people can take steps in ecumenical learning through the partnership, even if they have no direct contact with the partners during their visits nor work actively in the partnership committee. But in order for this to be the case, those who are responsible for the partnership must perceive this ecumenical relationship much more as a place of learning for the congregation and actively structure it in this way.

SYSTEMATIC EVALUATION

In contrast to the widespread assertion that ecumenical learning takes place in partnerships, as a result of my findings I have established that processes of ecumenical learning take place much less in interchurch partnerships than is generally assumed despite the fact that these offer excellent opportunities for ecumenical learning in intercultural encounters.

This hypothesis is supported by the observation that first, learning processes in partnerships are not methodically structured; second, of all the people questioned hardly any could name any lessons that had been learned; and third, at a congregation level no changes, or only very isolated changes, in attitudes, behaviour or actions could be named or observed.

If anything at all can be said, it is that individuals involved in the partnership experience had personal learning processes of their own over the years. These individual learning experiences frequently cannot be transmitted to the congregations. Many of those actively involved are of the opinion that the congregation members are not interested in their experiences. The people that I talked to confirmed the hypothesis that hardly any impetus for ecumenical renewal in congregations and churches stemmed from the partnership work. As a rule, partnership work is understood in German congregations as one field of church work among many others. That is why almost all the structural characteristics of other fields of church work are also applicable to partnership work (such as number and structure of those involved). The fundamental aim of ecumenical learning, that "oikoumene, the worldwide Christian church" should become an integral part of church and congregational existence, has not been achieved by the partnerships.

My observations allow me to conclude that ecumenical partnerships are generally not understood as a means of ecumenical renewal in the church and its congregations. This idea is neither to be found in the motives of the people actively involved nor is it stated by the regional churches and their mission departments in their descriptions of the role of partnership. For this reason there is no purposeful and methodical structuring of ecumenical learning in the partnership encounters. Neither do the regional churches or the mission departments or institutions of the church development service offer appropriate educational support in order to initiate such learning.

Ecumenical learning aims at renewal of the church and the congregation. It intends to make the congregations more receptive both to an ecumenical exchange on questions of personal faith and also on questions of influencing responsibly their personal environment. It is a question of learning about and celebrating the worldwide community of the body of Christ and at the same time striving for justice throughout the world.

When ecumenical learning is understood in this way it comes into conflict with the fundamental apparatus of the existing majority church both in Germany and in many African countries. Overcoming parochial boundaries, turning towards the world, actively taking on responsibility for the way our society and our environment are structured, but above all the bias of ecumenical learning towards the poor, the weak, the oppressed and those with no rights, are very difficult if not impossible to combine with the desire for harmony and the wish to protect vested interests of the wider German church. Ecumenical learning includes potential material for conflict not only for partnership relations but also for the congregations themselves. Clinging to structures and forms of congregational life influenced by the majority church situation seems to me to be the greatest obstacle for the effective practice of ecumenical learning in ecumenical partnerships.

IV. Practising Ecumenical Existence

Considerations for a New Orientation with a Systematic Perspective

The fourth and final chapter of this study serves mainly to offer a perspective and search for new forms of partnership practice. I shall progress from basic considerations about a new orientation for partnerships to practical suggestions for new forms they can take. The forms of partnership work I shall consider emphasize three aspects that have so far been rather neglected: first, overcoming inequality and injustice between the partners; second, increasing thematic content in partnerships and promoting joint learning processes; and third, setting the goal of partnership work towards ecumenical renewal of congregations and churches.

During the course of this study my main points of criticism towards present partnership work have been as follows.

First, the structural differences between the partners that encourage "one-way partnerships". The partners' differences reflect the existing political and economic North-South divide to the usual disadvantage of the Africans, but also have roots in an unreflected dominating role of the German partners. "Partnership work" takes place almost exclusively in Germany (committees, seminars, activities). Financial means for partnership are almost entirely raised in Germany. The real "fields of work" (projects!) of partnership are, however, in the churches of the South (on the former "mission-fields"). Finance, initiatives and ideas flow from the North to the South. But... hardly anything comes back! Partnership groups do not feel themselves responsible for looking into their own situation. They do not see it as their role to take up ecumenical challenges at their own German front doors, either privately or as a church, nor do they expect anything in this direction from their partners in the South.

Second, partnership encounters seldom have thematic content to give them depth, and often become an end in themselves. Partnership encounters have, in fact, become the reason for many partnerships, but they have no special themes. They do not consider special topics, nor do they serve any special aim or fulfil any of the partners' joint tasks. They are simply encounters. This leads to superficiality and a thematic weakness in the partnership relations. Learning processes are avoided rather than being activated.

Third, partnerships do not help towards ecumenical renewal of congregations and churches. Only a very small circle of people are actively involved in partnerships in congregations and churches. While individuals may experience important things that lead to personal changes, they do not succeed in transferring them to the congregational level. Congregational life is not changed by partnerships. (This is most likely where a single congregation maintains an intensive partnership over many years.) Among other things, encounters lack depth as they have no thematic content.

Fourth, sometimes the ideology of closeness between the partners prevents them from realizing their foreignness and from working out any conflicts. Partnership encounters suggest a closeness of the (foreign) partner, an understanding for each other, which in fact is not the case. Emotionally, a state of harmony within the partnership is valued highly and can only be maintained due to the more occasional character of the encounters. Misunderstandings and conflicts between partners are felt as threats to their closeness instead of being seen as opportunities for learning; therefore they are suppressed. It often takes many years before the partner's otherness is really recognized and accepted.

Fifth, the majority of projects supported by partnerships have no relevance to development, and thus sustain a dependency of the African partners on the North. The projects supported by partnerships neither serve primarily to fight poverty nor to support development: the most frequent projects are church buildings and vehicles or wage subsidies; only more recently has there been an increase of investing in training programmes. Neither do partners concern themselves with causes of worldwide poverty and injustice within the context of these projects. Hardly any of the partnership groups talk about long-term development concepts with their partners. Failed projects do not give cause for enquiry into the reasons for failure nor for a fundamental reconsideration of project work as such. There is no self-critical appraisal of the role of money and their own dealings with it. This strengthens the interest of many partners in the South in material and financial advantage, and creates and cements dependency.

In spite of such fundamental criticism of the present partnership practice, this study has proved that the specific approach of interchurch partnerships offers excellent opportunities for intercultural exchange and learning processes and for practice in ecumenical existence. Therefore the result of this study is in no way a fundamental rejection of congregation and district partnerships as such, but rather the specific criticism that the true possibilities of such interchurch relations are very often not made use of.

Indeed, there are many positive aspects of partnerships. Among them are the following.

First, in many cases partnerships offer the only opportunity for members of congregations to have ecumenical experiences in encounters with Christians from the worldwide church. Partnerships serve for the acquisition of ecumenism at a congregational level; they are often the only starting points from which the subjects of mission and ecumenism can be brought into congregational life.

Second, partnerships motivate people to concern themselves with the third world and strengthen their commitment and involvement. Partnership encounters give a "face" to the solidarity of the congregation members. Partnerships that are planned as long-term from the beginning develop much more staying power. The partners stick together in spite of all hindrances to contact and communication, even in times of annoyance and when contact "has dried up". Here there is no short-lived quick change of topics and activities, but rather the constant committed community on the way together.

Third, partnerships enable the practical solidarity limited to a specific place and group of people that is necessary for learning processes. It is not a question of general solidarity with those who are persecuted and oppressed but rather a relationship to known persons and groups. This offers special opportunities for motivation when talking about intercultural learning.

As impetus for a new orientation I shall describe possible ways of overcoming three fundamental deficiencies in partnership work in the following sections. In my opinion these three main deficiencies are: lack of relevance for renewal of the congregations and the church; lack of subject content and depth in the aims of partnerships; and insufficient ability to overcome injustice and inequality leading to greater dependency.

I believe these deficits can be overcome if the partners use the possibilities their relationship offers to enquire into the ecumenical missionary task of partnership in a new way. Partnerships should be strengthened for their importance in the search for church unity and also in enabling congregations and churches to be role models for an ecumenical missionary presence.

Also, a specific challenge to partnerships is that they should contribute to a deeper understanding of that which is foreign. And finally, I see a task for partnerships, as a form of North-South relations of the church particularly close to the congregations, that they should look for new symbolic rituals and forms of celebrating their partnership relations in religious festivities. I believe that in concentrating more on these aspects partnership work can find a fundamentally new orientation. Suggestions how this can be put into practice conclude my study.

1. The challenge to *Konvivenz*: partnerships as a way of practising ecumenical existence

The decisive starting point for a new orientation in partnership work and a reduction of the deficiencies established so far is to be found in the role the concept of partnership has in ecumenical history, and at the same time by recognizing the ecumenical missionary task of partnerships. It is not a case of redefining partnership work and its aims, but rather of remembering what ecumenical insights have already been gained and consciously making these ecumenical commitments our own.

The term partnership is frequently criticized because of its lack of biblical or theological qualification. However, attempts either to give more theological meaning to the term or to replace it with terms of stronger theological content (for instance, koinonia, brother- and sisterhood) have not been successful. In this study I have also consciously resisted developing alternatives to the term. In my opinion it is not worth trying to give the term partnership a particular theological content. The profane origin of the term, its economic and sociological connotations, even its roots in colonial history must be taken seriously when related specifically to North-South relations. They can be fruitfully used to determine what form relationships take. Equality and reciprocity are aspects which fulfil a particularly critical and constructive function here.

However, it is essential that partnerships between congregations and districts should be better qualified, both theologically and ecclesiologically, as interchurch relationships, in as far as they are the expression of the ecumenicity of the church. They remind us that the fullness of the body of Christ can only be realized in its worldwide form. In partnership we must think theologically about the reasons for ecumenical relations between churches, the form they take and their tasks. "Ecumenism" is not primarily an organizational "superstructure" or rather a limited field of work for a few experts, but rather "it is a fundamental aspect of all church existence and all that the church does". Ecumenical partnership should and can remind congregations and districts that they are part of "a holy catholic and apostolic church". The specific factor of ecumenical partnerships is that they can lead the congregations to a deeper understanding of the ecclesiological attributes: unity in diversity, holiness in suffering, catholicity in conciliar conflict and apostleship in discipleship:

The church can and should be and become "a holy, catholic and apostolic church", in face of the discrepancies under which people suffer today, in face of the conflicts that tear through her and through world society. However, its unity has not the character of uniformity but rather of manifold riches. Its holiness has not the appearance of radiance, of an ideal, but is rather most likely to shine in suffering and distress. Its catholicity is not reflected through hierarchical compulsion but rather in a joint search for the right way, in conciliar struggle for the truth. Its apostleship is not to be found in self-satisfied reference to tradition but rather in obedient discipleship in service to everyone.

Partnerships between congregations and districts are not merely a means to an end, either to achieving a mission goal or to carrying out development projects at a local level. They gain their ecclesiological quality from the vision of the church, which can only be ecumenical within the worldwide community of brothers and sisters in Jesus Christ. The church can only participate globally in God's mission. "The church today is the ecumenical movement." From the beginning the ecumenical movement has been determined by the search for church unity both locally and globally, and by fervent efforts to create a more just and viable society. Partnerships offer an important starting point for putting this into practice in the local context of a congregation or a district. This is the ecumenical missionary challenge they face.

For partnerships, or rather the individuals involved in partnership work, this means getting away from seeing it only as a bilateral relationship and therefore from an ecumenically limited perspective. At the same time, it means moving away from simply concentrating on the situation of the overseas partners, the perspective of many German partnership groups. Such an extension of their task compels them to consider the ecumenical situation at their own front door. Partnership, then, means that partners help each other to realize ecumenical and missionary responsibility in their own context. This task is by no means new. However, in most of the existing partnerships it is neglected.

Theo Sundermeier formulated the ecclesiological term *Konvivenz* (English, "living together") for this ecumenical way of existence, which has been taken up many times since. The term *Konvivenz* is based on experiences and the way of living in Latin American basic ecclesial communities. At the same time the concept of *Konvivenz* integrates insights and findings of the study on "The Missionary Structure of the Congregation" carried out by the WCC in the 1960s. Sundermeier criticizes the concept of the "church for others" as put forward by Dietrich Bonhoeffer and Ernst Lange and dominant in this study, and points in its place to the "church with others". "Being there for others", the attitude of wanting to help, is an attitude of those who feel themselves superior. The "helper-syndrome of Christian pro-existence" prevents people living together. This in itself makes it clear that it is not just a case of a new programme, but rather of a fundamental change in the place and perspectives of church communities and thereby also a change in their attitudes and actions. The conceptual proximity to ecumenical learning is obvious. *Konvivenz* means becoming the church of the poor, not as a copy of Latin American models but as a contextually relevant application of the same. *Konvivenz* is the community of those who help each other, who all learn from each other and who celebrate with each other life and community "in the horizons and from the perspective of the poor and those on the fringes of society".

The idea of *Konvivenz* is helpful for the partnerships in that it reaches out and includes thematic aspects of interchurch relations that are not as such included in the term partnership. This means firstly the essential connection to the context of the poor. Here we are not talking about charitable aid, but about taking sides, the change in perspective and position towards becoming a church of the poor.

Partnerships are well acquainted with the aspect of helping or sharing, but it is usually limited to material and financial aid. In my opinion, within the framework of their partnership relations, the German partners must face the serious question, what help they really expect from their African partners. My observations have shown that this requires far-reaching changes in attitude, which cannot be just limited to the German side but must finally include the African partners. The Namibian theologian Kameeta has described two important aspects of sharing and helping in *Konvivenz:*

> It cannot be a one-sided entry into the life and needs of the other! A one-sided entry into the life of the other and his needs is an assault on his life, is oppression.... The oppressors come arrogantly into our lives and claim to be experts for us and our needs. But on the other hand we are not allowed to enter into their lives....
>
> In this process of making others rich we do not in the first place need to cross borders. If I am afraid of the exploited, the foreigners and the refugees in my society and not willing to take sides and to act together with them, it is hypocritical to go out and only to act in faraway places. However, limiting my involvement for justice and peace only to my closer surroundings is just as narrow-minded and egoistic.

It is quite obvious that the German partners interfere in the lives of their African partners in a massive way with their project aid. The testing question is where they expect and where they are prepared to accept the tangible interference of their African partners in their own lives. It is often postulated that partners learn from each other. My studies, however, have shown that mutual learning in partnerships has so far not been sufficiently put into practice. I have pointed out the main reasons for this: the lack of thematic direction in the partnership encounters prevents joint learning experiences; learning processes are not consciously initiated and influenced; conflicts in partnerships are rather suppressed than seen as opportunities for learning from each other. However, I must also name two further reasons. On the one hand, while there is no lack of high-flown aims and far-reaching demands in the theoretical concepts for learning in intercultural encounters, yet there is a great lack of clear didactic suggestions as to how they can be realized. Secondly, it must be said that in general congregations are not essentially suitable "places of learning". The difficulties partnerships experience "only" reflect the conditions of majority church structures. These make learning together and action to bring about change very difficult, as they prevent the conflict necessary to decide on priorities and take sides with the poor and the excluded. As a direct consequence, churches and institutions so far have not set up any structures to make intensive educational assistance available to partnerships to help them initiate learning processes. It is expecting too much of the individuals and congregations involved in partnership work to carry out this task, and they urgently need support and supervision. To explain this a little more I shall look again at the criticism levelled at the learning concepts for intercultural learning. I shall concentrate on ecumenical learning although the comments are equally valid for intercultural and development-oriented learning.

While it is easy to formulate the reasons for ecumenical learning and its desirable aims, it is very difficult to put them into practice in specific situations. Horst Siebert speaks in this context of a "postulation pedagogy" that fails to analyze what chances it has of realizing its suggestions from an educational point of view. General demands such as "justice, peace and the integrity of creation" are not goals for learning modules. Siebert pleads for teaching models within a more specific range. Similarly Wolfram Weisse demands a reduction in the expectations made of ecumenical learning in order to make attempts at it somewhat easier. Otherwise, on the one hand there is the danger of overloading it, and on the other hand taking the bite out of it by just using empty slogans. Weisse pleads that the tasks and possibilities for ecumenical learning should be described in a more differentiated way, so as to relate to the different social forms within the church context. Both suggestions by Siebert and Weisse can be related effectively to the partnership work. At the same time I believe that partnership relations between German and overseas congregations and districts could play an eminently important role in developing and testing practical models for learning together, and in this way bring some of the high-flown theoretical learning concepts "down to earth".

But first I must point out that at present partnership groups have an unusual status as far as their position in the social structure of the church is concerned; they are usually viewed somewhere between that of the "action group" and the "local congregation". They share several things with the action groups: their involvement limited to certain subjects and places, the greater homogeneity of the people actively involved, their interests, and their great commitment. Beyond that there is some thematic overlap, for example, between the German-South African partnerships and the former anti-apartheid and covenant groups.

At the same time, however, the partnership groups are bound institutionally into the local congregations – quite differently from the action groups – and thereby structurally and financially secure and part of the normal life of the congregation, especially the services of worship. In comparison to the action groups this lessens the partnership groups' ability and willingness to enter into conflict with the local congregation, but at the same time it gives them greater opportunities for exerting their influence and it increases their chances of initiating learning processes in the congregation and of contributing to learning experiences. This situation of the partnership groups also puts them in a position where they are able to develop limited learning models as demanded by Siebert, for the committed involvement of the action groups can be related to a local context, that of the local congregation. In this limited field of action it is possible to mark out limited fields of learning and to make contextually related learning experiences.

It should not be forgotten that as long-term commitments in personal encounter such partnerships offer special starting points for limited, contextually related and action-oriented learning experiences. However, this assumes that both the congregations and the partnership groups are willing to extend and re-orient their way of looking at things. The partnership groups have to discover themselves as a place of learning and as a place for practising ecumenical existence, and the districts have to do the same with the interested congregations. They must discover those areas in each local situation where concrete action is required in the search for church unity and efforts for a more just and sustainable society. Their relationship to overseas partners can and will help them to identify these areas more clearly. The congregations should recognize that the partnership groups do an important service in helping their congregation to an essential ecumenical existence.

The aim of interchurch partnerships is the growth of local "convivial congregations". This *Konvivenz* cannot remain only in relationship to the bilateral partners but must also include the local ecumenical and missionary situations, in other words, the relationship to other Christian congregations and religious communities, and also the fellowship with the poor, the suffering and those pushed to the fringes of their own society. In contrast to present practice in the partnerships this would mean considerable changes, not only in the way of looking at things but also in the use of means, strengths and abilities available. But above all this would change the partners' relationship to each other. It would offer an opportunity for overcoming the existing imbalance between the partners and breaking down the one-sided aid relationship from North to South. Project orientation would no longer be in the foreground; the partners would have new questions to put to each other. The German partners would no longer need to ask their African partners: "What are your problems, and how can we help you?" Instead, both sides could report to the other: "These are our challenges and our troubles! How do you think you can help us?"

Partnerships have a great contribution to make in order that churches may become learning communities and communities of service and witness. I believe that this form of partnership encounter and relationship would have a much stronger influence for change, and that it would have a far greater effect on the independence of the African partners than the project aid so far.

2. The foreign partners: how we see the others in interchurch partnerships

This study has shown that an important element for motivating people actively involved in partnership work is the direct and affectionate friendship with their overseas partners. The partners' friendliness and warm affection for each other, their closeness and above all the unity they experience in their joint faith as Christians in various continents, are sustaining elements in all partnership relations between congregations and districts. Yet partnership encounters are encounters between foreigners, encounters between people from different social, political, cultural and ecclesiological contexts. This raises the question whether in the present partnership practice real awareness of what is foreign and real encounters with the other actually take place. Although partnership visits offer opportunities for this without any doubt.

At the beginning of this chapter I formulated the theory that the closeness claimed in partnerships, expressed by such sentences as "now we are partners", is often a closeness that merely veils the real foreignness. The danger in many partnerships is that a rash identification with the partners takes place as a result of the positive attitude taken towards the partners and the partly ideologically motivated emphasis given to being the same. The actual foreignness, the experience of inequality and difference and of doing things at different times and speeds are easily suppressed in order to avoid conflicts. However, in this way learning processes are prevented and no use is made of opportunities for overcoming the North-South divide, at least partially or for a short time. Accepting and being aware of the other, the foreign partner, as really other and foreign to me means also accepting him or her as a subject, as my opposite number. Identifying too quickly with the partner as "one of us" means just as much not taking him or her seriously as my opposite number as defaming or excluding him or her.

Following on from the work done by Tzvetan Todorov, it is possible to identify two basic positions of human perception and behaviour in encounters with foreigners: either the emphasis is on being the same or the starting point is the differences. Todorov develops his typologies of "discovering the other through what I am" using the example of the "discovery" and conquest of America. The most important people of the Spanish Conquest (Colón, Cortés, Las Casas and others) represent special types in the encounter with foreigners, who all however have one thing in common, that they do not perceive the others as individual subjects. For Todorov, the reason why the Spaniards did not succeed in recognizing the foreigners was because of the conquerors' own "egocentrism"; an attitude which sees one's own values as being universally valid. If we take as given that foreigners are principally not the same, this often leads to a negative disqualification of the foreigners. The perception of differences leads to the hierarchical differentiation between above and below, between good and bad, between master and slave; it leads to a relationship of superiority and inferiority. The other is seen to be of inferior status. The Spanish *conquistadores* did not recognize the Indians as humans of equal value to themselves; they put them on a level with animals, or even lower, as merely objects.

However, Todorov also points out that the postulation of being the same in no way leads to a better understanding of the foreigner – a point that is of particular importance for this study. One must particularly be aware of the danger of rash identification, assimilation or projection. The example of Cristóbal Colón shows that he did not really discover this America and its inhabitants, "but rather he found it exactly there where according to his 'knowledge' it had to be". Colón interprets what he sees within the framework of what he knew already. Within the framework of this "finalistic interpretation system" it is "no longer a case of searching for the truth but rather of confirming an already known truth". Communication on a human level could not succeed with the foreigners, as Colón was not interested in it.

Todorov also considers Bartholomé de las Casas to be a representative of the postulation of being the same. He goes a step further as he tries to understand the other from himself. Las Casas achieves both a change in perspective and also "distributive justice": the values of the others are recognized as such. The emphasis on being the same however implies the cultural "indifference" of people. Cultural differences are not understood; instead a cultural identity is postulated based only on idealized perception and projection.

Todorov points out particularly that Las Casas did not recognize the Indians because he was a Christian and he projected onto them the idealistic traits of Christian piety.

> Las Casas loves the Indians.... Can one really love someone if you do not know their identity, if instead of this identity you only see a projection of yourself or your own ideals?... How is this related to the encounter between different cultures?... Is there not a danger of wanting to change the other into what one wishes him to be and as a result to oppress him?

I believe that there are questions in this direction that must also be levelled at partnership work. Todorov concludes from this that while "indisputably the prejudice of superiority is an obstacle on the way to recognition, one must also admit that the prejudice of being the same is an even greater one, for it consists quite simply in identifying the other with one's own 'ideal of oneself' or one's own self". In this way the postulate of being the same, which claims to know the identity, leads to "even less knowledge of the other".

According to Todorov the task of encounters between cultures is to see the others as similar and yet different, in "living the difference in the similarity". This does not mean abolishing all values on all sides in favour of a general relativism. That would lead to indifference and a renunciation of any concepts of values. What is needed far more is the "heterology that makes the variety of voices audible".

Todorov's final theory is that in the past centuries, "Western Europe has succeeded in assimilating the others, getting rid of the outer signs of difference and spreading their own ways of living and sets of values throughout the world". According to this concept, real encounter with others, an understanding of that which is foreign, has never taken place in the history of European expansion. Partnerships between church districts must also be seen in this historical line of tradition. Therefore it will be their task to search for new forms of encounter, which make it possible for both sides to perceive that which is foreign. But before I can show a few concrete steps in that direction, it seems fitting first to consider what the importance is of the encounter with what is foreign. Or, to put it in another way, why are efforts to understand foreigners at the heart of partnership work?

According to Henning Luther, "the self that takes the self of another in, and lets it stay hospitably in its house" becomes itself another. "Because the other is first self, (my) self becomes another." The other as subject is decisive for one's own subjectivity. The encounter with the other and being visited by the other (Levinas) both calls the subject into question and at the same time facilitates it. "Only when called into question by the other is the self evoked in its uniqueness and untenability," according to Luther. Only the encounter with the foreigner affects growth, renewal and change and enables us to become our true selves. The encounter with the foreigner changes both sides. Something new comes into being. This is what we call learning through encounter.

But what is foreign in this sense? It is not simply the unknown, but far more that which is the opposite of what one has learnt to expect, the opposite of what one is accustomed to, that which is awkward and offensive. As such, it calls things into question and at the same time motivates an exploration of the foreign reality. Quite correctly Klaus Berger points out that only the "accompanying foreignness", for example, the otherness that is close to one's own or neighbouring traditions, can have the greatest consequences. As far as the subject of this study is concerned this is expressed by the term "foreign partners".

According to Levinas, "the other" has always been filled with content and had religious connotations. In others we see a "trace of the eternal". There is talk of nakedness in the face of the other, which makes it clear to us: the other is the stranger, the homeless one, the suffering other. In perceiving what is foreign, it is not a question of the exotic, not even of getting to know other people. Far more it is the case that:

> Foreign, as the accompanying otherness, has to do with all that is not seen, not perceived, that is pushed to the side and is not accepted. Foreign is that which is suppressed, that one does not want to see. Foreign means something outside ruling opinions and out of view of those in power. It is always a case of individuality gone off course.

Or as formulated by Henning Luther: "Only when I see the world through the eyes of the stranger and the outsider, look it in the face, does sense come into the senseless world, which so far has always overlooked the victims."

It is decisive that in the encounter with what is foreign, the difference and the otherness are not annulled. Foreign remains foreign, is not assimilated, should not be warded off or dismissed indifferently. Accepting the other is not neutrality but rather high esteem for individuality and particularity, both one's own and the other's. Foreignness endures as love.

The relevance of such an approach is obvious. Partnerships are essentially concerned with encounters with what is foreign, with the foreign partners. The task in the encounters is also to come to a perception and an understanding of that which is foreign. Especially in the early phases of many partnerships this aspect of foreignness is too frequently overlooked or ignored, bringing with it the danger of overstressing closeness and sameness and the assimilation and projection that go with this. Partnerships need to be encouraged to accept experiences of otherness; this can be unsettling and disconcerting, but people should not see them as a threat to their partnership.

It is also the case that individuals, congregations and groups need the encounter with that which is foreign in order to mature themselves (as subjects) in their subjectivity. Without the others we cannot exist, this is an old ecumenical biblical insight. The encounter with that which is foreign – this is the third insight – is the condition and prerequisite for change and renewal. Renewal of congregations and churches can only succeed if it is accepted as an ecumenical challenge. In the context of the renewal of the church lies the particular challenge but also the particular chance for partnerships. Finally, the encounter with foreigners from other cultural contexts always points to the foreignness that has been pushed to the side in one's own culture. The encounter with the foreigners can open one's eyes for the perspective from below in one's own society, for the outsiders and underprivileged in one's own country.

But how can we succeed in understanding what is foreign? To conclude this chapter I should like to sketch some methodical steps, whose consequences for the concrete form of partnership work I shall then develop in the further chapters of this final section.

To understand what is foreign demands first of all suitable external conditions; interchurch partnerships offer in my opinion a particularly suitable situation. Part of this is the basic willingness to have something to do with the foreignness of the other, to perceive and accept the similarities and the differences. A second condition is participation in the life of the other not just for a short period of time. Living with the other and sharing their daily life makes it possible to come to a deeper understanding than if just passing through. This has far-reaching consequences, for example for planning the programmes for delegation visits. The third condition for understanding is the willingness to go beyond just collecting information from the other and to begin a more intensive exchange, which aims at understanding the different ways of thinking and the different models of interpretation and communication. The fourth and final condition for understanding that which is foreign is joint action.

Sundermeier has worked out four stages in understanding that which is foreign, which can be of assistance in shaping partnership encounters. At each level a specific stage of perception takes place. Each level is linked to a certain attitude or action of the perceiver. The order of the steps describes the process of perception. No step may be left out or skipped over if the perception of what is foreign in the encounter is to succeed. The transitions are fluid; understanding is a circular process at the end of which the understanding of what is foreign begins again.

The first step: phenomena level. In this step, factual perception takes place, the objective descriptive analysis. It is a question of seeing the other as he or she is. An attitude is needed which abstains from any value judgment whatsoever. Sundermeier uses the term epoche for this: "Every bias either positive or negative, every prejudice obscures the image. The first encounter must occur 'avoiding value judgments'. That which is revealed to me, or he or she who reveals themselves to me should be perceived as they are." This attitude assumes a certain detachment, for one cannot perceive at close quarters.

The second step: sign level. Here the aim is ordering what has been perceived into its historical and cultural context. With an attitude that is markedly sympathetic, it is a case of observing the foreign context in an active way. The signs of the other (language, gestures, behaviour) are perceived as characteristics of his or her otherness. It is not a question of identification but rather "of understanding the other in his context, leaving his signs of identity in his context and not rashly trying to interpret them from one's own habits, let alone to universalize one's own experiences". Such perception has to be practised; it has to be learned.

The third step: symbol level. This step has to do with the symbolism of the other. Symbols are culturally determined, they have many meanings and can be interpreted in different ways. In encounters with foreign cultures they can make understanding more difficult but, Sundermeier says, they can also open up new dimensions, as soon as their meaning has been understood. Being willing to get involved and to feel one's way serves towards grasping the world of symbols of the foreign culture. To do this requires study, the acquisition of knowledge, but just as importantly it requires intuition and empathy. By interpreting and comparing what is foreign with one's own context, difference and similarity can be weighed up against each other. In this part-identification, that which is foreign is not neutralized but rather remains as it is.

The fourth step: relevance level. Finally, new forms of behaviour grow out of the encounter. "The aim of intercultural hermeneutics is successful living together, in which everyone can remain as they are, no one will be assimilated and yet an exchange takes place which respects and strengthens the dignity of the other." This attitude of respect for that which is foreign and that which is one's own leads to a translation, a transfer of the new experience and thereby to a new form of joint action, of living together, of *Konvivenz*.

The four-step model described here in abstract terms can be put into practical terms in partnership encounters. The steps described should be used in the methodical planning of the encounters and in the evaluation sessions of travel experiences. The most important thing is to encourage and empower people to learn to observe in a neutral way, free of value judgments, and to encourage the detachment necessary to do this in partnership relationships. The respectful closeness of *Konvivenz* comes at the end of the process, not at the beginning. Secondly, as far as the reflection and evaluation level of the partnership are concerned, understanding what is foreign requires the contextualization of the foreign perception, the challenge to a change in perspective, the ability to think oneself into the situation of the other. Only in this way is it possible, thirdly, to understand the meanings and the patterns of interpretation utilized by the other. The fourth step throws both partners back into their own situation. What relevance has this encounter for their own situation? Where do they see challenges for (joint) action and for change?

Sundermeier summarizes his model of steps to understanding what is foreign in a table:

The foreign opposite number	Subjective attitude	Objective correction	Action level
Phenomenon level	Epoche	Descriptive analysis	Detached perception
Sign level	Sympathy	Contextualization	Active observation
Symbol level	Empathy	Comparative interpretation	(Part) identification
Relevance level	Respect	Translation/transfer to ourselves	*Konvivenz*

The purpose of using this hermeneutic model in partnerships is to offer orientation for planning and evaluating encounters. It also offers opportunities for analyzing obstacles to understanding what is foreign in the encounter. I believe that many misunderstandings in partnerships could be explained with the help of this model, in as far as possible steps in the encounter are skipped over or left out. Negative experiences in project work can be evaluated using such a model and in this way lead to a better understanding. For example, frequently steps of analysis and contextualization are left out when a project is realized. Far too quickly the interpretation is there ("a situation of poverty in which help must be given") and action (projects), which are not appropriate for the given situation. But the other way round similar things can be discovered to do with the transfer of experiences from the partnership work into the German situation, for example with regard to the spontaneous expressions of faith and piety by the African partners.

Here too the levels of analysis and interpretation are often ignored or left out. Being moved emotionally and from a rash identification with the African partners, attempts are made to take over the African partner's way of doing things directly, which usually fails and is given up. It would be necessary to look at it very closely (what is actually happening there?) and then to think about what has been seen and experienced and put it in context and evaluate it. (What sort of piety do we experience? What cultural and religious traditions does it reflect?) Only then can comparative interpretation begin. That which is foreign can be understood as such, overlaps and differences become clear, the awareness of one's own situation is increased. (What sort of a situation do we live in, what do we need, what can we do?)

Finally the translation and transfer of what has been learned (the search for contextually appropriate forms of piety of one's own) enable practice in the community of *Konvivenz*. The hermeneutic model even fits for the partners' understanding between themselves of the meaning and content of their partnership relations. The description of a visit to a Tanzanian teacher in section 4 is a good case study.

3. Festivity and celebration: reflecting on the identity of the community

The following section is concerned with one aspect of partnership relations: joint celebration. This was already mentioned in section 1: joint celebrations as part of ecumenical *Konvivenz*. Why then also a whole section? There are three reasons for this. First, the theory that celebration, as an interruption of the routine of daily life and as an "intrusion of a quite different truth", makes community with the other possible in a very special way. The question is what importance religious celebrations have for the partnership community or what they can have. Second, the observation that partnership visits in African congregations are often the occasion for large festivities. No efforts are spared to welcome the visitors; they are entertained and catered for lavishly and with great ceremony and the visit has almost show character. Many German visitors do not feel at ease in this situation, they even experience the whole thing as a show. In contrast, it is remarkable that the visits of African Christians to Germany have hardly any festive character at all. The following section will try and contribute to an understanding of this phenomenon. Third and finally, I shall consider my observations that in most partnerships the way the so-called Partnership Sunday is celebrated causes many problems and many members of partnership groups express their dissatisfaction with the forms that have been found so far. Greater consideration of the meaning of festivities and celebrations for the joint identity of the partners can open up perspectives for new forms of cele-bration. These in turn can set learning processes in motion that are not primarily rational and oriented towards discourse, but appeal to the many facets and dimensions of human existence.

Jan Assmann describes the religious festival as "a medium of cultural remembrance", as a central place for orientation and reflection on the origins of a social group. The festival is the place of "the other", the opposite number to daily life. If daily life is marked by chance and shapelessness (contingency), by shortage and strife (shortage) as well as by automization and habit (routine), then the festival will be a produc-tion of abundance, a reflection on fundamentals and the "surge of emo-tions" (effervescence). The festival, with its position as a contrast to daily life and something that goes beyond it, has its main function in the "constitution and reproduction of the group identity". By reflecting on the origins of a social group and its recurring representation (perpetra-tion), the identity of the group is expressed in symbolic form (rituals). "Man, who remembers the 'other time', reflects on his belonging to an extensive community."

There are clear echoes here of the worldwide ecumenical community. And yet it is not possible to create a direct link from Assmann's state-ments to practical suggestions for forms of interchurch partnerships. Any application made must be done with strong reservations. It must be pointed out that Assmann developed his theory with regard to archaic societies with no written languages. For such groups it is true that they live in a unity of time and space. But neither of these applies for inter-church partnerships. Quite the opposite: the partners do not share the same habitat, but rather each of them belongs to a quite different world quite a long way away from the other. There is no permanent joint con-text in their lives; the delegation visits are just occasional events.

Furthermore in interchurch partnerships one cannot speak of a social group identity, but only of an identity founded on theology. Interchurch partnerships are manifestations of the community of the body of Christ based on mutual faith. They gain their unity and their identity from this source. And here in my opinion is a starting point for making the idea of the festival or religious celebration fruitful, also in the form that inter-church partnerships take.

In the context of the partnerships I examined, concentration on religious celebrations leads primarily to the way Partnership Sundays are celebrated. As I have already said, many partnership groups have great difficulty with the way Partnership Sundays are celebrated and are not satisfied with them. The forms and models tried out so far do not seem to have any power to create a feeling of identity. Ecumenical partnerships have therefore a specific task to search for forms of celebration and festivity that make it possible to "reflect on the origin and meaning of ecumenical community". Beyond that I believe this could be a starting point for the German partners to learn from the African Christians. For the German visitors the extravagant celebrations and show-like productions during their visits in African congregations will then lose their unattractive and embarrassing side. They will become a starting point not only for a deeper understanding of the situation itself and the motives of the African partners but will also challenge them to reflect on their own behaviour and their deficits in cultural communication.

As a result the task of Partnership Sunday will be to remember, recollect and represent the ecumenical identity of a congregation through the medium of a religious festival and religious celebration. This means specific changes of accent against the present practice of partnership services. First of all, the aim of Partnership Sunday is altered: it is no longer primarily concerned with passing on information about the partners or the partnership. Nor is its central concern recruiting activists or project support. Far more its intention is that the local congregation reflect on its ecumenical existence. "Man who remembers the 'other time' reflects on his belonging to an extensive community," Assmann says. This extensive community is the ecumenical community of churches for the local congregation, lived out in an exemplary manner through its partnership with an overseas congregation or church district. The celebration of Partnership Sunday should therefore not primarily serve to present the bilateral partnership relations to the congregation, as is presently the practice, but rather to remind them of the ecumenical church community, of which the bilateral partnership relationship is a part, not more and not less. The central question for Partnership Sundays is to determine what it really means for the local congregation that it cannot be church without the others.

Various consequences follow from this as far as planning is concerned. Firstly it will become relative whether up-to-date information from the partners is available on that Sunday or not. Attention will be focused much more on the situation of their own congregation, where it is integrated ecumenically and what ecumenical responsibility it has taken on. Attention will also be turned on local ecumenical partners: neighbouring congregations, action groups concerned with similar topics as allies, foreigners, people on the fringes of society. Finally, they will be able to take up that which is foreign in their own context and the missionary challenges in their own country. The partnership as such will certainly be a focusing point of Partnership Sunday because it is exemplary of living ecumenism, but in its exemplary function that points to the greater community of the body of Christ.

Essential for any festivity or celebration is stage management, perpetration and ritual or repetition. Partnerships can hardly draw upon existing traditions, as they are not in the ethnographic sense groups or social units; rather they will be compelled to develop something new. And this can very well be understood as an exciting learning opportunity: is it possible that the partners develop symbolic forms together, which represent their specific relationship, recall their origins and constitute their identity? Over the past few years the ecumenical movement has tried to develop and try out forms of celebration that can contribute to identity building and meaningful worship. Partnerships can make use of these, and yet each partnership will have to develop its own form. This can mean fundamentally calling into question the forms of worship we know so far, should we establish that they are not capable of transcending daily life and creating a communal identity. And again this can be an important impetus for the ecumenical renewal of the congregation. Developing and testing such forms of service and celebration can only take place through a long process of mutual exchange and learning between the partners. But this could become an important subject for both sides during the visits back and forth.

Two aspects must be paramount: reflection on what the worldwide ecumenical church really is and should be, and exchange with each other about how from their own specific cultural context each of the partners really understands their partnership relationship. In the following section I shall make several suggestions of an exemplary nature on both these questions.

4. Foreigners become brothers and sisters: towards an African understanding of partnership

I have already mentioned that the concept of "partnership" is a Western concept and foreign to African Christians. This is apparent from the historical review, which also shows the historical roots of the concept in British colonial policy. It was representatives of the North who first spoke of partnership and continued to do so; the churches of the South were more interested in organizational unity. During the course of my study African partners indicated that "partnership" was something that had come to them from outside, but which they had learnt to accept and value. Do the African partners have their own approach to interchurch relations? In the following section I shall highlight some insights gained from my encounters and conversations with African partners during the course of my investigations.

This section does not claim to develop an African understanding of partnership. Nor can there be such an understanding, for the churches and persons concerned are very different from each other and will each set their own emphases. Above all it cannot be my task, as a German, to develop an understanding of partnership from the point of view of African Christians. What I can do is to pass on what I have seen and heard, draw attention to what the African partners are saying, raise greater sensitivity to it and far more than has so far been the case make it part of all considerations on the subject of partnership. I limit myself quite consciously to what I have experienced during the course of my study. I do so in order to show that each partnership encounter offers sufficient opportunities and "material" for joint considerations about the nature of partnerships and specific interpretations of the existing relationship; considerations that can be fruitful for learning processes and thereby help to overcome the dominance of the North in partnership relations.

A starting point for my considerations is to look at the words the African partners use, apart from the English word "partnership", when talking – possibly among themselves –about these interchurch relationships. In English they preferably used the terms "friendship" or "fellowship", although, when asked, they explained that the latter emphasized the spiritual character of the relationship.

The Swahili terms used by the Tanzanian partners all have a singularly clear background. In the Karagwe district they mainly use *undugu* or *urafiki*. The former means "brotherhood" (relations, brotherliness, friendship), the latter "friendship" (comradeship). On account of the political overtones of the word *undugu* in the concept of Tanzanian socialism, the Christians in the congregations of Arushachini and Chemchem were hesitant to use this term. They preferred to use the word *usiano*, which essentially has the same meaning of "friendship". The term "partnership" was used much more frequently by the South Africans than the Tanzanians as a consequence of the much greater use of English there.

Even when the South Africans spoke to each other in their mother tongue they often used the word "partnership" instead of a term in their mother tongue. Only when asked did the partners suggest possible translations, which mainly stressed the aspects of friendship and community in the relationship, among these the Sotho word *kopano,* which is used for the gathering of people in a community. Another word frequently used in Sotho is the term *setswalle,* which can be translated as friendship, whereby the aspect of cooperation and working together also plays a role. The Zulu words used to describe partnership are also quite similar in their meaning: *hlangano* means "gathering together" or "linking up"; the word *ubungane* means "friendship, friendliness and comradeship".

A further approach to understanding the African partners better is by means of the proverbs used, especially by the Tanzanian partners, when called upon to describe the meaning of the relationship and its importance for them. Two aspects are mentioned frequently: the particular closeness and solidarity of the partners which cannot be destroyed, and the ability of both partners to help each other and to achieve much more together than they would have been able to do alone. Here, as in many other statements by the African partners, the most important point of comparison is that of a relationship between family members or friends.

Thirdly, let me recount a single occurrence during the visit of the youth brass band from the Lübbecke district to Bweranyange, which shows how the African partners express their particular understanding of partnership. It also raises the question how much room there is in the partnerships for evaluating "in a learning and understanding way", and whether the German partners are prepared to let themselves in for this form of expression, to understand it and to learn from it.

While visiting a congregation in the Bweranyange district, the group was invited to the house of an elderly church councillor and teacher, who had been involved in the partnership from the beginning. He had been a member of the first delegation from the Bweranyange district to visit the Lübbecke district, and a close personal relationship had developed between him and the family of the chairman of the partnership committee at that time, who was also the person in charge of the trumpet group. After giving a short open-air concert in front of the house, the band was invited in and offered juice and roasted coffee beans – in Karagwe a sign of peace and hospitality. They were then invited to take the usual tour around the host's *shamba* (banana plantation) and finally to sit down on mats woven from banana leaves and a few chairs under the spreading branches of a large tree. In the meantime it had got dark and relatively cold, which caught the young trumpeters in their light summer clothing unprepared.

What followed was a "ceremony" carried out by their host, in which he demonstrated the particular closeness between his family and the family of the pastor in charge of the visiting group. First a huge cake was brought out, reminiscent of a wedding cake, which the pastor and the host cut into with both their hands on the same knife. At the request of the host, this act was "witnessed" by one of the children from his house and the visiting pastor's daughter. Then the host and the pastor gave each other a piece of the cake to eat, before cutting up the rest and distributing it among the other visitors present. This custom is part of the wedding celebrations in Kagera. The host then directed the distribution of several gifts. For example one of the host's sons together with the pastor's son (both his son and his daughter were members of the visiting group) handed over a bow and arrow to the pastor. The pastor's daughter accepted the gifts for her mother, who was not present. Finally a grandchild of the host handed over a wooden model of a house to the pastor's son as a sign that both families were now "one family", as the host explained. He also explained the significance of the other gifts. That evening "brotherhood" had been established between the two *mzees* (the old men) and both families had become *one* family.

Just how intensive such relations between strangers can be was demonstrated during the visit by Prof. Katoke, a historian who himself came from Karagwe. During his lecture to the trumpet group he talked about the religious tradition of blood brotherhood. Here the coffee bean also plays an important role. Katoke described the situation where two people from different clans have become friends and now wish to cement their friendship:

> We must establish a contract of brotherhood.... So I take the coffee bean, smear it with my blood. And he takes one, he smears it with his blood. He gives me the bean which has his blood, I swallow it. And he swallows the one with my blood. Now we have become blood brothers.

In this way, Katoke explained, a true brotherly relationship comes into existence between the two. For example, from now on the same marriage taboos apply to him as apply to other members of the clan. The property of the one is also now the property of the other. Katoke illustrated this with an example that is unusual for European ears:

> His property is mine and mine is his. Even when we had polygamous marriage, several wives, if he came to visit me and it is a cold night like these days, I have the two spare wives, he could take one of them and sleep with her, because she is his wife.

In his talk Katoke also pointed out how close this was to the understanding of Christian community made possible through Christ's death and resurrection:

We as Christians, we know that we are calling ourselves brothers and sisters, whether you come from Europe, Asia and so on, because of the blood of Jesus.

Here are aspects of a genuine understanding of interchurch relations. Implicitly they contain structures of thought and interpretation that give special meaning and importance to partnership. These must be talked about together in order to discover them and understand them. However, it is significant – and this reflects my previous comment about the willingness to learn on the part of the German partners – that the German group did not talk together at all, or in more detail, about the unusual and in my opinion very important occurrences of that evening. There was no discussion within the group about what they had experienced. On the contrary, the young people were far more indignant, for they had been frozen the whole evening and felt themselves to be of only secondary importance in comparison to the very special position of the two families. While the joint group-journal mentions the visit as such, it does not go into any detail.

In remarkable conformity African partners interpreted partnership relations as relations between friends and kin. They did not mention the economic level of meaning at all that is common in the North. It is quite possible for such an intensive friendly or brotherly-sisterly relationship to exist between people who are foreign to each other at first, or between members of different families and clans. It is therefore not difficult to see how African Christians take up this traditional attitude and give it a specific Christian theological interpretation. For the African partners the whole range of kinship relationships are contained in the understanding of this word: care and concern for each other, help for each other, sharing of possessions, sharing in joy and suffering, and celebrating together.

These observations made during my case studies are supported and consolidated in concepts for African theology. Several African authors, while trying to draft a theology based on African experience, also give a central place to the African way of thinking in community and to categories of kinship relationships. In Christology especially many theologians have taken up the traditional understanding of the family unit in communion with the ancestors. Elements of this are also apparent in the consequences they draw for ecclesiology and ethics, which are important for interchurch partnerships. It is indisputable that thinking as a community is central for an "African way of looking at the world". A whole group of authors have worked on this in the meantime. In 1962 already the Catholic theologian Mulago gwa Cikalas described the "concept of the unity of life" as represented in family relationships as the focal point of traditional African thinking. John Pobee uses the example of the West

African Akan people to describe what he calls the *sensus communis*: if as Descartes claims *cogito ergo sum* – I think therefore I am – is valid for the people of the West, then *cognatus ergo sum* – I am a blood relation therefore I live – is valid for the Akan. Or as Pobee says: "I live because I belong to a family. And a family as a basic unit consists of the living, the dead and those yet to be born." This reflects just how fundamental the African system of kinship thinking is.

The Ugandan theologian John Mbiti also points this out. A deep-seated feeling of kinship has always been "one of the strongest driving forces in African traditional life".

> The kinship system is like a vast network stretching laterally (horizontally) in every direction, to embrace everybody in any given local group. This means that each individual is a brother or sister, father or mother, grand-mother or grandfather, or cousin, or brother-in-law, uncle or aunt, or something else, to everybody else... When two strangers meet in a village, one of the first duties is to sort out how they may be related to each other, and having discovered how the kinship system applies to them, they behave to each other according to the accepted behaviour set down by society.

However, these familiar connections do not only extend at a horizontal level within the social unit but also have a vertical dimension in the genealogy: "Genealogy transmits a feeling of depth and historical belonging, of having roots. It is therefore a sacred commitment to continue the genealogical line."

As a rule the kinship system is limited to members of one ethnic group. A stranger cannot be taken into a family unit without very special reasons. Here however the interpretations of African theologians are of importance. Charles Nyamiti and Benezet Bujo especially have developed the idea of the Christian community "as family" from an ancestral Christology.

In Africa the ancestors are the guarantee for the continued existence and vitality of a community. They share in the life of the community; they are the mediators between the deity and mankind. Nyamiti was the first to use the term ancestor for Christ. He makes a comparison between Christ and the brother-ancestor. Jesus' "blood relationship" with mankind goes back to the fact that we all stem from Adam. Through his death and resurrection he receives the new (ancestor) status, which binds him to both the earthly and the heavenly family. Christ is the mediator between his father and his earthly brothers and sisters; he is a model for Christian life and a guarantor of Christian identity.

While Nyamiti establishes the ancestorship of Christ in the Trinity, Bujo argues much more strongly for the historical Jesus: Jesus proves himself as the one who realizes perfectly the ideal of the black African ancestor cult and at the same time transcends it. This means "that there has never been nor can ever be another such ancestor who could possibly achieve such a realization and perfection". Christ is therefore the proto-ancestor, to use Bujo's terminology. He does not only guarantee life, he *is* life and he awakens to life.

For the community of the African family the expression of this is the ritually held meal, where some part is reserved and offered to the ancestors. African theologians make a bridge from here to an African understanding of the community of the church founded in Christ and its representation in the eucharist. In the eucharist people share in Jesus' life strength. The new community of the church, which is founded on this, crosses the traditional boundaries of the ethnic unit. The church as the new family overcomes geographical and ethnic boundaries.

These roughly sketched concepts can open up new horizons for learning together and understanding each other in partnerships. As far as I have observed it has so far mainly been a case of the African partners having to "learn" what the German partners considered to be partnership and how this was to be put into practice.

A new starting point in partnership work depends on a new willingness to learn and greater reserve and sensibility on the part of the German partners. However, learning, especially with regard to interpretation of relationships, cannot simply mean the transfer or assimilation of foreign patterns of thought. In the sense of understanding what is foreign it is possibly necessary to first work out the differences. It must be taken into consideration that terms such as family, kinship, brother- and sisterhood have quite different connotations and evoke quite different attitudes and feelings for German and African partners.

The aim of such a learning process is to get to know the foreign partners better, particularly in their interpretation of the mutual relationship, and to understand different attitudes towards partnership and different ways of behaving as a result. Efforts towards a more specific understanding of partnership – which assume at the same time more reflection on one's own understanding of partnership – can also contribute to clearing up misunderstandings and solving conflicts in partnership relations. These then do not have to be suppressed but rather the differences between the partners can be realized and accepted in respect and understanding for each other.

5. Practising ecumenical existence: perspectives for a new orientation of partnership work

In this final section I shall try to develop some practical suggestions for new ways of carrying out partnership work. The basis for all my suggestions is the idea that interchurch partnerships between congregations and districts must always be seen as a comprehensive opportunity for learning. This means that the congregations should be central and not just the individuals – although the personal character of partnership relations should not be given up. If partnerships are to be developed as places of learning in the way described, this very probably means a restructuring of activities. In no way should it mean putting extra burdens on the already active members. However, a new orientation of partnership work, if required, means pausing, reflecting on the work done so far and setting new priorities. The new orientation that I am talking about has two essential aims: partnerships should become reciprocal relationships with both sides sharing together to a greater extent than has so far been the case and in this way overcoming dependencies that still exist. Beyond that partnerships should gain greater relevance for the critical renewal of the congregations concerned. It is therefore first necessary to make a few comments on the institutional establishment of partnerships at congregational and district level.

THE INSTITUTIONAL ESTABLISHMENT OF PARTNERSHIPS AT CONGREGATIONAL AND DISTRICT LEVEL

Three of the four partnerships I examined are partnerships at district level and one is a congregational partnership. I have already indicated that the opportunities for learning have to do with the institutional level at which the partnership is established. A church district is, if at all, a very unsuitable place for learning in partnerships. A church district is essentially an administrative unit, which has no relevance for the identity of Christians in the congregations. The most important reasons for establishing interchurch partnerships at a district level are also chiefly of an administrative technical nature: greater financial means, assured institutional continuity and continuity of personnel, an "apparatus" capable of dealing with organizational procedures and projects. Partnerships at district level also mean that the regional churches and mission departments concerned have a better idea of what is going on.

On the other hand, I cannot simply recommend that in future partnerships should exclusively or predominantly be established at congregational level. That would be in direct opposition to the wishes of representatives of the African churches, who fear (quite rightly) even greater proliferation in their countries if large numbers of individual congregations establish direct contact with each other. Besides which, in many German church districts the North-South partnership is the only, or at least a very decisive, element that concerns the whole district and links them together so contributing to their identity as a church district.

Both the administrative and the contextual sides of partnership have to be considered as opportunities for learning. The organizational elements of partnership require connections at the highest possible institutional level within the churches. It therefore makes sense and is necessary to have agreements signed between the church councils and resolutions passed by the relevant churches and church district synods. In contrast, initiating learning in such a way that it is of relevance for the congregations is of course only possible at a congregational level. Partnerships must be rooted structurally in the congregations. Therefore I consider it necessary to search for ways in which congregations can be more directly structurally integrated into district partnerships.

An increasing number of church districts have established direct contacts between individual congregations on both sides for this reason, in some cases by linking all congregations in both church districts and in others, as in Osterholz-Scharmbeck, where only a few individual congregations are linked in direct partnership. Where such partnerships have been established within an existing church district partnership, they seem to have contributed to a more intensive awareness of the partnership in the congregations. However, they are susceptible to the same problems and difficulties as the district partnerships. Where such congregation partnerships are established they must be kept absolutely free of any financial and project aid *whatsoever*. Limiting this to small amounts, as is often the case, is not sufficient. Even small amounts of aid lead to inequalities and injustice and increase the danger of dependency. Direct congregation partnerships should therefore have one single aim, of putting what has been learnt in the partnership into practice in the congregation.

However, establishing direct bilateral congregational contacts is not always a suitable way of rooting a district partnership in the congregations or of initiating learning. Rather the opposite, such a model creates additional problems that can make learning more difficult or hinder it altogether. Above all there is the danger that the congregation partners will now concentrate entirely on themselves and the ecumenical horizon will be even more limited instead of it being extended. It is also problematic how to limit and connect congregation partnerships within district partnerships. Such a model – as shown by the partnership between the districts of Osterholz-Scharmbeck and Polokwane – causes considerable difficulties when choosing the members of the delegations and planning their programmes. If congregations with direct contacts wish to keep up their contacts through the regular delegation visits, those congregations without direct partners will soon drop out of the partnership altogether. Blanket coverage of the congregations will remain the exception on account of differing sizes of the districts, differing numbers of congregations in them, and their differing interest in direct contact. It must therefore not be presented as an alternative to establish partnerships at congregational or district level. Nor do attempts to establish partnerships more intensively in the congregations automatically mean that all individual congregations must make direct contacts. What is decisive is that partnership work is understood as learning and that it is directed and thought about at the congregational level much more than has so far been the case.

To establish district partnerships more firmly at the congregational level the existing district partnership committees should encourage the setting up of steering groups in the congregations that – inspired and motivated by partnership encounters – consider what ecumenical learning processes can be initiated in their own congregations. The task of such steering groups would go beyond the practice of a bilateral direct partnership. They would aim far more at an ecumenical orientation of the congregation. Ecumenical experiences made possible through the district partnership would then be important starting points for an ecumenical renewal of the congregation, but not the only ones.

In this model steering groups ensure that the district partnership is truly established in the congregations. However, it cannot be assumed that all congregations will have the same interest in active participation in partnership, and this must be respected. The district partnership committee should then be made up of delegates from these steering groups. It should coordinate the work in the congregations, enable them to learn from each other and take up new ideas and suggestions. This committee should continue to be responsible for the organizational side of partnership work.

Suggested tasks for such congregational steering groups are: to look at the ecumenical situation of the congregation (ecumenical parish audit); to report on the ecumenical missionary situation of the congregation in encounters with the partners (ecumenical congregation visitation); to identify subjects in the congregational situation that seem appropriate for partnership encounters (travel programmes better oriented to specific groups and on specific subjects); and to discover areas where the partners can act together (evaluation). Specific points of focus for the partnership visits will develop from the work of these steering groups. It is self-explanatory that carrying out projects and aid programmes does not belong to the task of such steering groups.

The objection that it will be impossible to find active members for these steering groups is refuted by experiences made in congregations with direct partnerships. The lack of active members has among other things to do with the establishment of partnerships at the abstract level of the church district. Where partnerships are linked directly to the life of the individual congregation and thus have an intense local connection, it is quite possible to win new people, who are interested, even without seeking a direct link to a bilateral partner.

I also consider the tasks of the congregational steering groups already mentioned to be elements of partnership work aimed at reaching the congregations and making learning possible. I shall now look at them one by one as starting points for a new orientation of partnership work.

ECUMENICAL PARISH AUDIT (ANALYTICAL SURVEY OF CONGREGATION CONTEXT)

The ecumenical parish audit or analytical survey is a method developed in conjunction with the project "ecumenical renewal of congregational life", and therefore goes beyond partnership work in the narrower sense, although partnership work can be a very good starting point for it. The prerequisite for carrying out such an analysis is that beyond a small group of people actively involved in partnership work there is a general willingness of others in the congregation to take part in a process of ecumenical renewal. An ecumenical parish audit – where one looks analytically at the social, economic and religious context of the parish and its work – is one, though not the only possible, starting point for an ecumenical renewal process of a congregation. Basic aspects and elements of such an ecumenical audit have been sketched in a project outline of the WCC from 1990 on "Ecumenical Renewal of Local Congregations: Mission as Transcending Boundaries". However, they must be adjusted to suit the individual congregational situation. Among the elements listed are participatory interviews of parish members, the formation of a steering group and a biblical and theological reflection on the missionary task of the congregation. One major aim is to strengthen the ecumenicity of the local congregation:

> They should be made aware of the social challenges of the context, of their cultural and mental barriers when encountering foreigners and non-believers, and they should consider how to overcome these barriers to communicating the gospel. By becoming newly aware of the situation in their part of the town and in their lives and learning to see it in connection with the biblical promises, people should begin to take on more responsibility for themselves and for their congregations. After carrying out such a project the congregation should be in a position to give more precise answers and to decide which activities it would like to continue, or to drop, which new activities should be started, which social challenges it will take up itself and which it wish to pass on to other agencies. In other words, to redefine its own priorities for its missionary work.

In the meantime there are tested questionnaires available for the parish audit which the core group or steering group for ecumenical renewal can partially answer themselves and which must partially be answered in congregation meetings, congregation groups or by interviewing other people and collecting individual answers. The questions, which have to be adjusted to the local congregation, are concerned among other things with the local situation, the make-up of the population, the structure and shape of the congregation as well as its life and practice, its visions and possibilities and what needs to be changed. The partnership steering group of a congregation, as described in the model for establishing district partnerships in the congregations, could form the nucleus and become the crystallizing point for such an extensive survey of the ecumenical situation of a congregation.

ECUMENICAL TEAM VISIT

The model of ecumenical team visits to a congregation has so far mainly been tried out at a church council level. Delegations of the WCC for example twice visited the churches of the Federal Republic of Germany, became acquainted with the main focus of church work and informed the churches on their part where they see strengths and deficits in taking on the ecumenical missionary challenge. In a similar way the United Evangelical Mission has instituted ecumenical team visits in congregations and churches within its domain.

The idea of an ecumenical visitation is to enable the partners to gain insights into each other's congregational and ecumenical missionary work. The partners each account to the other on the focus and priorities of their work, their aims, their strengths and weaknesses, their successes and failures. The visiting partners are invited to "look behind the scenes" from their perspective and with their perception. The partners being visited open themselves for the particular perspective of those visiting them and allow themselves to be challenged by it. As a result of such a visitation it is possible to discuss and agree upon new priorities.

In German congregations ecumenical exchange pastors have so far fulfilled a similar function, although in a less institutionalized way. In their reports they have held up a mirror to German Christians and pointed out uncomfortable truths. But frequently the German churches have not taken up the seriousness of such challenges; the criticism and suggestions made by ecumenical partners are often dismissed as not being to the point.

For partnerships I see a great opportunity for ecumenical learning if visits back and forth are at least in part conducted as ecumenical team visits. This would be a good way of combating the superficiality of the programmes. The partners would be able to consider the situation of the congregation more intensely, and the ecumenical challenges in the social context experienced, and in that way they would be able to deepen the meaningfulness of their partnership relationship. Above all the mutuality of the relationship would be strengthened; differences between the partners could be removed if the partners were really willing to take the others' observations seriously.

PROGRAMMES AIMED AT A PARTICULAR GROUP AND CONCENTRATING ON A PARTICULAR SUBJECT

Changes in partnership work can on the one hand, as described, be started by analyzing the ecumenical missionary situation of the congregation and the challenges that go with it. However, they could and should also come about essentially by finding new forms for partnership visits. My study has made the problems arising from the generally accepted form of delegation visits sufficiently clear. I only need to mention the superficiality of encounters under pressure of time, the lack of theme orientation on account of insufficient preparation beforehand, the avoidance or insufficient use made of learning opportunities and situations, the lack of evaluation. However, I do not mean to say that partnership visits should take a completely different form. The element of visiting congregations free from all other aims will and must remain a part of the visits, because this is necessary for encounters, for getting to know each other in a way that friendships can develop. There are ways, though, of planning the programme and setting emphases in it, which even if only taking up a short time can nevertheless influence the whole visit in a new way and so change the form of the whole partnership. I include here the idea of putting together the delegation with a particular aim in mind, and also setting meaningful priorities for the programme and the visit as a whole.

1. Programmes aimed at a particular group

This form of organization is sometimes used when a youth group visits their partners. They often take part in a work camp together. But there are also other examples to be found within the partnership between the Lübbecke and the Bweranyange districts. There the Evangelical Church of Westphalia's department for rural youth, social and educational work organized several such visits to the Karagwe diocese. They travelled once with a group of women farmers, another time with a group of male farmers and yet again with a youth group.

A programme aimed at a particular group means, first, that the delegation is put together according to certain criteria and is therefore much more homogeneous. It can be a certain age group (young people) or people with a certain profession (farmers, labourers, lawyers, teachers, social workers, and so on). It can just as well be people involved in specific areas of church work (parish councillors, Sunday school teachers, youth workers or people working with the elderly, people who visit the sick or do diaconal work), and it is possible to think of only women or only men in the group.

Second, the group should mainly meet with similar groups in the partner church. Third, the programme must take into account the specific focus of the group. This automatically means that this form of visit can only be tried out together with the partners, for both sides will have to work together on planning the programme.

The advantage of such a programme is that even the composition of the delegation offers starting points for the partners to exchange ideas. Deciding which priorities to set assumes a discussion among the partners about what priorities are necessary or could be necessary as far as the situation of the congregations is concerned. Such priorities can arise out of the parish audit or an ecumenical team visit. For example, if the partners decide they need to talk together and learn more from each other about the social problems in their surroundings, the delegation could be made up of church and non-church social workers and people doing diaconal work. During the visit they would then meet and study the subject together with people working in similar fields in the partner district and those affected by the social problems. This must not occupy the whole of the visit. It could be that just a special time is reserved for it, or that the subject is taken up at various places possibly in locally different contexts.

Such a particular group programme will enable participants on both sides to look and listen more carefully, to question more intensively and thereby to understand better their own situation and what is foreign in a new and clearer way. Such a programme will also enable the participants to pass on their experiences more intensely and with a clearer aim after their return. It goes without saying that such visits require particularly intensive evaluation both during the visit and after returning home. Finally, this form of programme may well make it easier for the partners to find links for joint action. There can be no patent remedies; partnerships are all far too different. Nor do I mean that every partnership visit should take this form. Here the partners themselves must find the form suitable for their situation and their stage of partnership.

2. *Programmes concentrating on a particular subject*

Even where the delegation does not consist of people chosen as a homogeneous group, the partners should nevertheless agree together on a thematic focus for the visit. I consider it necessary to give the journey such a topic in order to enable learning processes to take place, whether intercultural, development-oriented or ecumenical. Various possibilities and degrees of learning are possible here. What is most important is that the partners agree together before the visit on a mutual topic or set of questions. I am fully aware that this is made more difficult by communication problems. But as was the case with the particular group visit, the thematic focus must not be for all of the journey and every part of the programme.

It is conceivable that only one or two weeks of the visit should be concerned with the special topic. A further and perhaps more sensible alternative would be to take up the topic at various points during the visit. However, the partners should have the courage to really limit themselves to one topic and to consider it from various aspects as determined by the local situation. What is necessary is that sufficient time is allowed for getting into the topic. This demands careful restructuring of existing programmes that are always under great pressure as far as time is concerned. It will be necessary to limit and concentrate the programme; the thematic focus must under no circumstances be added on to an already existing programme.

Should, under exceptional circumstances, it not be possible for the partners to agree on a joint topic, there is always the possibility for individual members of the delegation to decide on their own special focus and the questions pertaining to it. This enables them to concentrate and intensify their experiences and impressions and makes it much easier to pass on what they have learned and seen on their return. New surprising discoveries that lead to change are only possible where there is a strong and well-directed interest in learning more. Practically this means that every participant chooses a certain topic, prepares herself or himself before travelling, and continues to learn more about it during the journey by individual research, well-aimed questions and acute observation. The spectrum of subjects is inexhaustible; they can take in any aspect of the whole field of intercultural, development-oriented or ecumenical learning. The mere fact of having chosen such a topic will quickly lead to intensive conversations of a meaningful kind. In the joint preparation and evaluation sessions it will be important to make sure that questioning should not only be in order to acquire information and become more knowledgeable, but also that help is given to understand what is foreign and to think more about one's own situation, so that real change can come about. In this way the well-directed desire to know more can be prevented from degenerating into a one-sided interrogation of the partners.

THE LIMITATION OF PROJECT WORK

In spite of many contradictions during the course of my study, I still maintain that a new orientation of partnership work, which aims among other things at overcoming the donor-receiver divide between the partners, cannot avoid making drastic changes as far as project and financial aid in partnerships is concerned. Some of the grave problems arising from project aid have become very clear during the course of this study. I well understand the arguments brought before me that the wealthy partners in Germany cannot ignore the poverty of their African partners and that there are certain advantages in direct aid as far as fund-raising and opportunities for learning are concerned.

Nevertheless: first, during the course and in the context of this study I have neither heard of nor come across any project within a partnership that can be proved to have led to or even contributed to independence of the partners. Second, on the contrary I have seen innumerable cases of failure or of projects that led to increased and continued dependence of the African partners on account of the subsequent costs. Third, I have observed that the project work of partnerships has not been sufficiently and critically evaluated and that the partners do not concern themselves enough with the causes of poverty and underdevelopment. To a certain extent their ability to concern themselves with these causes is diminished because all their energy is taken up in running the projects.

Therefore, my really urgent recommendation is to take project aid out of the partnerships altogether. As I see it, the effects of project aid, in the way it cements the donor-receiver divide in the partnerships, is more disastrous than any usefulness it may serve. I am of the opinion that the partners would talk to each other about various subjects on quite a different level if they were to give up direct project aid. At the same time I claim that in this way the dimension of development-oriented learning would not be lost. It is in no way coupled to the running of projects. On the contrary, the necessity for development-oriented learning would be strengthened if the German partners continued to be confronted with the poverty of their partners, but were no longer able to "remedy" it quickly and directly in a well-meaning manner, but rather were forced to seek together with their partners for other ways of changing the situation.

Since my experience tells me that such a suggestion will not be taken, I am of the opinion that, in addition to the rules and regulations written into many partnership contracts, the following basic restrictions should be added:

- *First, there should be no project or financial aid from congregation to congregation.* This is particularly the case when congregation partnerships exist within a district partnership.

- *Second, a limit should be introduced on the amounts of money trans-ferred that is in relation to the budget of the African partners.* For example, an African partner district's budget financed by the German partners at 80 percent would be preposterous! I consider a limit of 10 to 20 percent as appropriate.
- *Third, the German partners should only support a project where the African partners have first made their own clear contribution.* Only in this way is it possible to ensure that a project is really founded on the initiative of those concerned and affected. A possible sensible rule of thumb is for example that for every mark given by the African partners the German partners also give one mark.
- *Fourth, at the moment it seems most sensible to invest in educational projects and less in projects with technology transfer from North to South.* What is important is that the project is based on the use of indigenous resources, that through the project local existing know-how is activated.
- *Fifth, where the partnerships wish to support projects, they should seek much more the advice of experts in development organizations.* These organizations, especially those belonging to the church, have a wealth of experience and can help prevent mistakes from which they have learned being repeated at an individual and congregational level. Beyond this it could be a part of development-oriented learn-ing in partnerships critically to question the ideology of the greater effectiveness of direct aid. It would mean real progress if more peo-ple could get away from the idea that they wish to support exclu-sively or predominantly "their project", and instead support long-term structural development programmes from larger organizations.
- *Sixth, all project aid needs regular, careful and critical evaluation.* This does not contradict the idea that the African partners should determine themselves how the means are used, independently and responsibly. What is necessary is accountability on both sides. This means that the German partners are also compelled to demonstrate how they have tried to contribute to overcoming the North-South divide, for example through their development-oriented involvement and activities.

In general, German partners should direct their attention, their strength and their possibilities much more strongly towards the necessary devel-opment-oriented work in their own country. In face of the discussions on how to save money in the coming years, one of the most important tasks for German partnership groups in their own churches will be to stand up for ecumenical missionary activities and see that the presence of the churches at the crisis points of society is neither reduced nor neglected, and here among other things development-oriented educational work and political lobbying will be necessary.

INITIATING LEARNING PROCESSES THROUGH PREPARATION AND EVALUATION

If partnerships are to be seen as opportunities for intercultural, ecumenical and development-oriented learning, then preparation and evaluation, particularly of the delegation visits but also of all other partnership activities, must play a much more important role. I have made it quite clear that purposeful subject-oriented preparation and evaluation and reflection of what has been experienced play only a very subordinate role in the form partnerships take at present. It is therefore very important to allow more time for preparation and evaluation and also to develop and practise methodological steps, so that experiences in intercultural encounter made possible through the partnership may be transferred into changes in behaviour, both together and in each individual context.

All the elements of a practical new orientation of partnership work described so far require extensive reflection and consideration. Ecumenical parish audits, ecumenical visitations or visits aimed at a particular group or concentrating on a particular subject are unthinkable without methodically structured planning. It is exactly the same as far as project support in partnerships is concerned. The experiences, successes and failures must be evaluated together with the partners. The evaluation of the content of partnership experience must be looked at together with the partners as far as possible, for only in this way is it possible to really learn and take steps forward leading to different patterns of behaviour and to binding agreements between the partners. This does not, however, exclude each individual partner's specific evaluation for themselves. The demand to give more time for the partners to evaluate together so as to make learning processes possible has consequences mainly for the planning of the programmes for delegation visits. The present custom of talking together and evaluating for a few hours at the end of a several-week visit, which in addition is often overburdened with the discussion of joint projects, is insufficient. Evaluation sessions must take place at regular intervals as an agreed part of the programme throughout the visit.

They can take various forms. It would be sensible, if not always possible, to hold daily evaluation sessions, in which the experiences of the day could be talked through. In such cases it is important that the participants, both the delegation members and also their hosts, describe once more what they have experienced, speak of their emotions, about what surprised, puzzled, angered or frustrated them, and what background and attitudes influenced the way they experienced certain situations.

Methodological instructions such as the hermeneutic model in section 2 above would be helpful here.

Where it is not possible to evaluate daily, it should at least be attempted to talk about the experiences made on the visit once a week. This applies both for the delegates among themselves and for the discussion with their partners. I am of the opinion that once a week at least half a day should be kept free for this. Such discussions, both within the delegation and also between the partners, are easier if they are structured under a certain topic. It also pays dividends if the visit as such has a thematic focus, if the encounter as such is based on an interest in learning more. That is why I say that the work of reflection begins already in the preparation of a visit.

It is important for the evaluation, at least for the German groups, that it takes the form of the concept of learning in intercultural encounters described in chapter 3, as a form of thinking about one's own situation, of "looking into one's own culture". As I have already pointed out the methodological initiation of such learning processes often demands too much of the members of the partnership groups. Here it is very important that they are supported and encouraged by the mission departments and the educational institutions of the church.

ASSISTANCE FROM THE MISSION DEPARTMENTS AND EDUCATIONAL
INSTITUTIONS OF THE CHURCH IN INITIATING LEARNING PROCESSES

Those mission departments that coordinate and advise the partnerships should get involved more than has so far been the case in supporting the evaluation of partnership experiences and giving instructions on how to initiate learning processes. The work done so far, which offers help in organizing visits and projects and enables partnership groups to exchange information among themselves and learn more about a great variety of subjects in regular partnership seminars, continues to be meaningful and necessary. It is on the whole very well accepted by the groups.

But beyond that the individual partnership groups must be supported better in their local contexts. The United Evangelical Mission and the churches in the Rhineland and in Westphalia have at least created a structure for this with the regional positions for education for mission in the congregations. So far the Evangelical Lutheran Mission has no such structure. Here it would be possible to give these secretaries for education for mission the task of supporting the partnership groups, especially in their evaluation of partnership encounters and in the question how far the experiences made can bear fruit in empowering the individual congregations for ecumenical missionary activity. It is not possible for the partnership secretaries in the mission departments to offer such individual and contextually relevant advice aimed at initiating learning processes in all the congregations. Therefore it is necessary to create a decentralized structure, rooted more firmly at a local level in order to guarantee the necessary freedom and independence of the partnership groups.

Beyond the creation of institutional structures the mission departments must also do much more to develop methods and educational concepts for learning in intercultural encounters, or rather take up already existing concepts and fit them to the specific situation of partnerships. These individually tailored offers of assistance should make the members of the partnership groups more aware of the situation of their own congregation so that they can bring their experience to bear on it. As partnership groups have so far often met with considerable resistance to their efforts, it would also be the task of such an advisory structure to talk to many people in the congregations, to open doors and to bring partnership work into the wider field of the ecumenical missionary work of congregations and church districts.

It will also be necessary for partnership groups to make use of the assistance of expert organizations for development work or church educational institutions in certain fields and also to develop willingness to call up this assistance when required. So far partnership groups have mainly worked in a closed room, having at the most occasional contact with other partnership groups. Relations and contacts with other development-oriented action groups, educational institutions of the church or development organizations hardly exist at all. It is necessary to bridge this gap and overcome the reservations on both sides.